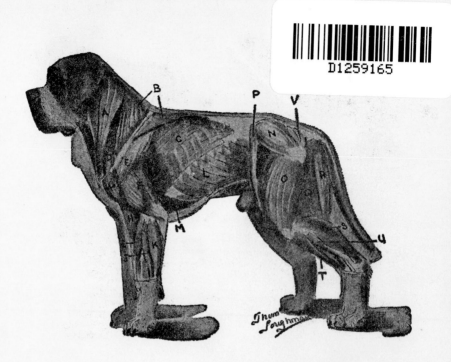

KEY

A	Sternomastoid	K	Flexor carpi Radialis
B	Trapezius	L	Obliquus abdominis Extensor
C	Latissimus Dorsi	M	Pectoralis Minor
D	Inferior levator anquli scapulae	N	Glutaeus Medius
		O	Quadriceps femoris
E	Deltoideus	P	Sartorius
F	Triceps Brachii	Q	Semimembranosus
G	Deltoideus	R	Semitendinosus
H	Extensor carpi Radialis	S	Gastronemii
I	Extensor digitorum communis	T	Tibialis Anterior
J	Extensor digiti minimum	U	Flexor Hallucis longus

These drawings were done by Thom Loughman, of Yonkers, N.Y., who was 18 years old at the time. A Saint fancier, he collected trophies as a junior handler, then entered the New York School of Design.

Above is his machine design of a working Saint Bernard. The muscles labeled O and S are prepared to do most of the work, corresponding to the thigh and calf muscles in the human leg. Muscle N lifts the leg and pulls it forward, as in your groin. The foot, from T on down, is an extended version of your instep and your toes. Muscle O does most of the work, with the rest of the Saint Bernard operating as a guiding and steering mechanism.

The drawing to the left illustrates leg action. Standing start becomes a walk, then quickens to a trot in Figure 4, with the sequence of movement remaining the same. Figures 5 and 8 show that the feet of a desirably short-coupled Saint overreach each other, compelling him to trot sideways. In nautical terms, this pictured dog is yawing a little to port. See chapter, **The Saint in Action.**

The New Complete
SAINT BERNARD

by

Milo Denlinger
Professor Albert Heim
Mrs. Henry H. Hubble
Gerda Umlauff
Joe Stetson

Edited and Expanded
by
Rex Roberts
and others

New Edition, 1966
with additional chapters and pictures

HOWELL BOOK HOUSE INC.
845 Third Avenue
New York, N. Y. 10022

A Saint Bernard puppy at four weeks old

The Statue of Saint Bernard of Menthon and "Pain de Sucre" 9517 ft.

The Hospital of Great Saint Bernard and "Pain de Sucre"

Contents

A Group of St. Bernards with Their Master
at the Hospice in Switzerland

Foreword

THIS edition of The Complete Saint Bernard is a major revision of the original book written by Milo Denlinger and others, and published in 1952. The historical portions remain substantially unchanged. Discussion of the breed as it exists today has been almost entirely revised, in order to keep pace with the increasing number of Saint Bernard fanciers, and with the widespread improvement they have created in the individual representatives of the breed.

Since the Saint Bernard was first recognized as a breed, there have been good, and great, representatives thereof. Along with the good ones, there have been many of the not so good. A breed so large, magnificent, surrounded by legend and beset by press agentry, true and untrue, and endowed with a size which magnifies every virtue and fault out of all proportion, is bound to have had trouble in achieving a definition as to what constitutes a good Saint Bernard.

This difficulty is now approaching resolution. Though it is neither cheap nor easy to have a Saint Bernard around the house, in the sense that it is neither cheap nor easy to have a wife, husband, son or daughter, the Saint has become a member of the family, a task for which he is well equipped.

During the past few years, Saint Bernard breeders and owners have grasped the vision of the ultimate dog, as big as canine structure will permit, as heavy of bone and body as his work requires, as gentle and yet indestructible as we hope all the members of our family will be.

We thank all Saint Bernard breeders and owners who have contributed to the support of this growing vision.

REX ROBERTS

5

The Hospice in Winter

6

Acknowledgments

Acknowledgments carried over from the first edition are:

To the Hospice of Saint Bernard and to the Saint Bernard Club of Switzerland for information furnished and for the use of illustrations.

To Miss Gerda Umlauff of Hamburg, Germany, for research in the Swiss and German history of the breed.

To Mrs. Henry Hubble, for the chapter on Saint Bernards in America.

Acknowledgments for the 1963 revision are:

First, to many secretaries of area Saint Bernard clubs who gathered information, names, and pictures relating to the modern fancy. Space permits the inclusion of only a small part of this material. The rest is being kept on file for possible use in later editions. Club secretaries who contributed significantly include:

Mrs. William Buell; Box 134, Canoga Park, Calif. (Southern California)

Mrs. Eugene Coulter; 17645 West 44th Ave., Golden, Colo. (Rockies)

Ulrich Engler; 13418 Second Ave., East Cleveland, Ohio (Ohio)

Mrs. Roy Gresham; 838 Lehigh Ave., Union, N. J. (Northern New Jersey)

Mrs. Harold Holmes; 434 Elm St., Bridgewater, Mass. (New England)

Mrs. Frank Lake; 1101 Laurel Road, Beverly, N. J. (Eastern)

Mrs. William McCausland; 5920 Bernhard Ave., Richmond, Calif. (Pacific Coast)

Mrs. Richard Seaman; R.R. 2, Markham, Ont. (Ontario)

Mrs. E. P. Wade; Box 151, West Chicago, Ill. (Northern Illinois)

Officers of the Saint Bernard Club of America made extensive contributions. Of special value were the information files maintained by the secretary, Edward A. Poor, R.D. 1, Acton, Mass. Mr. Poor also contributed lists, names, dates, and editorial advice. Other SBCA officers who assisted were Laurence Powell, Paul Wallbank, Richard Jackson, Boyd Shonkwiler, and Paul Cocanour.

Saint specialty judges Norman F. Keller and Dr. Henry E. Wedig, Sr., gave much time and thought to the problems of clarification, and made specific suggestions in writing. Mrs. Hubble once again must be thanked for her experienced suggestions and criticisms.

Also thanked are those individuals who, acting by request, made significant contributions. They include C. M. Cawker, Ed Dodd, Mary Lou Dube, Joan Edge, Cordelia Englund, Grace Harvey, Beatrice Knight, and William Roberts.

Professional photographers whose recent work was solicited for the revision include William Brown, Edward Harrison, Robert Jollimore, Frank Mazanec, Ruth Robbins, Evelyn Shafer, Paul Winick, Dave Wurzel, and Dick Yemma.

Many more secretaries, the record-keepers of a growing fancy, contributed to the 1966 edition. A partial list includes:

Mrs. Nancy Crane, Wilderness Lane, High Ridge, Missouri (Greater St. Louis)

Marian Sharp, Mine Hill, Dover, N. J. (Northern New Jersey)

Mrs. Jean Cox, 11 Partridge Lane, Agincourt, Ontario (Ontario)

Penny Little, 23596 Candace, Rockwood, Michigan (Michigan)

Mrs. Kaye Wessar, RD 3, Anderson, Indiana (Central Indiana)

8

Pat Thibedeau, RD 2, Antioch, Illinois (Northern Illinois)
Patricia Wiggins, 816 Sunkist Parkway, Minneapolis, Minn. (Minnesota)
James Yost, 501 W. 70th Place, Denver, Colorado (Rockies)
Photographers who contributed extensively were Jarvis Hunt, Jr., and James Howlett. Other contributors are literally too numerous to mention, but thanks anyway.

The Cross of Great Saint Bernard

The Hospital of Great Saint Bernard and "Pain de Sucre" 9517 ft.

The Hospice of St. Bernard

LOCATED more than 8,000 feet high in the Swiss Alps, the Hospice of the Great St. Bernard is one of the most highly elevated human habitations in Europe. As it sits in somber solitude, surrounded by the towering masses of snow covered mountain peaks, the Hospice through the centuries has remained what its name implies: a symbol of hospitality. Kings and beggars alike have found shelter and protection from the raging elements within its sturdy walls and the good deeds of the monks and their dogs have been highly praised in many languages.

Numerous legends surround the origin of the Hospice as no documents are available that contain the facts of its founding. The most credible story is that the original Hospice, a humble structure of several cell-like rooms, was founded in the 10th Century by Archdeacon Bernard of the St. Augustine Cathedral. Archdeacon Bernard was originally the son of a wealthy noble family which had its residence at the Castle of Menthon near the Lake of Annecy (Savoy). Upon completion of his education in Paris, Bernard began to teach theology, but his father requested his immediate return to Menthon. There he had, in the traditional manner, selected a bride for him. Bernard returned to Menthon but, contrary to his father's wishes, decided to remain in the theological profession. He fled to Aosta (Italy) where he entered the St. Augustine Cathedral as a Canon Regular and after the death of Archdeacon Peter became Preacher and Archdeacon of the Cathedral.

The Mons Jovis Pass, at which the Hospice of St. Bernard is located, had received its name from a temple that the Roman Emperors had built on the summit of the pass and dedicated to their god, Jupiter Penninus. At that time the pass was one of the principal roads connecting Switzerland with Italy. It was used primarily for commercial purposes, but several great armies of medieval emperors and, in 1800, that of Napoleon, used it to their advantage. As the Tomb of the Apostles in Rome induced a constant movement of salvation-seeking Christians, this road became also one of the main arteries for the Italian-bound pilgrimages. Merchants and pilgrims preferred the summer months for their mountain traverse, when daylight prevailed longer and the creeks were shallow and easy to cross. However, they were unable to foresee the dangers awaiting them as they proceeded.

Upon reaching the summit the travelers often were subjected to robberies and attacks by the heathen inhabitants of the mountains. These robbers were some of the wild Saracens who after a reign of terror and destruction had been driven out of the valleys and lived savagely in mountain caves. They cleverly took advantage of the mythological superstitions of that time and established their main hideout in the ruins of the old Mons Jovis temple from which they approached the exhausted travelers as threatening "ghosts."

Archdeacon Bernard in his efforts to eliminate the danger

12

A Monk and His Dogs at the Hospice of Saint Bernard

of robberies, went to preach to the heathen and finally succeeded in converting them to Christianity. He realized the need for a shelter at the mountain pass and in 1050 inaugurated the building of the Hospice. It was a simple structure resembling one of the refuge huts frequently found in the mountains. Bernard's parents who had been grief-stricken since his departure, visited him at the Hospice and donated a large part of their wealth toward its completion and maintenance. St. Bernard died at 85 years of age, having served as an Archdeacon for 40 years.

The Hospice served its purpose well. In the *Pilgrim's Guide of Saint Iago di Compostela,* printed in France in 1139, it was spoken of as one of the three great hospices in the world. We read: "The welfare of the poor rests on three strong pillars: the Hospice of Jerusalem, the Hospice of Mons Jovis and the Hospice of St. Christina at the Somport (Pyrenees). These Hospices were built at locations at which there is great need for them. They are sacred places, houses of the Lord, indispensable for the welfare of the holy pilgrims, the rest of the needy, the consolation of the ailing, peace of soul for the dead and assistance to the living."

During the centuries the Hospice received its operating funds from donations by English and German royalty, the Popes and other ecclesiastical dignitaries as well as neighboring bishops and clerics and the Family of Savoy, as they realized the importance of this institution. Pilgrims and merchants who had enjoyed the monks' hospitality demonstrated their gratitude by building other, smaller hospices which they gave to the monastery of St. Bernard. With its steadily increasing riches in lands and money, in the thirteenth century the Hospice was able to have its buildings enlarged considerably.

The Hospice operated under an independent administrative system and the Prior's authority in financial, as well as disciplinary matters, was generally recognized. As the Provost, who had final authority in all matters, resided at the mother-house of the Order in Martigny, the privilege of

"They always want to take my picture"
Young St. Bernard of the Hospice du Grand St. Bernard

Approaching the "Cantine de Proz", after travelling through the forests,
one finds still a Guest-house, where travellers can rest, in a
valley well adapted to pasture lands

self-administration was grossly abused by the Priors as well as the monks. Provost Jean d'Acres in 1417 attempted to counteract this abuse by setting up strict regulations for monks and Priors in which he demanded abstinence from worldly sins such as dancing, drinking, hunting, carrying arms and wearing fancy clothes. He also requested that a superior be appointed to teach and supervise the monks as many of them were illiterate and were not even able to administer the holy sacraments. However, little consideration was shown these regulations and they were soon forgotten after Provost Jean d'Acres retired in 1438. The new Provosts, who were elected by the House of Savoy, had little regard for the Hospice's welfare. They wasted its money and went so far as to sell properties belonging to the Hospice.

In 1555 a disastrous fire swept over the Hospice destroying the roofs and to a large extent the upper walls. For three years the monks were forced to live under most pitiful and primitive conditions before permission was granted to perform the necessary repair work. The first repairs consisted of clearing the rubbish, rebuilding part of the destroyed upper walls and building strong supports for the front of the building. The monks' rooms, as well as the church, received a new whitewash and the roofs were weighted down with large rocks and stone plates.

The Great St. Bernard, as the mountain was called from then on, seems to have held some kind of fortification. A sketch made in 1626 of the Church and the Hospice reveals part of an ancient parapet south of the buildings. Apparently, a crenelled barrier blocked the pass from the Swiss side and was connected with the Hospice buildings. Another battlement, similar to the parapet blocking the Valley of St. Themy on the Italian side of the mountain, seems to have been at the Plan de Jupiter. In 1476 this stronghold was the scene of bloody battles between the troops of the Count of Challant and the Valais soldiers. According to the legend, the old mortuary (which is still standing) was then built to take care of the enormous

16

number of casualties of the battle in the Combe des Morts.

During the seventeenth century the Hospice was completely remodeled and a new chapel added. The Bishop of Sitten, Adrian VI von Riedmatten, personally performed the consecration of the beautiful little building. Toward the end of the eighteenth century, Provost Ludwig Anton Ludder added the St. Ludwigs Spital on the northern side of the pass to the buildings of the Hospice.

Numerous priors were in charge of the Hospice in succession during medieval time. Most of them had the welfare of the Hospice at heart, others their own financial gain in mind. There was a constant struggle between the constitutionists who duly obeyed the fundamental laws of the congregation and the anti-constitutionists who failed to live according to their vows. In 1752 Pope Benedict XIV passed the "bull de separatione," a papal letter according to which all property on the Swiss side belonged to the orders of St. Mauritius and Lazarus. The anti-constitutionists were made Sardinian subjects, given the Valais property and left in charge of the Great St. Bernard Hospice with the stipulation that the monks were to elect their own provosts. However, this was a very unfortunate solution and caused the Hospice large losses in land, money and personnel. Most of the monks returned to the valleys.

The Hospice had hardly recuperated from the consequences of the separation when the Canton of the Lower Valais declared its independence and started a chain of political events at the end of which was the fall of the old Helvetian Confederation and the invasion of Switzerland by French troops.

Climate

Rock, snow, and ice are the principal elements in the vicinity of the Hospice. No vegetation is able to withstand the extremely cold and most undesirably variable climate. Some lone, weather-beaten pines clinging to the rocks about 2,000 feet below the pass are the last sign of organic life. Even during the months of July and August, frost occurs daily and the monks know of only approximately twenty days annually that are free from frost and ice. The small lake in front of the buildings, which constitutes the boundary between Switzerland and Italy, is often frozen the year round. Many of the travelers, arriving at the Hospice after having been exposed to the sub-zero temperatures for the long hours of their ascent, suffer frozen extremities. This applies particularly to the seasonal laborers crossing the pass insufficiently clothed. Frequently it becomes necessary for the monks to supply these people with warm clothing, as well as to provide dry clothes for all comers that have encountered drenching rains, snow storms, or the dankness of the mountain fog.

Many of the monks' experiences tell of the unpredictable weather conditions on the mountain. Travelers starting out on a bright, sunny morning may after a few hours be overcome by violent snow storms that not only eliminate visibility but, accompanied by falling temperatures, cause the snow to freeze on hair and clothing.

During the winter months the snow reaches a depth of thirty feet and causes the Hospice to become almost completely isolated. The tremendous winds to which the buildings are continually exposed change during the winter months into treacherous snow storms. A few people, most of them laborers seeking employment in the warmer Italy, venture across the mountain during the winter. It is a perilous undertaking, as the way is partially covered by large snow drifts and the passage at the summit becomes almost inaccessible. Posts that are connected with a strong rope have been anchored in the rock to guide the traveler over the steepest part on the summit.

One of the greatest dangers the traveler may encounter is the avalanche—a mass of ice, rock, and snow, which viciously thunders from the cliffs carrying with it destruction and certain death. Even those familiar with the dangers of the mountains are not always able to escape. Only recently three of the monks were buried by an avalanche while they were searching for lost travelers.

The Sanctuary of the Church which was built by the Master-Mason,
Jean-Antoine Marcoz, of Brissogne and in 1698 was consecrated by
Adrian VI of Riedmatter, Bishop of Sitten
Choir Stall of the Year 1681

19

The Monks

Approximately fifteen of the seventy members of the Order of St. Augustine reside at the Hospice. The monks are selected from their mother-house at Martigny for service at the Hospice at the age of eighteen or twenty years. Particular attention is paid to the monks' physical condition in selecting them for service at the Hospice. While monks of excellent constitution have been able to withstand the undesirable climate for longer than fifteen years, others have averaged only twelve years. Almost all of the monks continually residing at the Hospice acquire ailments of the rheumatic type and heart conditions.

Under the supervision of the Prior, three monks perform duties as Master of the Novices, Sacristan, and Host to the Travelers, while a fourth one is in charge of the financial and economic details. Until recently, the older monks at the Hospice taught student priests in the fields of philosophy, literature, history and theology. These educational functions have now been transferred to a Hospice-owned farm at Encone, near Riddes.

The present Provost of the Hospice is the Honorable Monseigneur Nestor Adams who was elected in 1939. He carries the insignias, miter and crosier of a Bishop as first bestowed upon the Provosts of the Hospice by the Pope in 1762.

Brothers of the Order of St. Augustine under the supervision of a Prior also serve the Hospice at the Simplon Pass and nine different Church communities in the valleys.

The Dogs

The dogs of the Great St. Bernard which have been bred, raised and trained by the monks for the past four centuries, have remained one of the main attractions of the Hospice. They are powerfully built dogs of fawn or mahogany color with white markings. Their heads are impressively large and their noble expression gives them an air of dignity. Even though a variety of long haired dogs exists, a short, dense coat is preferred as it does not interfere with the dogs' work in the snow.

The manifold stories relating the rescue of snow-bound travelers by these dogs have added much to their glamour and legendary reputation. The first indication of their existence is a painting by the Neapolitan Salvator Rose of the seventeenth century. Many contradictory views have been expressed regarding the origin of these dogs. It is assumed that they result from cross-breedings of English Hounds and Spaniels, and there is also some legendary belief that they stem from a mating of a Great Dane and a Valais Alpine female. Another assumption is that the St. Bernard dog originates from a large type of hound which the Romans used in their military establishments or that it is a cross of bulldogs and Pyrenean sheep dogs.

Twelve or fifteen dogs are usually kept at the Hospice and trained for rescue work. The training requires approximately two years and the older and more experienced dogs aid in the training of the younger ones. During the dangerous winter months the monks, accompanied by some of the dogs, used to leave the Hospice every morning and search the pass for exhausted or lost travelers. On occasions the dogs were sent out by themselves and frequently located snow-bound travelers whom they guided safely to the Hospice.

One of the most miraculous rescues was performed by Old Barry, one of the best specimens ever bred at the Hospice. As the story goes, Barry found a small boy in the snow and by some mysterious means got him to climb on his back and carried him to safety. With Barry's death in 1814 the Hospice lost one of its most famous guide and rescue dogs. During the twelve years of his life he had rescued more than 40 persons and his work has not been equalled since. The Museum of Berne preserved and mounted him and today, after more than one century, he is still the object of respectful admiration. The monks honor Barry by naming after him those dogs bred at the Hospice that are beautiful in appearance and of excellent character and ability.

Among the deeds of rescue well remembered in the history of the Hospice is one which occurred in the winter of 1874. Some Italian laborers insisted on crossing the pass on a most dangerous and unpredictable day. As the monks felt it was their duty to assist the travelers, seven of them and one dog accompanied and guided this group of eight persons. After three hours of strenuous climbing in the quickly falling snow, a huge avalanche fell, burying beneath it three of the monks, five of the Italians and the dog. The remainder of the party immediately and fiercely began to dig and search and was able to free five of the victims. The dog, which had freed itself, returned to the Hospice and by its excited behavior informed the Superior of the accident. A rescue party was sent out immediately and for several hours worked laboriously at freeing the persons buried under the avalanche. Unfortunately, the victims had been exposed to sub-freezing temperature so long that they died shortly after being found.

Amazing is the ability of the dogs to discover lost persons even though they are covered by a thick blanket of snow. In 1907 a lone traveler was overtaken by a sudden snow storm. As he had fallen down from exhaustion, the quickly falling snow covered him completely, wiping out his tracks. A rescue party was sent out; and the dog, immediately picking up the scent, led the party to the snow covered victim.

The monks value the service of their dogs very highly and seldom leave the Hospice without them. The dogs easily find their way back to the Hospice by their instinct while the human eye is often unable to penetrate the quickly descending mountain fog.

Even though the dogs are of a sturdy, hardy constitution, their life span is reduced to about ten years by the severe climate. Like their masters, they suffer from rheumatic and heart diseases as well as asthma, as they increase in age.

True to the tradition of the Hospice, the monks have continued to breed these fine dogs even though their services are no longer needed. The Hospice is now easily accessible by automobile and the dangers formerly encountered by the lone traveler on foot are greatly reduced, if not completely eliminated.

The Hospice Today

The Simplon Tunnel (built from 1898 to 1905) now connecting Switzerland and Italy, worms its way 12¼ miles through the mountain northeast of the Great St. Bernard Pass. In seven years, human ingenuity has converted the formerly perilous mountain traverse of several days' duration into a pleasant, smooth half-hour trip. However, it has also robbed the passage of its glamour and romance, the Hospice of its purpose, and deprived the traveler of an experience unexcelled in grandeur and impressiveness. No longer need the traveler exert himself in the strenuous ascent, exposed to the hazards of sudden snow storms, avalanches and freezing temperatures; but no longer, also, will he enjoy the grand and wild scenery and the sublime feeling of closeness to eternity inspired by the loneliness of the ice-bound mountains.

Lacking the picturesque loveliness of many other mountain passes, the Great St. Bernard impresses one with its rugged panorama and the massive proportions of the surrounding mountains. Until the end of the nineteenth century the Hospice was the only sign of humanizing influence in this barren canyon. With the completion of a road in 1890, however, the pass became easily accessible. The road has been so improved that it is now travelled by thousands of motorists annually who reach the Hospice in several hours' drive from Martigny. This, however, applies only to the summer months, as during the winter months the road remains closed on account of the danger of avalanches and snow drifts. As the last part of the road is too narrow to permit traffic from both directions, upgoing traffic is restricted to the morning hours, and descending traffic, to the afternoon of each day.

The road now available has also eased considerably the burden of transporting supplies to the Hospice. The countless travelers as well as the monks require large quantities of food to be stocked at the Hospice during the winter months. These supplies were formerly carried up the small path by horses or mules in a laborious ascent. A herd of nearly one hundred cattle and a large flock of sheep enable the Hospice to keep in stock considerable quantities of smoked mutton and salted beef, which in recent years has been frequently supplemented by fresh meat.

The buildings, consisting of the Hospice with connecting Chapel, the St. Ludwigs Spital and the old mortuary, though massive stone structures, seem dwarfed as they huddle against the masses of naked rock rising behind them to a height of 9,400 feet. The Chapel, in which the monks sing Mass daily and perform their hourly prayers, is one of the greatest attractions. Built in the seventeenth century, it still contains its original murals and choir stalls of beautifully carved walnut wood. In the Chapel the Tomb of General Desaix is reminiscent of the battle of Marengo in 1800 when Napoleon defeated the Austrians in Italy.

During the years, representatives of all creeds, ranks and religions have gathered in the large entrance hall of the Hospice and decorated it with the tokens of their gratitude. A message of gratitude to Napoleon was inscribed on the wall by the people of the Lower Valais who through him had gained their independence. The piano which King Edward VII presented to the Hospice is also displayed here.

A museum, containing countless objects of great value and interest, occupies the ground floor. The monks have assembled remarkable collections of insects and stones, and they as well as antique coins, votive tablets and statues discovered at the site of the old Mons Jovis temple, are now on display at the museum.

The west wing of the house is occupied by the monks and not open to the public. The upper floors contain the guest rooms which are simple and clean and contain from one to four beds.

One of the most valuable assets is the library in the loft of the main building. More than 30,000 volumes, some of them hand-written and hand-pressed, make up this marvelous collection of both antique and recent editions in many languages.

With a capacity of 400 beds in its approximately 100 rooms, the Hospice has often accommodated more than 500 overnight guests by converting hallways and the dining hall into sleeping quarters. On occasions like this, all of the monks assist in the preparation and serving of meals and other chores necessary to provide a comfortable stay for the transients. The Hospice does not operate on the basis of a hotel but in accordance with the principles of a religious order. As it was built in the eleventh century for the "welfare of the needy and for the rest of the pilgrims" it still serves this purpose to some extent by giving shelter and food to those in need of it. Everyone who so desires has access to the Hospice. Upon ringing the door bell he will be welcomed by the Father Aumoniér who receives with equal cordiality all guests regardless of nation, rank, or religion.

Unfortunately, curious and thoughtless tourists have greatly abused the monks' generous hospitality; and it is now limited to the truly needy travelers, who are permitted to stay one night during the summer months and as long as necessary during the winter months. (A hotel opposite the Hospice has facilities for 180 overnight guests. It is open the year round.)

Approximately one half of the 20,000 persons annually visiting the Hospice are Italians, 6,000 or more are Swiss, approximately 2,000 are British tourists, and the remainder

25

are composed of members of all nations of the world. Most of the Italians crossing the pass are needy people or workers in search of employment. They cross the St. Bernard in spring to work during the summer months in Swiss valleys and return to Italy in the fall.

British, German, and Italian royalty have enjoyed the hospitality of the monks. Queen Victoria of England, who spent one night at the Hospice, later presented it with her portrait. At the age of eighteen years, the Prince of Wales, later King Edward VII, was guest of the monks. Upon his departure from the Hospice the Prince was presented with a beautiful St. Bernard puppy. The Prince was deeply upset when the puppy died before the royal party even reached the valley. Soon after his arrival in England, the Prince repaid the monks' hospitality by presenting the Hospice with a piano, and later, when he became King of England, he had another piano shipped to them. In 1883 King Edward's sister, the late Empress Fredericke of Germany, also visited the Hospice with her husband, the Crown Prince. Frequent visitors during the summer months were the King and Queen of Italy, who traveled by automobile from Aosta.

It seems that the monks' hospitality is enjoyed not only by mankind but by all of the Lord's creation. Twice annually, the swallows on their flights to and from the South rest at the Hospice. As soon as the first ones are noticed, the monks open wide all windows for the graceful little birds to enter. They remain quietly in the building and even permit the monks to caress them. As soon as the weather permits, they are on their way again, chirping a song of thanks to their hosts.

Through the installation of a telephone the Hospice is now in a position to inform those starting their ascent of the weather conditions in the upper regions. On the other hand, the monks can now receive word of travelers approaching so that they may be on the lookout for them in foul weather. Coach service is now provided from Martigny during the months of July and August, and tourists are able to reach the Hospice by automobile, though the trip is time-consuming and arduous.

Some years ago the Hospice was threatened by undesirably large and noisy crowds of tourists. Fortunately, the rugged remoteness of the setting and its difficulty of access soon persuaded the casual tourist to seek his amusement elsewhere. Although a small hotel is now available through part of the year, the serious-minded visitor is content with the sense of austerity and dedication.

At the time of this revision in 1963, the breeding of Saint Bernards continues at the Hospice. The principal purposes of this work now are love of the breed and the continuation of a grand tradition.

Flüelen, Switzerland
St. Bernards of the kennel, Zwinger Zwing-Uri

Water Color by Job
Napoleon with his Army, scaling the Alps in May 1800

The Crossing of the Alps by Napoleon

THE crossing of the Alps in 1800 which won Napoleon the admiration of his contemporaries was so great an accomplishment that even in our days of modern warfare it impresses us.

At Dijon, France, General Berthier was put in command of the army which he later led to victory at Marengo. Captain Coignet, an old warrior, relates the details of the mountain traverse of his unit in his "Cahiers" as follows:

"From Lausanne we ascended the wide Rhone Valley to Martigny, a small settlement in extreme poverty. At this point the Rhone River receives the Dranse and we entered the Dranse Valley which in a series of ascents and descents leads up to the mountain pass. We finally halted at St. Pierre, a small community on the foot of the mountain. Even though the houses of this village were small and poorly constructed, the spacious barns provided sufficient room for us to sleep in and attend to our guns and equipment. Napoleon himself was present as all cannons were taken apart in preparation for the transport over the mountain. The tubes of the three cannons belonging to our artillery unit were placed into hollowed trunks of trees, but sledges and barrows were also employed as means of transportation. A strong, intelligent cannoneer with a detail of 40 grenadiers was put in charge of the transport. Being responsible for the safe transport of the material, he demanded strict obedience and tolerated no backtalk to his orders. No one was permitted to move when he shouted 'halt' and upon his command 'forward' everyone had to move on.

"Early the next morning we received our ration of rusk and two pairs of shoes per man and then started the ascent. Our cannoneer appointed twenty men to carry the trough containing the barrels of the three cannons, and while a number of other grenadiers shared the heavy burden of the body of the cannon, two men each were assigned to carry axletrees and wheels, and eight others bore the small arms.

"This ascent was one of the most arduous undertakings I ever engaged in. Silently, the men bore the heavy loads, obeying the short commands of 'halt' or 'forward' issued by our cannoneer. With the increasing steepness of the path the transport of the heavy guns became an extremely laborious and dangerous task. On one occasion we lost control of the heavy trough and it slid downhill rapidly. After hours of strenuous efforts we had the trough back in position and proceeded silently following the brief instructions and commands from our guiding cannoneer.

"Finally we were granted a moment of rest for the prime purpose of changing our shoes which ice and rocks had cut to shreds. 'Let's go, my horses,' said our cannoneer, and somewhat refreshed after hastily eating a bite of rusk, we continued our strenuous ascent.

"As we reached the regions of eternal snow and had just noticed with relief that our vehicle slid along with much less effort, we encountered General Chambarlhac. Arrogantly, the General ordered our cannoneer to increase the speed of our movement, whereupon the cannoneer harshly replied that the General was not in charge of this transport and that it was his, the cannoneer's responsibility. The General furiously stepped toward the cannoneer, who coldly advised that he would throw him in the abyss or use the loading stick on him if he interfered further.

"After several more hours of great strain and effort we viewed the roofs of the Hospice. When we were still four hundred paces distant from the buildings, we noticed a path in the snow and steps cut into the ice at the summit, which gave evidence of the presence of other troops who had previously arrived there. We put our guns down and after the rest of the four hundred grenadiers and officers had assembled at the pass, we entered the Chapel of the Monastery.

"The world-renouncing monks who occupy the Hospice have dedicated their lives to assist mankind and particularly those crossing the pass. Their large dogs are always ready to guide wayworn travelers away from the danger of avalanches and icy death into the care of the magnanimous monks. True to their tradition the monks provided sufficient bread, cheese and wine for all of us as we enjoyed the warmth of the fireplace in the large hall, and later generously prepared sleeping quarters in the spacious hallways for us. The good monks did everything in their power to make our stay comfortable and enjoyable and I believe that each of us in turn treated them with utmost consideration.

"Upon our departure the dogs accepted our caressing as if they had known us for a long time. We shook hands with the monks, unable to express sufficiently the admiration and gratitude we felt for these good men."

A Corridor of the Hospice Leading to the South Entrance

The History of the St. Bernard Dog

A speech delivered by Professor Albert Heim at a course for St. Bernard Judges in Berne, Switzerland, April 23, 1927.

"**K**NOWLEDGE increases our understanding of things and our sympathy for them." With this in mind, the St. Bernard Club requested me to speak to you on the history of the St. Bernard Dog.

According to Professor Studer and Dr. Sigmund, the Doggen type to which the St. Bernard belongs (large and powerfully built, large head, pendant ears, pronounced stop, short muzzle) has developed gradually from various breeds at different times and locations. Of numerous hypotheses that have been advanced concerning the origin of the St. Bernard dog, Studer supports that of tracing this breed back to the Canis Inostranzewi; Sigmund considers the Saints as an oversized type of the Canis familaris palustris (a domesticated animal of the Stone Age); and C. Keller, as well as H. Kraemer, represent the theory that all Doggen types originate from Asia, particularly from the Thibet Mastiff.

The fact has definitely been established that Doggen did not exist in Switzerland in prehistoric times. Old Egyptian literature also contains no indication of the presence of this type of dog, even though the Egypt of that era was one of the few countries in which the scientific breeding of dogs was highly advanced. The first dogs of the Doggen type were imported about 300 B.C. by Xerxes, the Greeks, Alexander the Great and the Phoenicians from Asia (Persia, Assyria, India, Himalaya).

A shipment consisting of 156 dogs was once imported by Alexander the Great for use in the arenas of old Rome. As these dogs allegedly originated at Molossis, Greece, they were identified as "Molosser" (Canis Molossus) until approximately A.D. 200. There were two types of the Molosser which differed in many characteristics. One of them, which was used as sheep dog, was of slight build and light color, with a somewhat long head and easy movements. The other, heavier type, was used as protection dog and war dog. Specimens of the latter type were of dark color, with broad heads, a short muzzle and generally more heavily built. The Illyrian Molosser had prick ears, the Babylonian Molosser pendant ears. Specimens of the lighter type still exist in small numbers in the mountains of Asia. The breeds traced back to the heavy type of Molosser are Mastiffs, the old Barenbeisser, and the St. Bernard.

In the beginning the two different types of Molosser were not distinctly separated and specimens showing characteristics of either type were quite common. The Romans used these dogs for driving and guarding the herds of livestock that accompanied the armies, as well as watchdogs for their garrisons and commercial establishments, which were located in isolated valleys and at mountain passes.

All available information produces the following picture: The Asiatic dogs arrived in Helvetia (Switzerland) via Rome and the Alps in two waves. The light variety

34

of the Molosser, the sheep dog, was the first one to migrate in the last century B.C. As they spread into the Fore-Alps they soon became animals of multiple use, serving as watchdogs at farms and homes in the valleys, as well as herding dogs and watchdogs at Alpine dairy farms. Through methodical breeding they gradually developed into a distinct breed of their own, the Swiss Alpine Dog, which, after 2,000 years, is permanently established in certain areas of Switzerland. As wolves and bears no longer jeopardize the Alpine herds, less emphasis is being put on breeding sheep dogs of white or cream color.

The second migration, during the first two centuries A.D., brought the heavier type of Molosser which remained primarily in the mountains, at pass stations and in the Valleys of Aosta and Valais. These dogs spread as far as the Bernese Oberland but remained few in number as the farmers there had acquired their dogs from the previous migration. Interested in these dogs were the wealthy aristocrats and the monks. This heavy type of the Molosser became the progenitor of the St. Bernard dog.

Literature of the past centuries contains only infrequent references to the existence of these dogs as the breeding of dogs was not cultivated in former times. The Swiss Alpine dogs, however, appear in some of the paintings by old Italian masters from 1550 to 1750. They apparently existed in the areas of Berne, Freiburg, Waadt, Unterwalden, Lucerne, St. Gallen and Appenzell.

No pictures of the St. Bernard dog are available until he appears in a painting by an unknown artist in 1695. The painting, which is now at the Hospice, pictures two dogs with typically exaggerated "Hospice" heads. They are both well built, however, one of them certainly has no double dewclaws. Their tails are quite long. A later painting, by Sir E. Landseer in 1815, shows Lion, a male imported in England from the Hospice. Lion was a very large dog of tawny color, with a sound head and no dewclaws on his hind feet. The two dogs painted in 1695, as well as Lion, resemble good specimens which could well compete with the St. Bernards of today. They prove that the distinct type of the St. Bernard was developed at that time and has remained unchanged.

Countless are the legends concerning the origin of the St. Bernard dog. One of them traces the St. Bernard back as an offspring of a dog which accidentally appeared at the Hospice. However, only one mating, or even several matings of the same type, do not create a new breed. It is also evident that the St. Bernard dog did not originate at the Hospice but was first known as the "Talhund" (Valley Dog) in the valleys and later taken to the Hospice. Years of inbreeding, with particular emphasis being placed on achieving qualifications necessary for the rescue work in the mountains, have produced the St. Bernard of today. However, the consequences of continual close line and inbreeding also manifested themselves in stillborn litters, bulldoggy heads and many other faults.

Père Roland Viot, Provost of the Order from 1611 to 1644, does not mention the dogs in his description of the Hospice and its duties. The first reference to the existence of trained rescue dogs at the Hospice was found in a rescue report of 1707 which mentions that "one dog was buried by an avalanche." In the course of his research work on the St. Bernard dog, Percy Manning, MA Oxford, discovered numerous old documents in British museums and Bodleian Libraries, among them a travel description by the Geneve Painter Bourrit. This description was written in 1774 and refers to the rescue work performed by the monks and their dogs as a fact that "has been known for a long time."

Apparently, the first dogs, descendants of the old Roman Molosser, were brought to the Hospice between 1660 and 1670 as watchdogs. The monks took them along on their walks in search for lost travelers and soon discovered their salient qualities of path finding and sense of direction. From then on the dogs were trained for guide and rescue work in which they have assisted the monks for the past 250 years with splendid results.

The records of the Hospice reveal that the dogs in 1787 protected the Hospice from a gang of burglars. During the years 1816 to 1818, years of severe snow storms, the dogs performed remarkable services and several dogs died in the course of their rescue work. In 1825 three monks, one traveler and three dogs were buried by an avalanche. The rescue work of the dogs has repeatedly been described and praised by travelers. The dogs leave the Hospice in groups, they search, find and report in groups, and many of them may have accomplished the same number of rescues (40) as Old Barry did. During the past 250 years a total of 2,000 persons have been rescued with the dogs' assistance.

It has at times been assumed that German, English or Danish Bulldogs have been crossed with the St. Bernard dogs. However, this is not true. The only occasion on which the St. Bernards were crossed with another breed was in 1830 when many of the breeding stock at the Hospice were lost due to an extremely severe winter and some disease which increased the mortality rate in puppies to almost 100 percent. In 1856 the Prior, Erw. J. Deléglise, wrote Mr. Friedrich Tschudi that the Hospice dogs were again threatened with extinction and said: "The two Newfoundlands we received last winter from Stuttgart developed very nicely, particularly the male who has started his duty in the mountains very well." (Friedrich Tschudi, *Animal Life in the Alps*). The Newfoundland here referred to was the old and very heavy type which was popular in England about 1800 and several years later was represented all over the Continent. Contrary to the St. Bernard, the Newfoundland had not been degenerated through in-breeding.

After 1830 the first long haired specimens of the St. Bernard appeared. It was believed that the long hair would protect the dogs better against the cold climate, however, it soon became apparent that these long haired dogs were utterly unusable for the rescue work. After wading in the deep snow, a crust of snow and ice would completely cover the dogs and make it impossible for them to advance. The monks sold or gave away the long haired dogs, the breeding of which was continued in the valleys. Their offspring included both the short and the long haired variety and several of the short haired dogs were again crossed with the dogs at the Hospice.

The breed had definitely gained, as far as strength, intelligence and character were concerned, by the temporary crossing with Newfoundlands, and after several generations the pure St. Bernard type was restored. The only indication which remained of the crossing is the long haired dog which began to exist in 1830.

The name of the breed is not old. The British named the dogs of the Hospice "Holy Dogs," "Alpine Mastiffs," "St. Bernard Mastiffs," also "Cloister Dogs," "Mountain Dogs," and "Hospice Dogs." The German canine experts suggested the name "Alpine Dogs" which, of course, would have invited the bastardizing and degeneration of the breed. In the Canton of Berne they were called the "Barryhung"; Old Barry's glory was still remembered. In 1823 Daniel Wilsen speaks of the "so-called St. Bernard Dogs," and in 1865 the name "Bernhardiner" or "St. Bernard Dog" was definitely applied. It caused much opposition as the name implied that all dogs were bred at the Hospice. This is not true since just as many or more dogs were bred in the valleys and only a few dogs had been sent to the Hospice and spread from there. The name was later interpreted more satisfactorily as "dogs, which are kept at the Hospice of St. Bernard." It was justifiable to name the dogs after the location of their rescue deeds through which they have gained world fame and popularity. The name was recognized in 1880. Brehm calls them scientifically, Canis familaris extrarius St. Bernardi; Fitz, Canis extrarius alpinus; Walther, Molossus Monti St. Bernardi.

The St. Bernard's qualifications that make him indispensable for the rescue work are the never failing sense of direction and the ability to scent (in clear weather they scent a human more than 800 feet, and against the wind

38

they scent for several miles. They are able to scent people buried 5 to 7 ft. deep in snow). The dogs also feel in advance the approach of a snow storm. About 20 to 40 minutes before the storm they become restless and want to go outside. The dogs further have the amazing ability of sensing the closeness of falling avalanches and have frequently proved this by detouring from the path which only minutes later was covered by an avalanche. Remarkable is the dogs' ability of endurance. They often remain outside for hours in temperatures 10 to 20° below and even violent snow storms do not seem to affect them.

The training of the dogs does not include punishment and orders; it is a mere matter of giving instructions; and no obedience training, as is necessary for Police dogs, is involved. The dogs soon sense when they are doing right and have confidence in their masters. They follow the example of those dogs that work well and seem to desire to share their joy of success.

Remarkable is the intelligence of these dogs in their way of cooperating. If several dogs find a lost traveler in the snow they try to get him in upright position. If this is not possible, two dogs lie down on each side of him to keep him warm while others return to the Hospice and summon help. As soon as the rescue party arrives, all of the dogs remain in the background so as not to interfere with the monks' work. As soon as the victim is placed on the stretcher, the dogs lead the way back to the Hospice. No orders need to be given the dogs.

It has been observed that the offspring of good rescue dogs need little training for their work. They learn much faster than those which stem from untrained parents. The ability for rescue work seems to be hereditary and can be intensified by inbreeding. Dogs which have never received any training, but whose parents were good rescue dogs, have frequently performed the services of a rescue dog in situations of danger.

"We are Seven"
Three weeks old puppies of the Swiss Kennel, "v. Lotten"
Owner: Mr. Otto Steiner, Muhen

GITA-OENZ SHSB 3629
Long haired St. Bernard Female
Considered an outstanding type in Switzerland
Owned by the Swiss Kennel "v. Lotten" of Mr. Otto Steiner,
Muhen, Switzerland

St. Bernard Breeders in Switzerland 1873 to 1904

R. KUENZLI of St. Gallen was one of Switzerland's greatest St. Bernard breeders. Through his friendship with Dr. Kuenzli, Mr. Richard Strebel, renowned German dog writer, became acquainted with this fine breed of dogs. Over a period of years he made visits at St. Gallen which usually lasted several weeks and provided an opportunity for Mr. Strebel to become familiar with Dr. Kuenzli's kennel and his breeding aims. Dr. Kuenzli, despite all discouragements, worked ambitiously toward his goal of breeding better St. Bernards—dogs with a good gait, and a perfect build; or, as he used to say, "They must stand like horses." He was trying with steady perseverance to create a new, more modern type of the Hospice dog.

As a breeder he favored his Young Barry and expected much of him. He also owned a male, Tell, a short-coated

41

dog, that, unfortunately in his old age, was suffering from facial atrophy. Besides these two studs Dr. Kuenzli occasionally used some stock of the old Hospice dog. It seemed, however, that the producing ability of Tell and Young Barry was not too good, as was usual with these two studs; only after three generations were satisfactory results noticeable. It was his aim to breed a large dog that combined a well balanced body with the desired height. Dogs of this type were owned by breeders Egger and Schumacher. He also tried matings with the Ivo strain but he did not achieve satisfactory results.

While Young Barry's offspring developed slowly, those sired by Tell showed much beauty at an early age. The Barry strain was distinguished by a shape that seemed to be pressed together at the sides. These dogs also showed extensive black markings which gave them a somewhat dark appearance. They had wide chests and well proportioned flanks. Outstanding dogs of the Young Barry strain were Orsino, Jenatsch I and II, Olaf, Garibaldi; outstanding females were the excellent Hero v. Hirslanden and Silva-Mehlem.

Tell's progeny showed a beautiful expression and lovely colors. They had broad bodies and their coat, especially on the hindquarters, had a tendency to curl. They carried their tails high. There are Kondor (doubtless the best one), Kean I and II, Grossglockner, Young Tell, and Willy Wood, that deserve mentioning as Tell's offspring. Ilse was one of the best brood bitches produced by Tell. Bello and Bella, two of Dr. Kuenzli's dogs, won first prizes at the Basel Dog Show in 1884.

Many difficulties and sad experiences were encountered during the latter years of Dr. Kuenzli's work. His stock of approximately 70 to 80 St. Bernards, which he boarded out at neighboring farms, had been greatly reduced as some of his best dogs had been poisoned. This fact caused him almost to discontinue his work, but nevertheless, he remains one of the most outstanding breeders in the history

One of the Monastery dogs, that saved many people from
the danger of snow and ice

of the St. Bernard and today receives the recognition he so duly deserves.

During the same period (1873-1904) there was another great breeder in Switzerland, Major Bloesch, at Biel, who bred for a new type of St. Bernards with imported English stock. He succeeded in improving the head in size as well as in expression. This point had been neglected by the English breeders. Young Marquis, Marquis I, and Hektor II v. Biel, were some of his best dogs. Marquis I, however, lacked in cheeks, a fact by which his English ancestry could be determined. The two other dogs showed the Swiss influence. Other outstanding dogs of his kennel were Lady Bloesch, Hektor I and Hektor II, Juno, Irma, Apollo, Herkules, Nero and Jung Bob of Biel. Several of them were sold in foreign countries for remarkable prices.

Of considerable influence in the background of many good St. Bernards was Ivo. He resulted from a mating of Leon, owned jointly by Grossrat Siegmund and Mr. Bauer, to Belline, owned by Mr. Duer at Burgdorf. Little is known of Leon's ancestors but apparently there is some Mastiff blood in his background. Ivo was a large dog with excellent colors, and a well wrinkled dark head gave him a good expression. His muzzle was well shaped without hanging jaws. His hindquarters were high and well built. Mated to his mother, Belline (later Champion "Sans Peur"), he produced the male Hektor v. Basel (later called Krupp's Hektor). This dog was sold in Germany, and even though he was not too frequently used as a stud, he had considerable influence on St. Bernards in Germany. Many offspring resulted from breedings to Ivo and it is impossible to mention all of them. Interesting is the fact that Ivo's brother, Rasco I, and his sisters, Flora and Lola Altels, developed into outstanding dogs. Flora won her championship in America.

Interested in breeding a better type of the old Hospice dog were Mrs. Deichman, wife of a Geheimrat at Cologne and later at Vaduz, Liechtenstein; Mr. Steiner at Arth;

44

Mr. Bubat at Hirslanden; Mr. Neumaier at Zuerich; and Mr. Kohler-Grueter at Basel. Mrs. Deichman owned Lola II and later obtained the stud Pluto directly from the Hospice. Matings of these two resulted in many a good St. Bernard. Later her kennel was sold to Mr. Bubat. In 1904 it was owned by Mr. Goerin-Gerber at Hirslanden.

Good dogs of the Hospice type that were outstanding at their time were bred by Mr. Carl Steiner at Arth. From his kennel Pluto v. Arth, Young Pluto v. Arth, Bergman v. Arth, and Berry v. Arth (later Viktor Plavia) have been top dogs.

Another breeder who deserves much credit for improving the Hospice dog was Mr. Neumaier of Zuerich. In 1877 he owned Flora, a female 31 to 32 inches high. The eighties seemed to be particularly favorable years for this breeder. Mars, a male, was born in 1889; and later in the same year he obtained Hektor from Mr. Bubat's kennel. Through Hektor, Mr. Neumaier's kennel received its first Hospice stock as Hektor's ancestors were Pluto and Juno Deichman. Also in 1889 he obtained from the monastery, Jupiter and Bellona. Jupiter was an excellent sire and among his progeny we find the well known Jupiter von Solothurn and Pluto Jupiter. Mr. Neumaier, however, soon realized that too much Hospice blood produced high and straight hindquarters as well as excessive white markings and uneven markings on the head (half-sided). By using Barry Fischertal he was able to outbreed these faults and then bred good dogs like Mars III and Hektor III.

Mr. Kohler-Grueter at Basel was another breeder who considered the monastery dogs the best type of St. Bernards. He tried to continue breeding in that line, and Rhyn and Barry v. Gundeldingen are to be mentioned as typical of his kennel.

John Bailey photo

W. Ernst and W. Staehli, officials of the Highland woodcarvers craft union in Brienz, Switzerland, place the date of this carving at somewhere between 1850 and 1890, judging from the carving style. They say there were several carvers doing "St. Bernhard" dogs during that time, among more than two thousand carvers working in Brienz. The number is now about four hundred.

This family of Saints is depicted in a single block of wood, 36 inches long, 18 wide, and 13 high. The figures are carved in full round, a task which must have required many hundreds of hours. All anatomical details are accurate, therefore it is assumed that the artist worked accurately to scale. By present-day standards, the mother is small in relation to the size of her pups. Muzzle shape would seem to be earlier than the 1894 painting shown on page 52, but the puppies' body shape and leg action does not seem to have changed much in a century.

The carving, still in excellent preservation, was rescued from the attic of a curio shop by Saint fancier Charles Sorenson, of Hull, Mass.

46

St. Bernards in Switzerland to Mid-century

UDGING by its dog shows, kennels and dog publications, Switzerland is one of the most dog-friendly nations. Swiss breeders refer to the strict kennel system, which is operated in many other countries on principles similar to that of a zoo, as "dogs' concentration camps." Swiss dog shows are always well organized and even though their preference is the home-bred dog, many foreign entries are accepted at the shows. Unfortunately, Swiss dog breeding, particularly of the larger breeds, has not remained untouched by the war. However, with initiative and optimism Swiss breeders quickly overcame the difficulties of that time.

While the activities of some St. Bernard Clubs in Switzerland are known to be somewhat limited, individual breeders industriously and seriously follow their breeding programs. One of the most popular St. Bernard kennels,

Von Lotten, was founded in 1925 and is owned by Mr. Otto Steiner at Muhen, Aargau. Medusa v.d. Birch, a long haired female, was purchased at the age of six weeks by Mr. Steiner. No information on her background or breeder could be obtained. She proved to be an international success in her first year and when bred passed on her excellent qualities to her progeny. It was Mr. Steiner's policy to eliminate inferior puppies at birth and thus he was able to follow his aim of raising well balanced, strong bodied dogs, that developed a good gait, had well formed heads, a noble expression and good colors. Meta von Lotten combined all these excellent qualities and was considered the ideal St. Bernard. Besides her faultless appearance she was a good watch dog and had a most faithful disposition. At international dog shows at Den Haag, Freiburg im Breisgau, Strassburg, Muehlhausen, Zuerich, Bern and Basel, she won first prizes, and at Frankfurt-am-Main she received the title "World Champion." Her breeder, Mr. Steiner, was honored with the title of "World Champion Breeder." Meta's offspring were sold in Germany, Netherlands, America, Italy, France, North Africa, etc., and, like their famous mother, won many an international first prize. Jupiter, a Meta son, was entered at the Chicago World Dog Show.

Today's proven brood bitch at the Lotten Kennels is Gita von Oenz, a daughter of Ch. Erga-Oenz, 94631 (mother of the smooth coated Ch. Figaro-Oenz and the American Ch. Gero-Oenz). Gita's mother, Erga-Oenz, was a powerfully built female with strong bones, a deep chest, a good body, excellent angulation and a kind expression. Gita has inherited all of her mother's good qualities and is credited with several wins at international shows. The fact that she has a slightly arched back and is somewhat lacking in height, does not harm her excellent reputation as a brood bitch and she is considered a most valuable asset to the Lotten Kennels.

Famous among the Swiss St. Bernard Kennels is Zwing-Uri, owned by Mr. Charles Sigrist at Flüelen. Conveniently located to trains from all directions and at one of Switzerland's most romantic spots, the Lake of Lucerne, the kennel attracts many tourists. During the 27 years of its existence Zwing-Uri has produced a number of good dogs, many of which were exported to England and the U. S. A., as well as to Netherlands, Belgium, Italy and France. Horsa v. Zwing-Uri was sold in America where in the course of winning his championship he won a "Best of Breed" over 16 competitors, and a "Best of the Working Group." One of the best dogs owned by Zwing-Uri is Olif, by Nero v. Zwing-Uri, out of Alma v. Zwing-Uri. Olif recently spent three months in France where he participated in the film, "Barry." In order to inject some new blood into his stock, Mr. Sigrist imported two St. Bernards from Germany.

Besides its fine dogs we believe that the unique setting of the kennels deserves mentioning. The kennel buildings resemble the typical Swiss frame structures and are decorated with the Coat of Arms of the Uri Canton. The buildings are located atop a rose-covered cliff, and the most amusing event of each day takes place when the serious-faced puppies climb up the steps to their houses at night. The tree-shaded kennel grounds with a small body of water provide an ideal place for the dogs.

Other St. Bernard kennels in Switzerland today are: Von Rigi, Von Sood, and Von Immenberg.

At the 1949 International Dog Show, "Excellent," "First Prize," and "Champion" title were awarded to the following St. Bernards:

Figaro-Oenz (1680), male, long haired
Erga-Oenz (94631), female, long haired
Clodina v. Schwanen (98381), female, smooth.

At the 1950 International Dog Show held at Langenthal, Switzerland, first prizes and champion titles were awarded to:

Asco v.d. Pfaelzerhuette (16311), male, long haired

Erga-Oenz (94631), female, long haired
Freier-Oenz (1681), male, smooth
Madi v. Immenberg (14049), female, smooth.

The 213 St. Bernards registered in 1948, compared with 104 registered the previous year, are an indication that this breed is gaining popularity and that the future for Swiss St. Bernard breeders is bright and promising.

The President of all the dog clubs in Switzerland reports that in 1951 the Saint Bernard Club in Switzerland had 115 members and that each year approximately two hundred puppies are registered. The smooth coated variety outnumbers the long haired and enjoys greater popularity.

During the years since this chapter was written, a cordial relationship through Saint Bernards has grown between Switzerland and the North American continent. With the latter offering wide interest and wide markets, and the former offering excellent examples of the breed, it is not surprising that a mutually profitable exchange of interest now exists.

Space does not permit a listing of the many fine dogs brought from Switzerland in recent years. Most recent imports to North America have been through the offices of Eduard Rodel, Ottenbach, Zurich, Switzerland, who operates the Sauliamt Kennels, and also acts as a bi-continental agent between the many active breeders in Switzerland and the many interested importers in North America.

The Swiss Saint and the American Saint have become very much alike. American families who acquire Saints from Switzerland find no difficulty in recognizing the appearance and habits of their imports. They discover only one major problem; that the new members of their families must be taught to speak English.

The Swiss government is interested in maintaining the excellence of Saint Bernards, as a source of national pride. Much of this work is being done at the Monastery, with the help of the Breeders Association, whose secretary is Hans Zimmerli, of Langenthal, Switzerland. Mr. Zimmerli, one of the fancy's most respected breeders, has sent many fine Saints to North America.

FIGARO VON SAULIAMT, whelped June 15, 1959, breeder, Eduard Rodel. A big, impressive rough-coat with excellent movement, Figaro became the top winning Saint Bernard in Europe. Among a long list of titles appear best-in-shows in five countries, plus the coveted Best Dog in Italy. Figaro was brought to North Attleboro, Mass., early in 1963, by William Sweet and Donald Dube. Mrs. Dube is the handler in this picture.

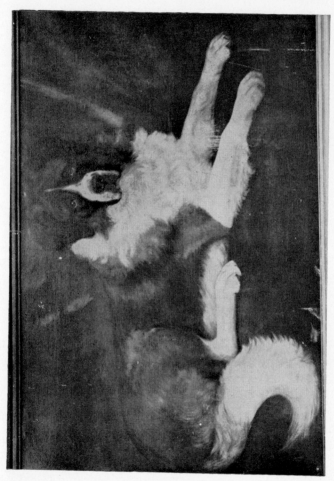

This oil painting, done in 1894, hangs in the living room of the Donald Dube home. It would seem to demonstrate that as far as the better Saint Bernards are concerned, there has not been too much change since that time. A present-day judge might say only that this dog's muzzle was a little narrow and his ears set a little too high.

St. Bernards in Germany

With research by Gerda Umlauff

ERMAN breeders had been interested in this breed several decades before the Special Club for St. Bernards was founded at Munich in 1891. More than seventy years ago these dogs were frequently referred to as "Alpenhunde." A dog magazine published in 1882, tells of considerable difficulties that were encountered by breeders at that time, among them the impossibility of tracing the ancestry of stud dogs, the lack of sufficient funds to carry on good breeding programs, and the spiteful way in which St. Bernard breeders were referred to as "Specialty Breeders" who used inferior and inbred material which they sold as St. Bernard for the sake of financial gain.

Soon, however, even those in strong opposition recognized the excellent qualities of the St. Bernard as a companion and watchdog. He was considered to be particularly useful as a companion dog to theologians on their lone walks and, because of his pleasant temperament, seemed much better qualified for this type of work than the Great Dane.

Instrumental in the inauguration of the St. Bernard in Germany were three breeders: Dr. Caster of Winkle/ Rheingau (also a breeder of Great Danes) ; Prince Albrecht of Solms and Braunfels-an-der-Lahn; and the retired Premier Lieutenant Fink of Berlin. Even though the number of dogs at that time owned by these three breeders did not exceed twelve, they deserve much credit for the promotion of the breed in Germany.

Prince Albrecht's Wolfsmuehle Kennel was one of the largest on the continent. His first import was Courage, an almost faultless male, who was later used as the model in setting up the standard for his breed in Germany. He placed first at the 1878 Berlin Show as well as in four other shows held in the Netherlands and England in 1880. Well beyond his prime he was awarded another prize at a Hannover show a few years later. A truly great show dog, his stud career seemed somewhat limited. He is known to have been bred to only a few bitches and his get was of poor quality. No records are available on his ancestors. Courage stood 35½ inches high and weighed 140 pounds; his forehead measured 28.8 inches. He was of the smooth variety and slightly feathered only on legs and neck. Contrary to the much preferred white markings on a dark basic color, Courage was of a grayish-white color and showed yellow markings.

Bred and owned by the Prince of Solms were also the males Gessler, Courage II (a Courage son out of Hedwig), and Courage III (a Courage II son out of Alp), and the females Bernina II and Hospiz, while the females Alp and Berna II had been imported from Switzerland. Exemplifying the law of alternate inheritance Courage III, at the age of 15 months, showed a strong resemblance to his famous grandsire, Courage. Even though he lacked Courage's height, he was a powerfully built dog of excel-

GONNY V.D. EILSHORST 16370
Bred and owned in Germany

ZENO VOM GROSSGLOCKNER 12767
Long haired German Saint Bernard

lent appearance. Matings of Berna II to Courage II resulted in remarkably good offspring. There were two litters in which the puppies resembled each other almost identically, all of them having equally good markings and perfect colors, broad, expressive heads, and well developed, powerful bodies. At a Kleve Show, the Kennel Club of Aarburg showed two litters out of Bernina (a litter sister to Berna II) by a stud of the Wolfsmuehle Kennels. (The stud's name is not mentioned here and it is known only that the same dog was later sold to Switzerland.) Several of the Wolfsmuehle dogs were sold in Switzerland, as good stud dogs had become scarce there.

While English breeders were able to exhibit some good St. Bernards at that time, Germany showed only specimens of the long haired variety. The smooth coated type was hardly represented. Among the questions pertaining to the standard of the St. Bernard was the one as to whether a reddish-brown nose was acceptable. Mr. Hartenstein, a well-known breeder, imported a female from Interlaken, Switzerland, and bred her to two different studs. Each of the two litters showed the reddish-brown coloring of the nose and even though the puppies were good in many other points, Mr. Hartenstein decided to eliminate them. (The color of the nose was at that time not mentioned in the standard but received recognition at a later time.)

According to Dr. Caster, none of the large breeds at that time were in as much a state of decline as was the St. Bernard. In his opinion there was not one St. Bernard in Germany that came up to the standard, and he did not expect the available mediocre dogs to be good producers. Referring to British St. Bernards, he stressed the large number of beautiful dogs entered in the shows and the fact that British breeders had for some time been using only the very best stock, for which they paid enormous prices. It was Dr. Carter's suggestion that a Club or several interested fanciers join in the purchase of an outstanding female which was to be bred to one of the best studs in England and the resulting offspring then would constitute a fine breeding stock for Germany. Dr. Caster based his advice to import British St. Bernards on the fact that many of the long haired St. Bernards imported from Switzerland were beautiful in appearance but seldom the result of good breeding and in most cases of poorest heredity.

At the 1882 Hannover All Breed Dog Show, 36 dogs were entered as long haired St. Bernards—"Alpenhunde." In addition to these, several Newfoundlands of untraceable ancestry were put in the same group. Of these approximately 40 dogs, nine males and three females, received prizes. However, only six of them were considered purebred St. Bernards. The others resembled the Alpenhunde or some equally large breed. The presentation of prizes to these dogs met with considerable astonishment and disapproval on the part of the breeders and promoters of the purebred St. Bernard. The large, long haired dogs were known as "Leonbergers" and their ancestry could easily be traced to several different large half-breeds. Some of these dogs, which were raised chiefly in Wuerttemberg, had impressive, powerful bodies, but it was quite obvious that there had been no St. Bernards in their background. For several years consistent efforts had been made to eliminate this type of dog, and we can understand the anger and disappointment of the serious breeders when these mongrels received prizes at a show and were classed as St. Bernards. Foul play was suspected, but the judge, an Englishman, insisted that he was in no way involved in any disreputable actions.

First Prize at the Hannover Show was awarded to Cadwallader, a large male of excellent color and strong bone. Particularly impressive were his mighty head and the well proportioned muzzle, but also his fine reddish color and the white markings. Gessler, a male owned by the Prince of Solms, placed second. He showed gray markings on a white basic color and had a beautiful large head and a noble expression.

Two more Wolfsmuehle dogs were entered in the show

but they did not place. They showed the results of excellent grooming, but incorrect carriage of their tails disqualified them. Courage III was entered but was faulted on account of his narrow forehead, his somewhat pointed nose and lack of stop. His father, Courage II, also did not place at this show. This seemed somewhat unusual, as Courage II was indeed a good dog; and even though his head lacked broadness, it was much better than that of his son Courage III.

Showgoers were most favorably impressed by the smooth coated St. Bernards for these seemed to be well behaved dogs of a kind disposition. Because of these qual-

Shorthaired and Longhaired St. Bernards, Germany

HECTOR V. BASEL	BRUTUS
v. Barry 'a. Gemmi 1889	v. Young Barry a. Irma 1888
Breeder: B. Siegmund-Basel	Breeder: Dr. Künzli-St. Gallen
Owner: Krupp-Essen	Owner: A. Lasz-Fuskirchen

ALTONA'S ALF 13923

CHAMPION GISA V. LUDWIGSTEIN 16952

Gisa received Champion title and "excellent" first prize at Munich
in 1948, at Mannheim in October 1948, "excellent" first prize
and Mannheim, May 1949, "excellent" first prize

59

ities they desired to help the St. Bernard gain more popularity, and it was felt that they soon would constitute a serious competition for the Great Dane.

The average of the St. Bernards shown at Hannover in 1882 left much to be desired, particularly as far as gait and hindquarters were concerned. Careful selection of breeding material and the necessity of physical exercise for young dogs were stressed in an effort to improve the breed. It was known that at the same time the average Swiss St. Bernard was of much better quality.

During the years following the Hannover Show, more breeders became interested in St. Bernards and started breeding programs with good stock. They willingly paid high stud fees for the best foreign studs and also invested considerable money in importations. Besides the Prince of Solms, who later imported the male Barry Braunfels from Switzerland and several other St. Bernards from England, Mr. Hartenstein of Plauen enlarged his kennel through imports. In 1884 in the Rhone Valley he purchased Rocher, an excellent stud; and later he imported from Switzerland Finette II, Fels, Phaedra, Prinz v. Burgdorf, Torone, Tamina, Victor Plavia, Jungfrau, and Grossglockner. Prinz v. Burgdorf was considered the most outstanding of all these importations. Unfortunately, only a few years later the Hartenstein Kennel ceased to exist, as did also the Wolfsmuehle Kennel upon the death of Prince of Solms in 1901.

Other breeders carried on the work. Of them we know Dr. Calaminus of Langendiebach, Mr. Probst and Mr. Pingerra, both of Munich. Mr. Pingerra imported from Switzerland Rawyl v. Atburg (SHSB 16), Watzmann, Pilatus, Beresina, Belisar (16), Queen (287) and several others. However, he seemed to have little success in raising good dogs. As St. Bernards were much in demand at that time, he apparently tried to breed for quantity rather than quality and started crossing his St. Bernard stock with long haired mongrels. This was a grave and unforgivable mistake. While the St. Bernard ancestry was still distinguishable in the first few litters, the mongrel blood soon predominated. Fortunately, the St. Bernard Club came into existence at that time and made the continuation of this type of breeding impossible.

One of the oldest and most successful St. Bernard breeders was Mr. G. Schmidtbauer of Munich, who imported from Switzerland Herakles (31), Saentis, Barry (49), a half brother to Krupp's Hektor (29), Berna, Troja (146), Priest (218), Meta II (615), and Barry Frauenfeld (213), and with these dogs founded his famous kennel, Munichia. Isis, a female by Krupp's Hektor out of Queen, and Troja, were the kennel's best brood bitches. Isis was later sold to Dr. Zeppenfeld and mated to Young Meder. While Isis was a typical descendant of the Ivo strain, Young Meder was the result of a most fortunate mixture of English and Swiss blood. The best offspring produced by Isis and Young Meder was Othello. For a long time the Munichia kennel held the first place among the St. Bernard breeders in Germany. Its dogs, the famous Ch. of Munichia Lord (842), Ch. Munichia Pierette (1593), Munichia Ivo (1302), Munichia Rival (2266), Munichia Sparta (279), have laid the foundation for the St. Bernard breeding in Germany and are found in nearly all of today's German pedigrees.

Dr. Toelle, at Muehlheim/Baden, was another German breeder of good St. Bernards. He owned Peter v. Muehlheim, Gesserl, Tell-Pirna and Bello-Kalk, all belonging to the same litter out of Turka by Grossglockner. One of Dr. Toelle's famous dogs, the smooth coated Bergmann, died of injuries received in a dog fight with Peter v. Muehlheim.

Other well known breeders of that time were the painter R. F. Curry of Munich; Bubat of Mehlem; Guerteler of Munich; Kohn of Ravensburg and later of Augsburg; Boppel of Canstatt, and Max Naether of Munich. Famous dogs like Wodans Rasko (1409), Wodans Barry (1091)— one of the greatest St. Bernards that ever lived—Wodan v. Schwabing (701), Wodans Saturn (1969), Wodans

People ask, "How big are they when born?" SANCTUARY WOODS SO BIG
and one of her recent whelp, NOT SO BIG, attempt to answer this question. Picture taken at their home in Drain, Oregon.

Stella (2982), Wodans Heidi (3019), came from the Wodans Kennels owned by Mr. Naether. All of these fine dogs resulted from well planned matings between the Hospiz, Deppeler, Munichia and Herkules v. Bern strains.

Not to be forgotten as one of the popular kennels at that time is the Urach Kennel, owned by Mr. Kempel. It seems that incorrect pedigrees interfered very unfavorably with Mr. Kempel's carefully planned breeding program, and he had to overcome many discouraging experiences before he established his kennel's bloodline. He was particularly interested in obtaining dogs with a good disposition, a goal which he finally achieved. Some of his best dogs were Athos, Tell, Ch. Barry Urach, and the females Flora v. Basel, her daughter Gemma, Blanka Urach (dam of Barry Urach) and Norma Urach (a Rosette daughter), which later produced the famous champions Wotan v. Elberfeld and Ada v. Plankstadt. After twenty years of breeding, Mr. Kempel, in an effort to revive the old Hospice strain, purchased the male Jupiter (Sire: Tuerk, Dam: Liaune) from the Hospice.

Of the ladies interested in breeding St. Bernards we know Mrs. Johanna Nickau, wife of a brewery owner; Mrs. Deichmann of Mehlem; the Countess Larisch of Munich; and Baroness v. Moll at Villa Lagarina in Austria. Mrs. Nickau's kennel was located at Gohlis near Leipzig and besides St. Bernards she raised some toy breeds. Other breeders of that time were the gentlemen: Bostelmann of Meckelfeld, Fehn of Erlangen, Groos of Wiesbaden, Hoffmann of Hannover, Krause of Dresden, Landfried of Obergerlachsheim, Latz of Euskirchen, Probst of Munich, Teufel of Tuttlingen, Wachendorf of Steglitz, and the Austrian breeders Schinle of Meran and Puch and Seidler of Graz.

Famous St. Bernards at the end of the 19th Century were Barry v. Goeppingen II (452), Barry Saulgau I (152), Barry Saulgau II (465) and Barry Canstatt.

At that time several breeders in Netherlands endeavored to breed good St. Bernards. We know of Mr. Steensma,

Dr. Lange and Mr. P. Attema, who purchased their stock from Swiss and German kennels and produced a number of fine dogs which, in turn, at a later time, were bought by German breeders of the Rheinland.

The first *St. Bernard Stud Book* published in Germany in 1894 contained 301 registrations, 175 smooth coated and 126 long haired St. Bernards. These figures prove that the St. Bernard, hardly known in Germany a few years back, now had become the most popular of the large breeds. In fact, the St. Bernard outranked the Great Dane. Also listed in the 1894 *Stud Book* are the purpose and aims of the St. Bernard Club which primarily deal with the improvement of type, body, size, color and markings.

Many a famous kennel was founded before the close of the 19th Century, with Bavaria taking the lead over Baden, Wuerttemberg and Northern Germany. To mention a few of these kennels, there were Von Moeckern, Von Kronental, Von Dessau, Von Langenstein, Von Duesseldorf, and Von Altona. Still in existence today, the Altona Kennels are considered the oldest St. Bernard kennels in Germany.

The Guetsch Kennels, owned by Mr. Mannuss at Lucerne, were founded in Switzerland at that time, and with the importation of the stud Rigi von Dessau, Mr. Mannuss intended to bring some new blood into his stock. The majority of the Swiss breeders resented this transaction, but the fact remains that the Guetsch kennels produced famous St. Bernards.

Outstanding stud dogs in Southern Germany at that time were the litter brothers Ch. Troubadour v. Duesseldorf (1397) and Barry v. Fuerth (1324).

In the minutes of the monthly meetings of the Verein der Hundefreunde (Association of Dog Lovers) reference is made to the most common faults of the St. Bernard of that time. Apparently, most of the dogs were too light in muzzle, lacked broadness of the head, carried their tails incorrectly and were generally too small and too long in body. The St. Bernard Club tried in many ways to educate its members and assist them in raising better dogs. Mr. Boppel, who in his long experience as a judge had obtained extensive knowledge of this breed, sketched and published the four different types of head that appeared most frequently around 1905.

From 1906 to 1909 some of the best St. Bernards shown were Prinz v. Stadtilm (2249), Ch. Argos v.d. Hammerburg (2269), Ch. Wola v. Stadtilm (2248), Ch. Prinz v. Goeppingen (2782), Ch. Barry v. Goeppingen (2350), Pyrrhus v. Lauben-Urach (2728), Lola v. Bernhardinerheim (2351), Ch. Thalattas Iduna (2569) and Ch. Nonne v. Fuerstenfeld (2085). German breeders deserve much credit for improving the St. Bernard in type and body. Their untiring efforts were rewarded when finally German St. Bernards had achieved the same degree of perfection as those in Switzerland. Of course, they encountered many reverses during World War I when the breeding of St. Bernards almost came to a standstill. Lack of food during the war years necessitated the elimination of a large number of dogs and only the very best specimens were kept alive. Compared to the 800 studbook entries from 1912 to 1914, the number of dogs registered from October 1914 to February 1922 seems alarmingly small. In this eight-year period only 202 litters (a total of 1,108 puppies) and 217 single dogs were registered.

All such discouraging experiences did not keep Mr. Ludwig Kasten from continuing his work toward improving the St. Bernard. Mr. Kasten who had founded his Altona Kennels in 1897, was one of the most successful breeders in Germany and was appointed judge by the St. Bernard Club in 1909. As the size of the St. Bernard in Northern Germany after World War I left much to be desired, Mr. Kasten began his search for a large stud dog with which he intended to accomplish some improvements. After numerous efforts he finally located in Bavaria Ch. Xenos v. Taubertal (9715), by Ch. Kavalier v. Grossglockner (7741) out of Ch. Leda v. Taubertal (8040). However, at first his offers to buy the dog were refused, and only his persistent efforts and several trips to Bavaria finally made the purchase of the dog possible. Ch. Xenos' influence on St. Bernards in Northern Germany was remarkable, and he brought the breed to new heights. Many of his off-spring won champion titles—to mention only Ch. Greif v.d. Helenenburg, Ch. Gretel v.d. Helenenburg, Ch. Nelson v. Falkenstein, and Ch. Dieter v. Norden who later was sold in Southern Germany. After Xenos' death, Mr. Kasten leased for two months Ch. Aegir v.d. Scheerenburg who, like Xenos, was a Ch. Kavalier v. Grossglockner son. Aegir sired the male Altona's Alf (13923), a fine dog that won many an "excellent" at the shows but unfortunately was poisoned and died at an early age. One of the fine qualities of Mr. Kasten's dogs was their kind disposition. As an example of Xenos' good disposition Mr. Kasten relates the following incident: One night he was awakened by the furious barking of Xenos. Looking outside for the cause of the disturbance, he saw his pet cat trapped. When the cat was freed, Xenos immediately took him to his dog-house and licked his little playmate's injured leg.

Another well known kennel in Northern Germany was Mr. Zillinger's Von Falkenstein, founded in 1909. His stock consisted of the imported bitch Toja Guetsch (43406), and the stud Ch. Theo's Minka v. Falkenstein (3396). Matings of these two produced a number of famous St. Bernards, among others Ch. Wanda v. Falkenstein (3582) and Ch. Kora v. Falkenstein (10493) who won her champion-ship in 1933. After the 1935 World Dog Show at Frank-furt, a Dutch specialist, Mr. de la Rie, wrote in the *Swiss Dog Magazine* that the success of the German St. Bernards would have been much greater if the long haired dogs of Mr. Zillinger had been half a year older. He said: "These young dogs have been the greatest surprise at the show and I am convinced that Mr. Zillinger will be very suc-cessful in the future. It must have been a great honor for him that at this show, where breeders from Germany, Switzerland, Austria, France and Netherlands met, all con-gratulated him." Mr. Zillinger died in 1943, and at present

Very much at home on old newspapers in the back room is CH. CARMEN SHOW GIRL OF OX YOKE, proving herself a family dog in more ways than one. Bred by Rita Holmes and Margaret Myers, and owned by Mary Lou and Donald Dube, Champion Show Girl is also something of a champion mother, with fifty-four living and healthy puppies in five litters.

all that is left of the Falkenstein Kennels lives in the memory of Mr. Zillinger's children who well remember the times when they rode to school in a small cart which was drawn by one of the St. Bernards. However, it seems that the Falkenstein Kennels will experience a renaissance, because one of Mr. Zillinger's grandsons has the desire to become a breeder of fine St. Bernards and will no doubt do so after he has finished school.

Founded shortly before the outbreak of World War I was the Grossglockner Kennel, owned by Mr. H. Glockner, at that time president of the German St. Bernard Club. In 1914 Mr. Glockner purchased the stud Rigi v. Hessen (4565), by Ch. Tangua v. Rheinland (31315) out of Ch. Rene v. St. Michael (3300). Rigi later won his championship. Outstanding males of the Grossglockner Kennel were Armin v. Grossglockner (5041) who later sired the famous Ch. Bernd v. Mitterfels (6031); Art v. Grossglockner (5031); Baer v. Grossglockner (5105), a Rigi son; Dumar v. Grossglockner (5683); Ch. Kavalier v. Grossglockner (7741); and Rasco v. Grossglockner (10310). Mr. Glockner preferred to keep not more than twelve dogs at a time at his kennel as he liked to observe them individually and remain in close contact with them. Not too many of his dogs were seen in the show ring, as his frequent assignments as judge prevented him from entering his own dogs. One of the outstanding dogs of the Grossglockner Kennel after World War I was the smooth coated Wito v. Grossglockner (12457), whelped in 1932 and sired by the famous Ch. Fritz Drei Lilien (9782), whose ancestry can be traced back to the Swiss Ch. Emir Jura (SHSB 15532), Susi v. Grossglockner (10625), Kavalier v. Grossglockner (7741) and Jutta v. Grossglockner (6989), thus carrying the strain of Ch. Bernd v. Mitterfels (6031) and Baer v. Grossglockner (5105). The long haired male Zeno v. Grossglockner (12767) was another fine stud dog. He resulted from a mating of the famous Eros Guetsch (SHSB 32205), an

Emir Jura (SHSB 15532) son out of Netti Deppeler (SHSB 27623), to Ulla v. Grossglockner, a Jutta v. Grossglockner daughter. In 1934 a repeated breeding of Eros Guetsch and Ulla v. Grossglockner produced some excellent smooth haired Saints.

Other kennels which started their breeding programs before the war and continued during and after the war were Von Alsatia, Von Freudenfels, Von Asyl, Von Rheinland, Von Elberfeld, Von Crimmittschau, Von der Vorstadt, Vom Taubertal, Von den Drei Lilien, Von Eistobel, etc. Ch. Tangua v. Rheinland (3135), Ch. Castor v. Freudenfels (6653), Ch. Tasso I v. Freudenfels (5147), Ch. Rigi v. Hessen (4565), Ch. Estor v. Taubertal (5424), Ch. Bernd v. Mitterfels (6031), and Ch. Elmire v. Rheinland (3140), were some of the excellent dogs produced by these kennels. There were many admirers for these dogs, particularly from Switzerland and other foreign countries. A Swiss dog magazine admitted that the German St. Bernards exhibited at the Munich Show in 1926 were of much better quality than those available in Switzerland at the same time. Top stud dogs of the year 1923 were Samson v. Eistobel (4772), Barry Jura (5195), Arth v. Grossglockner (5032), Barry v. Memmingerberg (5026).

Northern and Southern Germany were in friendly competition with each other in raising the better dogs, and in 1925 Northern Germany took the lead with fine dogs like Argos v.d. Blattgoldstadt, Arno v. Helenenburg, Goswin v.d. Waldau and Minka v.d. Kollauburg.

In 1934, the fortieth year of its existence, seventeen volumes of the *St. Bernard Stud Book* had been published. A total of 13,200 Saints had been registered up to that time and 1,124 kennel names had been granted. With a total of 313 dogs shown during 1934, St. Bernards ranked in tenth position among the popular breeds. The 1,200 St. Bernards listed in Volume 17 of the *Stud Book* consisted of 940 long haired and 260 smooth haired dogs. Breeders expressed the desire to breed more smooth coated dogs in the future.

Also listed in the *Stud Book* are 11 stud dogs that had been used on five or more occasions during a two-year period. They are:

Ch. Fritz v. Drei Lilien (9782)
Arth v.d. Scherenburg (9830)
Rasko v. Grossglockner (10310)
Baldo v. Wiesental (9917)
Ch. Abs v. Gruenau (10406)
Armin v. Ranshofen (10590)
Falk v. Hemphorn (10670)
Henze Margothof (11135)
Iseg Margothof (11237)
Ch. Nero v. Uhlenhorst (12039)
Ingo v. Rigi (13052)

Falk (10670) and Nero (12039), both of Swiss parentage, were credited with the largest number of breedings. Fritz (9782) also had some Swiss blood in his background as his sire was the famous Ch. Emir Jura. Ingo (13052) was a Swiss importation.

The breed profited greatly from a decision of the St. Bernard Club which set the minimum age for a stud dog at two years and that of a brood bitch at 20 months. Two regulations released by the St. Bernard Club at a later date contributed much to the improvement of the breed. One of them limited the use of a brood bitch to once a year and the other limited to six the number of puppies to be raised in one litter. Not more than six puppies of a litter were eligible for registration in the *Stud Book*.

Seventy-nine St. Bernards were entered at the 1935 World Dog Show at Frankfurt-am-Main. This shows a considerable increase compared with 12 entries at Hamburg in 1869, and 42 entries in 1876. The largest number of entries ever recorded was 157 in 1907 at Munich. At the Frankfurt show in 1935 the German breed St. Bernards were of such excellent quality that only the best and fully matured Swiss dogs were able to compete against them. Sixty-one long haired and eighteen short coated dogs were entered.

70

The Nazis, in 1937 at the height of their success and dominating everything, tried to interfere with the breeding of St. Bernards. *Das Schwarze Korps,* a publication of the SS, attempted to convince German readers of the undesirable characteristics of the St. Bernard. They called attention to the shape of the St. Bernard's head and eyes as an indication of viciousness and at one time printed an article according to which a girl had been torn to pieces by a vicious St. Bernard that had then to be shot. The Nazis also prohibited the awarding of the titles Club Champion and International Champion (CACIB). The latter still cannot be obtained in Germany. At the beginning of World War II the Nazis planned to train St. Bernards as rescue and first aid dogs for Alpine units. The St. Bernard appealed to them for this purpose, as he combines a strong body and a good gait with the capability of endurance.

In this connection it may be mentioned that St. Bernards have been useful and reliable as seeing-eye dogs. One blind person had over a period of years owned various breeds of dogs and finally found in the St. Bernard the quiet, unexcitable, reliable dog fit for this type of duty. Another blind person who had previously owned a German Shepherd dog, purchased an eight-months-old St. Bernard which he, with the assistance of his Shepherd, trained as a guide dog. After a short training period the St. Bernard proved that his intelligence and ability were far superior to that of the German Shepherd and he never lost his tranquillity and kindness. As a salesman, the owner of this dog travelled extensively, and this placed a difficult task on his guide dog. However, the dog adjusted himself to new surroundings amazingly fast and was able on the first visit to a new city to lead his master safely back to the railroad station upon his request.

Unfortunately, World War II did much harm to the breeding of good St. Bernards in Germany. In 1939 only 172 were registered and 224 in 1941. However, the demand for reliable companion and watch dogs continued to

71

exist, and German breeders attempted to continue their breeding programs even though lack of food and other hardships inflicted by the war made it almost impossible. As money was practically worthless during that time, the dogs were bartered for food and other useful articles. The demand for purebred dogs did not cease to exist until June 1948 when the new German currency became effective. It was then lack of money that made the purchase of good dogs impossible.

From March 1944 to December 1946, 145 litters with a total of 646 puppies were registered. Forty-three of these litters consisted of at least 10 or more puppies. Baerbel v. Birkenberg (447) no doubt set the record with a litter of 20 puppies. She had previously whelped litters of 15, 18 and 17.

According to the *Stud Book,* the following numbers of litters were registered:

Name of Kennel	Number of Litters
Von Hannoverland	44
Von Bismarckturm	28
Von Lehnitzsee	27
Von Werdenfels	25
Von der Koenigsmuehle	21
Total	145

Four sires share in 90 (62 percent) of these litters with a total of 407 single registrations. They are:

Sire	Number of Litters
Ch. Dieter v. Norden (14502)	14
Omen v. Hemphorn (15375)	22
Ch. Kuno v. Sonneberg VKV 324	23*
Jochem v. Lautrach (13974)	11

*Bred in Czechoslovakia.

Other successful stud dogs were Cuno v. Ludwigstein
(15432), Boto v. Bismarckturm (15701), Dieter v. Bismarckturm (16135), a Cuno son, Page v. Hemphorn
(15814), Czar v.d. Falkenhoehe (16328), Pluto v. Sonne-
berg (17157), Lord v. Lautrach (15387), Kuno v. Werden-
fels (16423), Drusus v. Willkamm (15319) and Guenther
v. Kottmar (15369).

It was no doubt a remarkable achievement that was accomplished by the German breeders during those war
years as shortages of all kinds complicated their work to
a large extent. In 1945 the old name of St. Bernard Club
was restored after the Nazis had changed it to "Fach-
schaft fuer Bernhardiner." The Club has now 500 members, and close to 2,500 Saints have been registered since
1945.

These siblings began their lives in Germany, 1959, sired by Sieger Roy
von Neu Hepsburg, out of Celine von Morgenrot, and bred by Esther
Wurtenburger, of Rheinfelden Baden. As seen from left to right, Boris
von Salmegg went to France, Brita went to England, where she produced champion sons, Bill went to Switzerland, and Basko went to owner
Winifred Martin, of Roanoke, Illinois. For a later picture of Basko, and
his progeny, turn the page.

In 1965, CH. BASKO VON SALMEGG, late of Germany and now of Illinois, won the stud dog class at the national specialty.

Here are two more generations. CH. PRAIRIEACRES ROX V. ZWING BASKO, two years old, son of his German-born father and owned by Harold Ryburn, of Heyworth, Illinois, watches over grandson Thriller v. Rox, five months. You will note that the family strain is quite obvious.

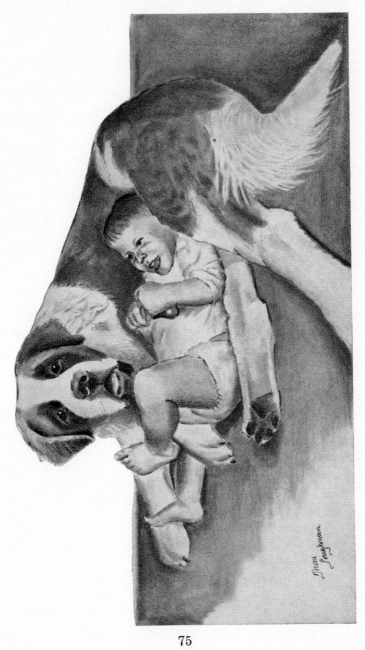

INTERNATIONAL CHAMPION (SIEGER) EMIR v. JURA
Born November 10, 1922
(S.H.S.B. 15,532)

Parents	G. Parents	G.G. Parents
Sire **Cuno v. Jura** (S.H.S.B. 10,341)	s Fleck—(Cardinaux) d Bella—(Waldvogel)	(Third generation names not available in America.)
Dam **Freya v. Leberberg** (S.H.S.B. 10,510)	s Rasco—Riesbach d Belline v. Leberberg	

Rough-Coated St. Bernard—Male

CHAMPION BERNA v.d. LUEG-WALDECK

Born October 30, 1931

(S.H.S.B. 45,779—A.K.C. 867,319

Parents	G. Parents	G.G. Parents
Sire **Bayard v. Riesbach** (S.H.S.B. 25,573)	s Sieger Emir v. Jura	s Cuno v. Jura d Freya v. Leberberg
	d Berna v. Schloss Blidegg	s Tristan v. Rafz d Wanda-Oenz
Dam **Freya v. Bergbruennli** (S.H.S.B. 35,149)	s Sieger Rasko v.d. Reppisch-Waldeck	s Sieger Emir v. Jura d Gerda—(Winzeler)
	d Berna—(Gruber)	s Bayard—Zytglogge d Dora—(Gruber)

Rough-Coated St. Bernard—Female

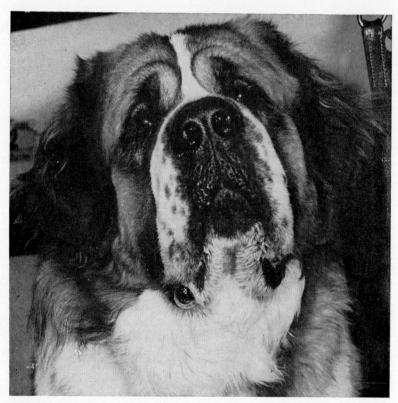

This is how a Saint looks when he is worried about why you are lying down. View from the floor submitted by Paul Wallbank, treasurer of the SBCA. The dog, sired by his Ch. Barre von Stanislaus, is KNAB-LAW'S FELIX VON BARRE.

St. Bernards in England

THE first St. Bernards, which were imported in Britain in the early part of the nineteenth century, were somewhat odd looking specimens. In 1815, Mrs. Boode of Leasowe Castle, near Birkenhead, imported a male, Lion, and a bitch (name unknown). Little else is known of Lion except the fact that he and two of his offspring so attracted the famous painter, Landseer, that he begged permission to paint them.

According to specialists, English breeders imported Swiss dogs with the intention of improving their English Mastiffs. However, they soon began to raise pure St. Bernards which, apparently, were quite a different type from the original Swiss dogs. One of the reasons for this difference in appearance was that the British preferred an almost self-colored fawn which to some extent resembled a Mastiff. The Swiss, being somewhat shrewd businessmen,

79

ST. BERNARD AND HIS DOG
This beautiful stained glass window in Feltham Church, Middlesex,
England, shows St. Bernard of Menthon and one
of his famous dogs

80

Arno v.d. Lohnmatt 58484

imported Mastiffs and crossed them with mongrels. The resulting half-breeds were well paid for by Englishmen and so were the red and fawn colored St. Bernards which did not appeal to the Swiss breeders. The British, however, became dissatisfied with these medium-sized imported St. Bernards and started breeding their own. They bred for large dogs and aimed for the much desired red color.

This newly created type differed in size and color as well as shape of head from the Swiss dogs. They had narrow noses with little push-up and not too well defined stops; their cheeks were less pronounced and even though their heads were well wrinkled, they lacked the typical St. Bernard expression. This fact is attributed to possible crossings with Bloodhounds. In more recent years, both Swiss and English breeders prefer the Swiss type and aim to breed large-sized dogs with good colors.

Mr. Albert Smith is said to have owned some Hospice dogs, but no pedigrees are available to support this statement. Imports of significance were Mr. Macdona's Tell (later Monarque) and Mr. Stone's Barry, who later appears in many of the best English bloodlines, among them that of Plinlimmon. Studs of equal ability were Mr. Charles Isham's Leo, once owned by Mr. Egger, and Mr. Gresham's Abbess. Some of the first British breeders were Mr. J. C. Macdona, Mr. Murchinson, Mr. Gresham and Rev. Arthur Carter. Outstanding St. Bernards, which were also well known on the continent, were Plinlimmon, Bayard and Sir Bedivere.

The appellation "St. Bernard" was adopted in 1862 when some of the imported dogs were exhibited at a Birmingham show. Up to that time they had been identified as "Alpine Mastiffs" or "Alpine Spaniels." (Major Hamilton Smith, 1827.) In the middle of the last century the size and beauty of the St. Bernard captured the fancy of many an exhibitor and within twenty years this breed claimed first place in popularity. Together with Collies they were responsible for inaugurating an era of high prices. According to a newspaper notice in 1880, a Sheffield dog,

Rector, had been sold in America for £300 which, at that time, was a considerable amount of money. However, this amount was completely dwarfed a few years later when Sir Bedivere was purchased by two Americans for £1,300. Sir Bedivere weighed well over 200 pounds and measured 33½ inches at the shoulder.

Further study of the St. Bernard history in England reveals that at the 1891 Charles Cruft Show (the first one open to all breeds) 34 competitors were entered in the Novice Class, 23 in Open Dogs, and 20 in Open Bitches. Soon after this show, however, St. Bernards began to deteriorate in quality as well as in number. Only the Bowdon Kennels, owned by Messrs. Inman and Walmsley, continued their breeding program. Referring to them, popular dog writer A. Smith is quoted as saying, "It is believed that these breeders introduced a Mastiff cross; but whatever they did, there is no doubt that they bred St. Bernards with remarkable consistency, and their dogs were noted for their soundness as well as type. It was a serious blow when their kennels were broken up, and the breed never recovered." Mr. Smith also stated that in more recent years Mrs. Staines of Abbots Pass Kennels at Leigh, near Reigate, established a kennel which was considered a model of its kind. The kennel buildings were among the best in the country and her dogs were noted for size and quality. Mrs. Staines imported several dogs from Switzerland which were expected to be of considerable influence on succeeding generations. Dogs of Mrs. Staines' kennel soon became a familiar sight at the shows and were distinguished by their size and nobility of expression.

The official standard for the St. Bernard in Great Britain is as follows:

The HEAD should be large and massive, the circumference of the skull being rather more than double the length of the head from nose to occiput. The muzzle is short, full in front of the eye and square at the nose end. The cheeks are flat and there is great depth from eye to lower jaw. The lips are deep, but not too pendulous. The stop is somewhat abrupt and well defined. The skull is broad, slightly rounded at the top and has a somewhat prominent brow. The whole effect should be to give an expression betokening benevolence, dignity and intelligence. The ears are of medium size, lying close to the cheeks and not too heavily feathered. The eyes are rather small, deep set and dark in color. They should not be too close together and the lower eyelid droops so as to show a fair amount of haw.

The CHEST is wide and deep, the back broad and straight, the ribs well rounded, the loin wide and very muscular.

The FORELEGS should be perfectly straight, strong of bone and good of length; the HINDLEGS heavy in bone with hocks well bent and thighs muscular.

As for SIZE, the taller the better, provided symmetry is maintained. They should have great substance and the general outline should suggest power and capability of endurance.

In the long haired variety the COAT should be dense and flat, rather full around the neck, thighs well feathered.

COLORS may be orange, mahogany brindle, red brindle, or white with patches on body of either of the above colors. Importance is attached to the manner in which the markings are distributed.

Puppies from the Kennel "v. Zwing-Uri"

INTERNATIONAL CHAMPION (SIEGER) RASKO v.d. REPPISCH-WALDECK

Born December 12, 1927

(S.H.S.B. 29,106—A.K.C. 867,315)

Parents	G. Parents	G.G. Parents
Sire **Sieger Emir v. Jura** (S.H.S.B. 15,532)	s Cuno v. Jura	s Fleck—(Cardinaux) d Bella—(Waldvogel)
	d Freya v. Leberberg	s Rasco—Riesbach d Belline v. Leberberg
Dam **Gerda (Winzeler)** (S.H.S.B. 18,322)	s Tristan v. Rafz	s Barry—Oenz d Freya—Neuhof
	d Diana—(Bachmann)	s Stolz—Gutsch d Berna—Alt Mars

Rough-Coated St. Bernard—Male

85

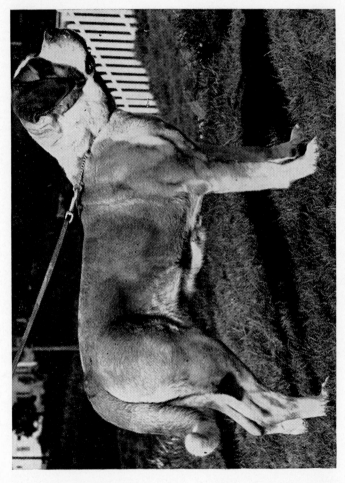

BELLINA VOM RIGIBUHL (smooth coated bitch)
Sire: Astor v. Reitnau (Helios v. Grafensteiner x Edith v. Bauerheim)
Dam: Ella v. Rigi (Sieger Emir v.d. Lohnmatt x Siegerin Berna v. Rigi)
Breeder: Willy Geschwind   Owners: Mr. and Mrs. Lars Lind

86

CHAMPION GERO-OENZ VON EDELWEISS (rough coated dog)
Sire: Sieger Emir v. Melina (Erco v.d. Lohnmatt
x Siegerin Belline v. Emmenschachen)
Dam: Siegerin Erga-Oenz (Sieger Faust v. Zwing-Uri
x Belline v. Ringgeli)
Breeder: Alfred Wuthrich   Owner: J. H. Fleischli, Edelweiss Kennels

87

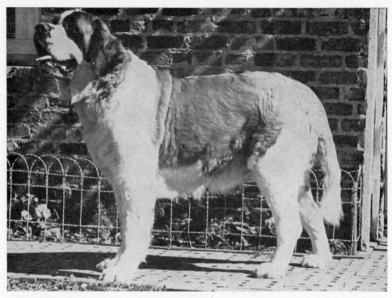

CHAMPION HELDA V. ALPINE PLATEAU (rough coated bitch)
Sire: Ch. Felix v. Alpine Plateau   Dam: Jung Frau v. Luthy
       Breeder: A. F. Hayes   Owner: Mr. Hugh Wood

CH. PELDATOR MARCUS, owned and bred in the 1960's by Mrs. R. L. Walker, president of the United St. Bernard Club of England. The English have been fond of large Saints. Marcus, photographed at three years, stands over 36 inches at the shoulder and weighs 230 pounds. Many of his offspring have been brought to the United States.

Early American Breeders

THE first St. Bernard to be registered in the National American Kennel Club, whose stud books were later taken over by the American Kennel Club, was CHIEF, a smooth coated male, owned by Mr. A. V. de Goicowria, New York City; Breeder, Mr. J. P. Haines, Toms River, New Jersey; whelped May 12, 1879; orange, tawny and white; by Harold, out of Judy; Harold by Sultan III, out of Dido II; Judy by Chamounix, out of Alphe.

In this same stud book the rough coated dog, Hermit, the rough coated bitch, Nun and the smooth coated bitches, Alma, Brunhild and Chartreuse, all owned by Miss Anna H. Whitney, Lancaster, Massachusetts, were registered.

Hector seems to be a popular name during the early years of the stud book. Volumes III, IV and V of the stud book were issued quarterly and in the last quarter of Volume V, Hector I, 11851 appears, owned by James Dunne, of

Brooklyn, New York; breeder, Colonel White, Long Branch, New Jersey; whelped April 26, 1887; tawny and white, black facings; by Neptune out of Nellie. From then on we have a series of "Hectors" until we reach Champion Hector, a smooth coated dog, whelped February 20, 1894, A.K.C. 4425. This dog played a prominent part in the bloodlines of the early St. Bernards. He was bred by Henry Schumacher, Berne, Switzerland, and imported by Mr. K. E. Hopf of the Hospice Kennels, of Arlington, New Jersey. His height at the shoulders was 30½ inches.

In criticism, Mason states that the head was well formed but would be still better if wider; muzzle also of good formation and could only be improved by having more width; ears correct in size, shape, position and carriage; eyes well set and exactly the right color; stop excellent; expression most pleasing indicative of dignity, courage and good nature combined; neck muscular and of ample length; shoulders well placed; chest truly formed in every direction; loin firm and nicely arched; hindquarters well set and supported by rare good legs and feet; hocks clean, strong and well bent; elbows not very well placed; legs straight and strong; feet of the very best kind; coat could not be better; his stud fee was $100.

Writing in the American Dog Book, published in 1891, Mr. F. E. Lamb tells us, and we quote: "The development of St. Bernard interests in America has been remarkably rapid during the past ten years, and is illustrative of that enterprising spirit and that marked liberality with which Americans always engage in any work that enlists their sympathy. As illustrative of the magnitude of this movement, it is only necessary to state that at the New York show of 1890 the St. Bernard entries numbered 151; at the Chicago show of the same year, they numbered 58; at Boston, 59; and at all the other shows the entries in this breed more than doubled in number those of any previous year.

The total investments in St. Bernards in this country then ran into millions of dollars, and some of the choicest blood of European breeding within a few years found its way into American kennels.

The following have been listed as among the many breeders and owners of St. Bernards in America:

Alta Kennels, Toledo, Ohio; American St. Bernard Kennels, Tomah, Wisconsin; Acme Kennels, Milwaukee, Wisconsin; H. R. Anderson, New York City; J. C. Anderson, Chattanooga, Tennessee; Alpine Kennels, New York City; C. W. Bickford, Boston Tavern, Boston, Massachusetts; Thomas Burke, Bridgeport, Connecticut; Charles T. Barney, New York City; Contoocook Kennels, Peterborough, New Hampshire; Chequasset Kennels, Lancaster, Mass.; A. Russell Crowell, Boston, Mass.; Cook Kennels, Detroit, Mich.; Dr. P. A. Dennison, Brooklyn, N. Y.; W. S. Diffendeffer, Baltimore, Md.; Lorenzo Daniels, Mont Clair, N. J.; Erminie Kennels, Mount Vernon, N. Y.; Elmwood Kennels, South Farmington, Mass.; George H. Eddy, Boston, Mass.; W. T. Fraser, Detroit, Mich.; Ed. H. Greiner, Buffalo, N. Y.; Halfway Brook Kennels, Glens Falls, N. Y.; Hospice Kennels, Arlington, N. J.; W. R. Huntington, Cleveland, Ohio; Mrs. H. Hughes, Joliet, Ill.; P. L. Hanscom, Oak Park, Ill.; J. C. Hobart, Chicago, Ill.; James F. Hall, Philadelphia, Pa.; Iroquois Kennels, Tonawanda, N. Y.; W. A. Joeckel, Jr., Hoboken, N. J.; John Kervan, Brooklyn, N. Y.; L. T. Kinney, Grand Rapids, Mich.; Eugene Kelmel, Boston, Mass.; Keystone Kennels, Pittsburgh, Pa.; Dr. C. A. Lougest, Jersey City, N. J.; J. B. Lewis, Belleville, Ohio; E. H. Moore, Melrose, Mass.; John Marshall, Troy, N. Y.; James Mortimer, Babylon, L. I., N. Y.; Meadowthorpe Kennels, Lexington, Ky.; Daniel Mann, New York City; Mrs. J. M. Nicholson, Albany, N. Y.; Namquoit Kennels, Boston, Mass.; Oakhurst Kennels, Chicago, Ill.; Prof. W. F. Osborne, Princeton, N. J.; Poag Kennels, Toledo, Ohio; Peninsular Kennels, Chelsea, Mich.; E. S. Pinney, Farwell House, Chicago, Ill.; A. F. Putney, Boston, Mass.; H. S. Pitkin, Hartford, Conn.; E. A. Rockwood, Buffalo, N. Y.; E. B. Sears, Melrose, Mass.; R. J. Sawyer, Menominee, Mich.; St. Gothard Kennels, Orange, N. J.; Mrs. E. E. Teague, South Farmington, Mass.; Dr.

Robert Taylor, Mount Vernon, N. Y.; Trojan Kennels, Troy, N. Y.; Otto W. Volger, Buffalo, N. Y.; John G. Venn, Chicago, Ill.; John Van Velsor, Buffalo, N. Y.; Charles G. Wheelock, Arlington Heights, Mass.; G. P. Wiggin, Lawrence, Mass.; E. H. Willson, Jordan, N. Y.; Wentworth Kennels, Utica, N. Y.; Woodbrook Kennels, Baltimore, Md.

The special characteristics of the St. Bernard are his immense size, his powerful muscular organization, his great frame, deep and broad chest, his massive head and spacious brain-pan, his heavy coat, his courage, his unswerving devotion to his human and canine friends, his kind, benevolent disposition, his sagacity and his aversion to or disregard of the attentions of strangers. Several specimens of this breed have reached a height of thirty-four inches or more at the shoulder, and a weight of two hundred pounds or over. Plinlimmon is thirty-five inches high, Sir Bedivere and Watch are each more than thirty-four inches, and many others are over thirty-three inches.

Volumes could be filled with anecdotes and incidents of the remarkable instinct, the superior judgment, the almost human intellect, of the St. Bernard. The heroic services rendered by these dogs in rescuing and aiding snowbound travelers in the Swiss Alps are too well known to require further mention here. Hundreds of instances occurring in our own country could be cited had we the space for them. As showing the steadfast devotion of the St. Bernard for his friends, I may recall the case of a boy who was drowned in a lake in New York while skating. The body of the grand old St. Bernard dog who had been the constant companion of the boy was found at the bottom of the lake, near that of his young master, and the indications pointed plainly to the fact that the boy having broken through the ice, the dog had gone to his aid, had caught him and tried to pull him out; that the ice had broken and the dog had fallen in. Then he had released his hold, climbed out on the ice, seized his master and tried again to drag him out, but again the ice had broken. These struggles had been repeated again and again until the noble brute, exhausted by his efforts, had sunk and died by the side of his young friend.

Mr. G. W. Patterson, writing of a St. Bernard bitch that he had formerly owned, says:

"My little girl was enjoying a slide last winter, back of my house, and Sylvia was accompanying her down the hill by running alongside. When she reached the bottom of the hill, the little girl held out the rope, saying: 'Here, Sylvia, you must draw me back up the hill' and although the dog had had no training, and was only eight months old, she performed the task admirably, if not as quickly as she did afterward. Carrie never took a slide after that without having Sylvia with her to draw her back up the hill. I never could tell which enjoyed it most—both growing strong under the influence of bracing air and exercise."

It has been claimed by some of the opponents of the St. Bernard that he is dull of comprehension and difficult to train. My experience and observation teach me that such is by no means the case. I have known many St. Bernards that have been trained to perform some truly wonderful tricks, errands, and services, and that with as little time and labor as would have been necessary to train the brightest Spaniel to do the same work. Col. C. A. Swineford, of Baraboo, Wisconsin, had a St. Bernard that would at his bidding, stand on his hind feet, place his fore feet on the office railing, and walk from one end to the other of it in this position. Then, at command, he would place his hind feet on the railing, and with his fore feet on the floor, repeat the operation.

He would place his hind feet on a barrel, and standing with his fore feet on the floor, roll it back and forth across the floor. His master could send him with a note or package to any house or office where he had ever been, and the dog would return promptly with the answer. A few hours had been sufficient in which to teach the dog either of these tricks.

The St. Bernard is one of the most useful and valuable of all breeds as a watch-dog. While not vicious or savage, he is

BEAU - GESTE

Born January 18, 1928

(A.K.C. 650,034)

Parents	G. Parents	G.G. Parents
Sire **Emir v. Altachen** (A.K.C. 558,368) (S.H.S.B. 22,528)	s Dino v. Jura	s Cuno v. Jura d Kamilla v. Eistobel
	d Dana v. Sprengelbach	s Barry Oenz d Kathi v. Olten
Dam **Alma Gutsch** (A.K.C. 567,058) (S.H.S.B. 23,043)	s Pascha v. Drei Lillien	s Grunda v. Drei Lillien d Barry v. Grossglockner
	d Jung Stella Gutsch	s Monch Michel Gutsch d Stella v. Eistobel

Rough-Coated St. Bernard—Male

94

alert, courageous, faithful, sagacious, and his great size renders him an object of dread to wrong-doers. Few men would care to disturb property of which he had charge. Besides being an excellent guardian for children, he is also an affectionate and patient companion for them. He may not romp or run with them, but will, if harnessed and hitched to a toy wagon, draw them as faithfully and patiently as an old horse. He will allow them to ride him, wool him, or impose on his good nature in almost any way they may choose, and never resent or object. Many of the noble qualities of the race are illustrated in the case of SAVE, a noted St. Bernard formerly owned in England, of which a contributor to the *American Field* wrote as follows:

"Mr. J. F. Smith mourns the loss of a dear friend and most faithful companion. This was Champion Save (E. 10626), one of the most notable St. Bernards ever seen. He was bred by Rev. G. A. Sneyd, being by Othman (E. 6422)—Hedwig. He was born in March, 1879, and was the only survivor of a litter of fifteen. It was on this account that he was called Save. In color and markings he was admittedly the handsomest dog ever shown here. His strength was such that he would carry his master with ease, although he weighed fourteen stone, and no two men could hold him with a chain or slip, if anyone whom he knew called him. Yet he was so gentle that the smallest child could do anything with him. He was very fond of the company of ladies, among whom he was known as Gentleman Save. He was also passionately fond of children, and delighted in their company. For some years a cot has been maintained in the Children's Hospital, at Sheffield, solely by money collected by Save, who always carried a small cask attached to his collar. He used to go to the hospital twice a year, in January and July, to pay in his contributions, and his visits were looked for eagerly by the little ones, as all that were well enough in the ward which contained the 'Save Cot' had a ride on his back.

"He died calmly and painlessly on July third, and this grand old dog is sincerely mourned by his late owner and his family, as well as by all the children of Sheffield and many of their parents. Probably no other dog had so wide a popularity, for his portrait, first published in 1882, afterward figured in almost every illustrated journal; and the story of his life, his strength, his intelligence, his docility, and his love for children, has been told hundreds of times."

The St. Bernard has frequently been utilized as a retriever, and it is believed by many that with proper training he would excel in this class of work. A writer in the *Kennel Gazette* gives interesting and valuable testimony on this point.

He says: "I had just put together my belongings preparatory to starting for Scotland in the evening. My friend with whom I was staying had kindly promised that during my absence he would take care of a valuable St. Bernard bitch (sister to Plinlimmon) which had recently been given to me, and, as though conscious of our impending parting, Midge, who had become greatly attached to me, lay at my feet, from time to time casting upward such beseeching glances as only our affectionate dumb pets are capable of. As the afternoon wore on, and during the early evening, the dog closely followed my every movement, almost appearing to ask that she might accompany me, until at the last moment I decided to take her.

"The first outburst of cordial greeting which welcomed me as I drove up to the house of my friend was somewhat toned down upon the appearance of my pet. I saw at once I had brought a visitor by no means popular in a sporting establishment, but trusted that time might make matters smooth; nor was I mistaken, for the dog's very looks soon worked wonders. Days went happily by, and with Midge for my companion, I rambled by the river, rod in hand, she upon occasion leaving me to flog some pet stream while she took small hunting excursions on her own account. I noticed on several occasions that she became wondrous keen at the sound of a gun, and found one had only to raise a gun to one's shoulder to put her at once upon the alert.

"One day I had gone up to a loch for a day's trouting, and while I was thus occupied two friends went to the upper end of it in quest of ducks. It was with some difficulty that I prevented Midge from following them, and later on her uneasiness at the sound of each shot and her efforts to jump over the side of the boat gave rise to such anathemas as might well have sunk a less sturdy craft. After some time we were nearing the spot where the shooters were, and when we got to within some three or four hundred yards of them a duck was duly brought down, at sight of which Midge broke away from me, swam to the bird, a considerable distance, retrieved it in perfect form, without disturbing a feather.

"Later in the day other chances presented themselves, the results being always satisfactory, and especially so in one or two instances where a less powerful dog would have been utterly unequal to making his way through the thick reeds and sedge. Now, to me it seems that with very little training these really well-bred St. Bernards might be most useful in the field in such situations as I have mentioned, and over heavy, marshy ground, and I send the above account, not desiring to claim more for them than they deserve, but to meet the assertions many people make that these large dogs are treacherous and useless pets to have about a place. I may, in conclusion, say that to her other accomplishments Midge adds that of poacher-hunting, having on one occasion knocked down and held a man until the keeper with whom she had gone out on the quest came up; and the prisoner was only too glad to surrender his arms and accouterments on condition of the dog being called off, though she had not bitten him, but had merely held him down by the moral persuasion of a pair of heavy paws and an ominous growl when he attempted to move."

FOUR-BELLS GOYA, 6 months old male
Sire: Four Bells Darig   Dam: Debbie v. Ridgewood
Owner: Walter E. Tartar, Jr., 3½ years old

The Saint Bernard in America to Mid-century

by Mrs. Henry H. Hubble

I SHALL attempt in this chapter to give a brief outline of the history of the Saint Bernard in America. I shall point out the high lights of the Saint Bernard Club of America's activities since its origin, mention briefly some of the most outstanding bloodlines of the past, and lastly and most important, discuss some of the more outstanding dogs of today together with their bloodlines and who owns them.

Introduction to America

The exact origin of the Saint Bernard fancy in America is not known. We do know, however, that some time around 1880 the Saint Bernard or a large dog called by that name was introduced to American theater audiences.

Founding of Breed Club

The later 1880's, namely 1887 and 1888, were very important years for the Saint Bernard breed in both this country and Europe. It was in June, 1887, in Zurich, Switzerland, that the international congress was held to establish a standard for the Saint Bernard breed. The Swiss standard of the breed was adopted and called the International Standard.

In the year 1888, a group of Americans met and organized the Saint Bernard Club of America. On February 22 of that year, they adopted the International Standard established by the Zurich congress to govern the breed in this country. It should be noted that all countries except England accepted the International Standard.

As one might expect, the above conditions established the basis for a great and long continued controversy in this country because the adopted standard was not compatible with the then more prominent in America, English type Saint Bernard. However, at that time most of the American owners were content with the English type dog, since the majority of their dogs had come from England. We know that the original club was still operating in the year 1892 because in May of that year a small booklet containing the adopted standard, constitution and by-laws of the club as well as the membership roster was published. In this publication 68 members were listed.

The officers and governors of the club at that time were as follows: W. H. Joeckel, Jr., Bloomfield, N. J., president; Miss Anna H. Whitney, Lancaster, Mass.; R. J. Sawyer, Menominee, Mich., and Jacob Ruppert, Jr., New York, N. Y., vice presidents; E. B. Sears, Melrose, Mass., treasurer; and J. C. Thurston, New York, N. Y., secretary.

Other governors were:

William C. Rieck, New York, N. Y.; R. T. Rennie, Newark, N. J.; W. A. Wells, Brooklyn, N. Y.; E. H. Moore, Melrose, Mass.; B. P. Johnson, New York, N. Y.; K. E. Hopf, Arlington, N. J.; W. H. Walbridge, Peterborough, N. H.; Otto W. Volger, Buffalo, N. Y.; and I. A. Sibley, address unknown.

BARRY VON DEHNHOFF
Year old female, from Imported Swiss Stock
Sire: Hannibal Von Norell   Dam: Gretchen Von Ludwigstein
Owner: Walter E. Tartar, Sr., Seattle, Washington

Nothing more is heard of the club until December 30, 1897, when ten men journeyed to Grand Rapids, Michigan, to organize another Saint Bernard Club of America. The meeting was held in the office of Dudley E. Waters, who from that time until his death on January 19, 1931, served as secretary-treasurer of the Club.

The minutes of this Grand Rapids session make no mention of any previous Saint Bernard Club of America, but the constitution and by-laws adopted were substantially the same as those drawn up by the original club. Again, the International Standard was approved and adopted, and a new slate of officers and governors elected. The new club started off with a charter membership of 58.

Col. Jacob Ruppert, Jr., was elected president and Mr. Waters was named secretary-treasurer. The ten men who attended this second organization meeting were George P. Savage, Spring Lake, Mich.; W. S. Hall, Grand Rapids; R. L. Hills, New York, N. Y.; B. C. Cobb, Grand Rapids; W. G. McKennan, Sioux Falls, S. D.; Nat. Robbins, Grand Haven, Mich.; W. O. Hughart, Jr., Grand Rapids; Mr. Waters, A. W. Hine and Fred McCarthy, all of Grand Rapids.

Following secretary-treasurer Waters' death in 1931, Mr. M. T. Vanden Bosch of Grand Rapids acted in his place and assisted in the re-organization of the Saint Bernard Club of America for the second time in its history.

In March of 1932 Mr. Joseph T. Mulray of New Town Square, Pennsylvania, and Mr. Leroy E. Fess of Williamsville, N. Y., served as the re-organization battery in the capacity of president and secretary-treasurer, respectively. The re-organized officers were in charge of the Club's affairs to February 13, 1933, when the first meeting was held at the Hotel Victoria, New York City. The Club then began to function in the "mail-order basis." In the New York meeting the officers and governors of the Club were elected and took office. The Saint Bernard Club of America again took its seat among the American Kennel Club's big family of specialty clubs.

STOYIL OF BLISS FARMS and her five-month old son Rabutin, at the home of owner R. W. Wilson, in Old Westbury, N. Y.

Platnick photos

Three age groups wait for a handout at the Bliss Farms kitchen window.

The officers and governors elected in the New York meeting were as follows: President, Joseph H. Fleischli, Springfield, Ill.; Vice Presidents, Paul R. Forbriger, William Gartner, Paul G. Tilenius, all of Brooklyn, N. Y.; Secretary-Treasurer, Mrs. Eleanor J. Dalton, Stamford, Conn.; Governors, Eleanor Cavanagh, Eleanor J. Dalton, Joseph H. Fleischli, Paul R. Forbriger, Alice H. French, William Gartner, Arthur Hesser, Agnes Kemp, Joseph T. Mulray, Robert Nicholson, Jessyn S. Robinson, Paul G. Tilenius, Leo C. Urlaub, Gottlieb Zulliger.

The Saint Bernard Club of America had been inactive for a long period between the years 1897 and 1932, during which time the breed was greatly degenerated. This degeneration was due primarily to the fact that there was no organized effort to maintain and improve the quality of the breed in this country, and many of the dogs were bred by "dog dealers" instead of by persons having a full knowledge of the breed or having its best interest at heart.

About the time of the re-organization of the Club in 1932, and shortly prior to that date, several Saint Bernard fanciers in the United States imported Swiss and German bred Saint Bernards. These dogs were then used for breeding purposes, and a revitalization of the breed was started.

Breed Progress 1932-1945

I should like to mention a few of the outstanding dogs which were used in the comeback for the breed. These individuals are the basis for the bloodlines which were most prominent in the United States in the late 1930's and up to 1945. Prominent among the Saint Bernard Dogs imported after World War I, listed in chronological order, are the following:

Kavalier vom Grossglockner	rough German Champion
Nanni Deppeler	rough Swiss bitch
Barry von Oschwand	rough Swiss dog
Pluto von Altachen	rough Swiss dog
Tasso von Goppingen	rough German dog

FRANZI v. EDELWEISS

Born December 6, 1931

(A.K.C. 820,479)

Parents	G. Parents	G.G. Parents
Sire Ch. Barry v. Oschwand (A.K.C. 619,022)	s Barry v. Waldrand	s Sieger Emir v. Jura d Seline—(Ursenbacher)
	d Belline—Oesch	s Hektor v. Worblenthal d Belline v. Neuenegg
Dam Betty v. Edelweiss (A.K.C. 787,325)	s Ajax v. Alt-Heidelberg	s Arco v. Dreimaderlhaus d Dassy v. Freudenfels
	d Kyra v. Taubertal	s Ch. Bernd v. Mitterfels d Franzi v. Taubertal

St. Bernard (Smooth)—Female

Lola vom Rigi	smooth Swiss bitch
Rasko v.d. Reppisch	rough Swiss Sieger and international Champion
Berna v.d. Lueg	rough Swiss bitch
Dora Belmont	rough Swiss bitch
Odschi von Margothof	rough German bitch
Varus vom Grossglockner	rough German dog
Nero von Multenrain	rough Swiss dog
Tell von Lotten	rough Swiss dog
Rigo vom Rigi	smooth Swiss dog
Palace vom Rigi	smooth Swiss bitch
Vallo vom Rigi	smooth Swiss Sieger
Porthos von Falkenstein	rough German dog
Cid von Eiger	rough Swiss dog
Doldi vom Grossglockner	rough German dog
Esbo vom Grossglockner	rough German dog
Apollo von Rougang	rough Swiss Sieger
Armin v.d. Teck	smooth German dog

As individual specimens, most of the dogs imported were of good type and were able to contribute a great deal to the build-up of a more correct American Saint Bernard.

Importance of Smooth Breeding Stock

Most of the above individuals listed, as you will note, were rough coated. By examination of their pedigrees, one will find that all of those which are of an outstanding character and quality had a considerable amount of smooth blood in their immediate pedigrees. This is a very, very important factor in the continued breeding of the correct-type Saint Bernard, and has been recognized as a primary law of breeding by the noted authorities of Switzerland and Germany for many, many years. As one might expect, therefore, the continued breeding of rough to rough dogs resulted in a gradual degeneration of type. It was necessary from time to time to have importation of new primary stock from Switzerland or Germany, which had been developed from the breeding practices using some

CHAMPION GERD V.D. LUEG V. EDELWEISS (smooth coated dog)
Sire: Elmar v.d. Lueg   Dam: Bella v. Ringgeli
Breeder: Ernest Grossenbacher
Owner: Mr. J. H. Fleischli, Edelweiss Kennels

CHAMPION QUESTOR V. ALPINE PLATEAU (smooth coated dog)
Sire: Barri v. Hutwill v. Alpine Plateau   Dam: Helda v. Alpine Plateau
Breeder: A. F. Hayes   Owners: Mr. and Mrs. A. C. Boicelli

smooth coated dogs. After the start of World War II it was impossible to import any new stock; therefore, the loss of correct type was somewhat accelerated during those years.

The phenomena back of the fact that type is lost so rapidly by continued breeding of only the rough coated dogs without any refreshment by the smooth individuals is not fully understood; but it is a proven fact, one that has been demonstrated repeatedly in England and America. Regardless of how carefully the selection of progeny is made, this loss of type does occur. It was therefore a very noteworthy event when soon after the cessation of hostilities in Europe American breeders started the importation of new blood. It was even more important for the benefit of the American Saint Bernard that many of these imports were of the smooth variety, because this meant that we then had available in the United States the important smooth coated strains for the continued revitalization of the breed.

The majority of the imports since 1945 have been smooth coated Saint Bernards. We have had both males and females brought to this country, which is a very important point because this makes it possible to breed the true smooth lines without any dilution of the bloodline. In the forthcoming portions of this chapter, I shall discuss the various individual dogs which have been imported and give present owners' names of these dogs for the benefit of those persons interested in using them for breeding or obtaining this stock. It is not enough that a few good dogs be imported and used for breeding with existing stock, but these imported dogs must be interbred in the correct manner if real progress as to individual specimen quality is to be made in this country. There are many cases where such breeding is being carried out today and the results are most excellent. In short, the American Saint Bernard has never been in a more favorable position than he is today. There are a considerable number of direct imports of the highest quality and a large number of American-bred progeny of these dogs which are exhibiting the fine qualities of their ancestors. The smooth coated variety has become well established in the eyes of the breed fanciers who are interested in showing and breeding, as well as in the eyes of the general public, many of whom had not seen the smooth variety in this country before 1946.

I do not want to make it appear that the rough coated Saint Bernard should be dropped, or should not be considered an important type dog; but if the rough dog is to attain the highest possible status, it is by the correct breeding of roughs with smooths to establish the desired medium.

Leading Saint Bernards in the United States

In discussing the dogs and the kennels of the United States, I shall discuss only the recently imported bloodlines and a few of their immediate offspring. These are, in my opinion, the bases for the American Saint Bernard of the future.

Discussion of various breeders and their dogs is arranged by geographical location, starting on the east coast of the United States and progressing westward.

East Coast Breeders

On the east coast we have some very fine dogs and some top quality breeding in progress today. The Sunny Slopes Kennels of Mr. and Mrs. Howard P. Parker, Webbs Hill Road, Stamford, Conn., have two of our most prized Swiss imports, Swiss Siegerin Fortuna vom Rigi and her brother Champion Falco vom Rigi C.D. Both of these smooth coated dogs came from the world-famous Swiss Rigi Kennels, owner Carl Steiner, representing the hospice type Saint Bernard. Fortuna vom Rigi won the much coveted Swiss Siegerin title at 18 months and is the only bitch ever to reach our shores having this, the highest Saint Bernard title of excellence.

These dogs have been used for breeding and each has produced excellent progeny. Mr. and Mrs. Parker have raised Saint Bernards for many years and their Sunny

IMA CONQUEST, smooth coated bitch, at 9 months
Sire: Ch. Questor v. Alpine Plateau
Dam: Ina v. Alpine Plateau
Breeder-Owner: Ernest J. Van Matre, Ima Kennels

CH. TERENCE OF SUNNY SLOPES, bred by Howard Parker
and owned by Mrs. Nancy Wright, of Darien, Conn.

Slopes Kennels contain many top quality Saints. Mrs. Parker has gained eminence in the field of obedience training of Saint Bernards. Dogs of her training have won several C.D. degrees and at least one C.D.X. degree in obedience trials.

Mr. Kurt Diedrich, R.F.D. No. 1, Allandale, N. J., is the owner of the beautiful smooth coated son of Falco vom Rigi, named Diedrich's Armin, whose dam is Bella v. Sabesi, a Swiss type smooth bitch.

Mr. Stanley H. Bussinger, owner of Highmont Kennels, 211 Ashland Avenue, Philadelphia 27, Pa., is the owner of two excellent imported smooth Saint Bernards, Minka v. Immenberg and Champion Major v. Neu-Habsburg. Major was imported by Mr. Frank Maxwell, Lake Stockholm, N. J., and is a son of Fata vom Rigi (litter sister of Fortuna vom Rigi owned by Mr. and Mrs. H. P. Parker) and Hector v. Zwing Uri. As an example of the excellent breeding being carried out in the East, Fortuna was bred to Major, this litter representing line breeding of the highest caliber. Minka v. Immenberg is sired by Hasso v. Zwing-Uri, litter brother of Hector v. Zwing-Uri. Minka's dam is Nelda v.d. Lohnmatt, whose sire is Hector v.d. Lohnmatt and is out of Belline (Schar).

Mr. Victor Bittermann, owner of Peekamoose Kennels, West Shokan, Ulster Co., N. Y., has imported a fine German bitch Katja v. Ludwigstein.

Midwest Breeders

In the midwest we have one of the oldest and most widely known kennels in the United States. The Edelweiss Kennels, owned by Mr. Joseph H. Fleischli, 1111 Lincoln Avenue, Springfield, Ill., was founded in the United States in 1894 by the late Franz Fleischli, native of Luzerne, Switzerland, and is now operated by his son, Joseph H. Fleischli, who has raised Saint Bernards since 1908. Mr. Fleischli has imported an imposing number of excellent Saint Bernards from Switzerland and Germany during the many years of

CHAMPION FALCO-OENZ V. ALPINE PLATEAU (rough coated dog)
Sire: Ch. Gerd v.d. Lueg   Dam: Siegerin Erga-Oenz
Breeder: Alfred Wuthrich   Owners: Mr. and Mrs. R. C. Elliott
The young ladies are the daughters of Mr. and Mrs. A. C. Boicelli

DUTCHESS OF FORTUNE, bred by Roy Gresham and owned by Phyllis Black, feeds the family in dappled shade on a New Jersey lawn. At extreme left, buried under his siblings, is TAG-ALONG WADE, who later went to school, below.

Tag-along went to school with owner Helen Morgan, of Sparta, N. J., and gave the kindergarten class a discussion on nature study. His remarks went over big. Miss Morgan, who has taught there for 39 years, finds that the school now bears her name.

operating his kennel. Recent Swiss imports which are presently owned by Mr. Fleischli are the outstanding Champion Gerd v.d. Lueg v. Edelweiss, winner of 17 Best in Shows, Champion Gero-Oenz v. Edelweiss, winner of 4 Best in Shows, Helma-Oenz v. Edelweiss and Bella v. Menzberg.

Bella v. Menzberg's sire is Champion Gerd v.d. Lueg v. Edelweiss out of Freya v. Emmenschachen, whose sire is Faro v. Schmidigen and out of Alma v. Bornfeld.

Gerd v.d. Lueg and Gero-Oenz are being used widely at stud and are contributing greatly to the improvement of the Saint Bernard breed in the United States. There are also several Swiss bred sons and daughters of Gerd which have been imported to this country.

Mr. Hubert Heilman, Route 1, Vermillion, Ohio, is the owner of Champion Aline v.d. Roth, an imported smooth daughter of Gerd v.d. Lueg v. Edelweiss. Mr. Heilman also owns a fine bitch Maida v. Alpine Plateau (sired by the smooth Swiss import Barri v. Huttwil v. Alpine Plateau). She has produced an excellent litter sired by Gerd v.d. Lueg.

Mr. John M. Friend, Hartland, Wisc., owns the imported smooth male Champion Also v.d. Roth, litter brother of the previous mentioned Aline v.d. Roth.

In the Kennels of Odessa Llewllyn, Waukee, Iowa, we have the rough coated Swiss import Champion Joggi-Oenz v. Edelweiss. He is the same breeding as Gero-Oenz v. Edelweiss; however, from a later litter.

To the best of my knowledge these are all the direct imports in the Midwest today; however, there are numerous other kennels which have been using the above imports to improve their bloodlines. A few such kennels are: Janday Kennels, owned by Mr. and Mrs. Archie Shea, 2166 Bethel Road, Columbus 2, Ohio; Carl-Criss Kennels, owned by Mr. and Mrs. Carl E. Fritts, 7334 E. 34th No., Tulsa, Okla.; and Wedigston Kennels, owned by Dr. Henry E. Wedig, 150 Church St., Newtown, Ohio.

West Coast Breeders

The first kennel I should like to discuss on the west coast is one which unfortunately is not operating at this time; however, due to its great influence on the breed in the country today, it should be discussed in detail. The Alpine Plateau Kennels of Mr. and Mrs. A. F. Hayes, formerly of Portland, Oregon, were responsible for the importation of several excellent Swiss-bred Saint Bernards which have contributed greatly to the breed's improvement and recognition in the United States.

To Mr. Harold Jarvis, 35 Chesley St., San Francisco 3, Calif., goes the honor of importing the first Swiss-bred Saint Bernard to the United States after World War II. His import was the smooth bitch Champion Horsa v. Zwing Uri, C.D., a very fine specimen of the breed. Like Falco v. Rigi, Horsa made C.D. under Mrs. H. P. Parker.

Mr. Don Diessner, 201 Logan Avenue, Yakima, Washington, imported another of the much-sought-after Rigi-bred Saints from the kennel of Mr. Carl Steiner, the smooth bitch Mira vom Rigi. Mira is sired by Hector v. Zwing-Uri, who is by the Sieger Nero v. Zwing-Uri out of Siegerin Alma v. Reitnau. Mira's dam is Hertha v. Rigi, who was sired by Astor v. Reitnau out of Siegerin Berna v. Rigi.

A few of the others on the west coast having American-bred Saint Bernards of the above bloodlines are:

1. Mrs. Beatrice Knight, owner of the Sanctuary Woods Kennels, Gunter Route, Drain, Oregon.

2. Mr. and Mrs. Hugh B. Woods, owners of Ridgewood Acres Kennels, Box 116, Route No. 3, Blanton Road, Eugene, Oregon.

3. Mr. and Mrs. Adolph Boicelli, 1868 Grenwich, San Francisco, California.

4. Mr. and Mrs. E. J. Van Matre, owners of Ima Kennels, Route 1, Box 55, Pleasanton, California.

Historical note from the editors

Mr. and Mrs. Hubble were themselves well-known western breeders. In the years since this chapter was written, history-minded members of the fancy have concerned themselves with the question, "Who got there first in North America?" There are many different ways to answer this question.

The first Saint Bernard kennel to be registered with the American Kennel Club was probably Carmen Kennel, operated by T. E. L. Kemp, of Bridgewater, Mass., and licensed on April 22, 1903. Mr. Kemp, one of the first professional photographers, interested himself in taking pictures of horses, then dogs, especially Saint Bernards, then founded an early dog show organization which ran the first Eastern Dog Club show. His wife, Agnes, became the first all-rounder woman judge. His daughter, now Mrs. Harold Holmes, with her husband, continue to operate Carmen Kennel, which establishes something of a record for continuous devotion to the breed.

Franz Fleischli came from Luzerne, Switzerland and founded the Edelweiss Kennel, in Springfield, Illinois, about 1894. His son, Joseph, continued to raise Saints, founded an important dog magazine and dog book company, and wrote one of the first books on Saint Bernards, early editions of which are treasured by fanciers. Edelweiss is a name of special significance to Swiss and Austrians, and the Fleischli's, father and son, are of special significance to Saints.

Gottlieb Zulliger, from Canton Bern, Switzerland, has been preoccupied with Saints for about seventy years, which may make him the longevity champion of the breed. By profession a cheesemaker, Mr. Zulliger traveled through Europe and the United States, finally reaching Monroe, Wisconsin, where he began the Alpcraft Kennel in about 1910. Monroe, primarily a Swiss colony, became the source of many fine Saints. Gottlieb and his wife, Rose, were retiring at the time of this edition. For a picture of one of their Saints, turn the page.

117

Saints get around through time and space. Bachrach took the picture, about 1930, in Concord, Mass. It shows Mrs. George P. Metcalf with ALPCRAFT EIGER. Bred by Gottlieb Zulliger, this dog was a parlay from Switzerland to Wisconsin and back to Massachusetts.

KARLA OF OTTUMWAY, at eight weeks, is less interested in the location of Switzerland than is Eric Ottum, of Falmouth, Maine, at 13 years.

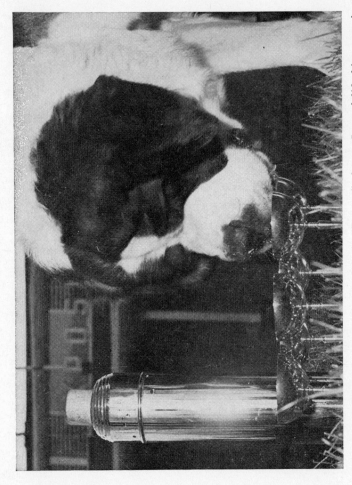

This is "Neil," widely seen on television's "Topper" show. In real life his name is SANCTUARY WOODS KRONOS.

The St. Bernard in North America into the 1960's

IN the years since the preceding chapter was prepared, the Saint Bernard fancy in North America has enjoyed a remarkable growth.

There are more Saint Bernards, both registered and unregistered.

There are better Saint Bernards, with top dog quality maintained, average quality raised, and the number of inferior specimens at the bottom steadily reduced.

The base of the Saint Bernard fancy has broadened to include large numbers of "minor" breeders and interested "pet" owners.

The smooth-coat Saint has been accepted in America as an essential and equal partner with the rough-coat.

The Saint Bernard Club of America has been revitalized and reorganized.

The area Saint Bernard clubs have increased in number and

121

in strength. The participants are principally families working together, which seems to be both a cause and a result of the realization that the Saint at his best is a working member of the family group.

More Saint Bernards:

With 2,459 American Kennel Club registrations in 1962, an increase of thirty per cent over 1961, Saints moved to twenty-seventh place, numerically, among the hundred and fifteen listed breeds. This increase may be more indicative of a growing interest in registration than a pure increase in numbers. Thousands of pure-bred Saints remain unregistered.

The fancy is content with this increase, and does not regard itself as engaged in a competition of numbers. Large dogs cannot and should not compete numerically with small dogs, for in many cases their care would then be inadequate. Saint fanciers, while striving for a slow but steady increase in numbers and a consistent improvement in quality, are in the competitive sense content to say that at least they have the most pounds of dog.

Better Saint Bernards:

With the Saint being treated as an honored member of the family, the Saint-owned family has gone to work in his behalf. The result has been improvement, not so significantly in top dogs, as in the average dog. Though the number of registered Saints is increasing every year, the number of "mutts" masquerading as Saints is steadily going down. The family pet has moved into the show ring, where he finds himself able to compete without embarrassment.

Top dogs remain top dogs, but more keep coming along. With Rasko and Gerd remaining the historical arch-types of rough and smooth, and while Berna, Bellina, Gero, Fortuna, and Questor are names to conjure with, the modern fancy can speak of Better Times, Fantabulous, Zwingo, Faust, Mighty Moe and many others without backing away an inch. For all that, the startling improvement made by the fancy is not in its top dogs, but in its hundreds of good dogs, any one of

Laurence Powell, of Pittston, Pa., President of the SBCA, could easily
fill a picture book with the champions he personally showed and finished. Chosen because of historical order alone, here is CH. KING LADDIE
RASKO WHITEBREAD, grandson of the famous Int. Ch. Rasko, and first
of five generations of champions shown by Mr. Powell, including from
"Laddie" on:

> CH. O'BRIEN'S KING RASKO
> CH. POWELL'S LITTLE JOHN
> CH. MORGAN'S ECHO OF HILLCREST
> CH. POWELL'S TRISTAN OF RIGA

Going outside this direct line of champions, here is pictured CH. LION D'OR, chosen from many others bcause this is the best picture the editors have of Mr. Powell himself.

which might well have been a consistent show winner in previous years. Judges report that in the past few years Saint entries of commendable quality have become the rule rather than the exception.

A Wider Fancy:

The "large" breeders have remained important, but the striking phenomenon of recent years has been the emergence of the small or "back-yard" breeder, and beyond that, the pet owner, as significant in the management of the breed. These people have educated themselves in the difference between good and not so good, have discovered the importance of the American Kennel Club and its rules, and have organized strong and active breed clubs.

Within this framework the Saint fancier has been interested not so much in competition for outstanding show winners as in improvement of the breed as a whole. In the world of dogdom, Saint owners are remarkable for their friendliness with each other. They are made unhappy by the sight of a poor Saint, and happy by the sight of a good one, no matter to whom he may belong.

The American Smooth:

Though the breed standard specifically states that smooths and roughs are identical except for coat, for many years the American fancy as a matter of preference leaned toward roughs. For a while many non-fanciers had difficulty in recognizing smooths as belonging to the same breed.

In recent years, among the large number of imports from Switzerland there have been many smooth-coats. Their use with the North American roughs has produced excellent results, and is responsible for much of the recent general improvement. Members of the fancy continue to exercise their personal preferences as to which type they wish to own, but any overall prejudice either way seems to have vanished.

Through the use of smooths with roughs, peak size is being maintained and average size increased, but with the breeders' intention concentrated much more on improving soundness,

125

intelligence, and good health. Again the important goal is to see that the Saint, smooth or rough, is equipped to become an honored and useful member of the family.

Saint Bernard Club of America:

Taking up where Mrs. Hubble's account left off in the preceding chapter; in 1943 the national club began to encourage the formation of affiliated local groups in many sections of the country. The parent club remained active, and by 1947 had over 250 members.

During the following years, the club conducted its business by mail, together with publication of breed brochures and its magazine, *The Saint Fancier*. While the local clubs grew and increased their activity, the parent club, unable to meet in any way except by mail, marked time. Finally it became apparent that the system of having a Board of Governors composed of representatives elected by individual affiliated clubs was not in the best interest of parent club or breed. The American Kennel Club urged reorganization.

During 1962 a new constitution was prepared and adopted in 1963 by an almost unanimous vote of the membership. It specifies that the Board of Governors be chosen in general elections rather than through affiliated club representation. In accordance with its provisions, the incumbent officers resigned, a nominating committee was selected, most of the previous incumbents nominated, and ballots sent to the membership.

The first annual meeting of the reorganized club was held on June 1, 1963, following the SBCA specialty show at Wellesley, Mass., with five of the nine newly elected national officers present. The new officers were: John Hemsath, president; Laurence Powell, vice-president; Edward Poor, secretary; Paul Wallbank, treasurer; and Richard Jackson, Mrs. Charles Rankin, Paul Cocanour, Mrs. A. E. England, and Boyd Shonkwiler, governors.

The Area Clubs:

These groups, originally sponsored by the SBCA, have been very effective in spreading and improving the quality of the

On his seventh birthday, Ch. Sanctuary Woods Gulliver poses between challenge trophies won at the Pacific Coast specialty show by son Fantabulous and daughter Nita Nanette.

127

Ch. Sanctuary Woods Fantabulous, a multiple best-in-show winner, is at home here with owner Beatrice Knight in his native Oregon hills. A more formal picture of the famous Fantabulous was selected to represent his breed in the book, *Visualization of the Standards*.

breed. Some of the area clubs are old in years; strong in activities and membership. Others are getting under way even as this edition goes to press.

The area clubs can and do meet regularly for discussion of breed problems, passing on of information and know-how to new members of the fancy, and for social pleasures among people from all walks of life who have been brought together by their common devotion to Saints. They hold AKC authorized specialty shows. They hold breed matches and training sessions. They engage in friendly competition with neighboring area clubs, and they assist in the formation of still more clubs.

Wider continental coverage has resulted from the recent formation of clubs in Canada, the Great Plains, and the Rockies. Reading roughly from east to west across the continent, the following clubs are now active:

> New England St. Bernard Club
> St. Bernard Club of Long Island
> St. Bernard Club of Northern New Jersey
> Eastern St. Bernard Association
> Middle Atlantic St. Bernard Club
> St. Bernard Club of Ontario
> Ohio St. Bernard Club
> Northern Illinois St. Bernard Club
> St. Bernard Club of Minnesota
> St. Bernard Club of the Rockies
> St. Bernard Club of Southern California
> St. Bernard Club of the Pacific Coast

Breeders:

The number of active breeders, "large," "medium," and "small," has grown to the point where it is no longer either fair or possible to single out specific breeders as being outstanding. The following list is published for the benefit of the non-fancier who wishes to find a nearby Saint breeder, therefore it is compiled roughly by locality, rather than by area club membership. To save space, each breeder is identified by one name only, omitting joint ownership and omitting kennel name. The address is included so that each may be reached either by mail or telephone.

New England States:

Bedard, Carla; RFD 2, Skowhegan, Maine
Boutilier, Donald; Hill St., Raynham, Mass.
Boynton, Amy; Ashland, N. H.
Crabb, Bruce; Baboosic Lake Road, Merrimac, N. H.
Dube, Donald; Hunts Bridge Road, North Attleboro, Mass.
Fisher, Gladys; Bypass 28, Derry, N. H.
Holmes, Harold; 434 Elm St., Bridgewater, Mass.
Jackson, Richard; North Windham, Conn.
McKeever, Edward; Hampton Road, Exeter, N. H.
Myers, Margaret; RFD, North Attleboro, Mass.
Natale, Benjamin; 835 Clintonville Road, Wallingford, Conn.
Parker, Howard; Webbs Hill Road, Stamford, Conn.
Parsons, Robert; 353 Elm St., Bridgewater, Mass.
Poor, Edward A.; R.D. 1, Acton, Mass.
Roberts, William; Baxter St., Tolland, Conn.
Saba, Alfred; Munsell Road, Belchertown, Mass.
Spahn, Richard; 5 Atlantic Ave., York Beach, Maine

Middle Atlantic States:

Andersen, Fred; 269 Maple Road, Woodbury, N. J.
Anderson, Marlene; Washington, Pa.
Black, William; Ryland Inn, Whitehouse, N. J.
Bos, Rudy; R.D. 1, Englishtown, N. J.
Bowen, John; Box 163, North Whales, Pa.
Bussinger, Stanley; 211 Ashland Ave., Philadelphia, Pa.
Deitch, Harold; 290 E. Main St., Smithtown, L. I., N. Y.
Eagan, Rev. Dominic; 179 Hussa St., Linden, N. J.
Gresham, Roy; 838 Lehigh Ave., Union, N. J.
Hauser, Dorothy; Box 462, Woodbridge, N. J.
Henry, Karl; Bayshore, N. Y.
Mallen, Louis; 46 Woodside Ave., Levittown, Pa.
McKeel, Robert; Box 143, Monaca, Pa.
Powell, Laurence; Sutton Creek Road, Pittston, Pa.
Prodziewicz, Florence; 49 Hutchinson St., Clark, N. J.

Even the lady Saints get big quickly. Here, shown with Robin Seaman, is the now CH. LADY RHONA DU GRAND ST. BERNARD, then nine months old. Owner is Richard Seaman of Markham, Ontario.

Reeh, William; 2 Ryers Ave., Cheltenham, Pa.
Reiland, Mrs. Donald; 39 Briarcliff Road, Larchmont, N. Y.
Ridgeway, Ben; 72 E. Main St., Columbus, N. J.
Ritter, Joanna; Thorncrest Drive, Butler, Pa.
Rose, Joseph; Ridge Road, Highland Hills, N. Y.
Taylor, David; 121 E. Buffalo St., Churchville, N. Y.
Yoder, Walter; R.R. 1, Meyersdale, Pa.

Ontario Area:

Bryder, Gordi; P.B. 38, Richmond Hill, Ont.
Cawker, Charles; R.R. 1, Foxboro, Ont.
Crumpton, Mrs. R.; R.R. 3, Stouffville, Ont.
Elliott, J.; Upper Saskatchewan Ranger Station, Rocky Mountain House, Alberta (not in the area but member of Ontario club).
Seaman, Richard; R.R. 2, Markham, Ont.
Widdis, Ruby, R.R. 3, Brockville, Ont.

East Central States:

Becker, James; 25 White Oak Drive, Hubbard, Ohio
Breyfogle, Dorothy; 1260 Taggart Ave., N. E., Massillon, Ohio
Cloyd, Robert; Lima, Ohio
Cocanour, Paul; R.R. 1, Whitehouse, Ohio
Cox, Shirlie; Box 56, Seville, Ohio
Douglas, Dirk; 235 Kilgore Ave., Muncie, Ind.
Engler, Frank; 1384 Brimfield Drive, Kent, Ohio
Englund, A. E.; Box 295, Bellevue, Ohio
Harvey, Grace; Syracuse, Ind.
Irwin, Lee; 32414 River Road, Rockwood, Mich.
Irwin, Anne; 5136 Cascade Road, Grand Rapids, Mich.
King, Marilyn; R.R. 1, Sheridan, Ind.
Morgan, George; Chagrin Falls, Ohio
Pangle, H. N.; R. 1, Wapakoneta, Ohio
Peabody, Herman; 744 Oliver, Sheffield Lake, Ohio
Poling, Dorothy; R. 2, Elida, Ohio
Sickels, Earle; 6773 Big Creek, Middleburg Heights, Ohio
Thompson, Robert; R.R. 1, Albany, Ind.
Van Osch, Andre; R. 2, Lynn, Ind.

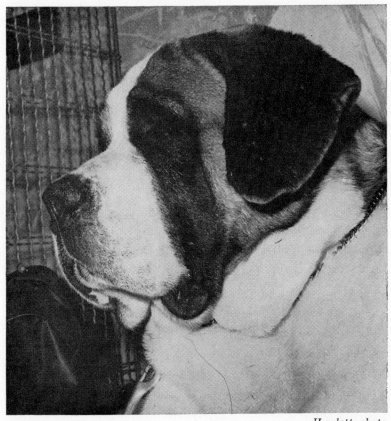

CH. SANCTUARY WOODS BETTER TIMES, already with many best-in-shows behind him, rests on the bench at Oakland, California.

Vigil, Bertha; 10580 Eighth Ave., Grand Rapids, Mich.
Worman, Charles; 122 Trailway Ave., Dayton, Ohio

West Central States:

Bartel, Joseph; New Holstein, Wis.
Justad, Mrs. M.; Cedar, Minn.
Koplin, E. D.; Litchfield, Minn.
Llewellyn, Odessa; Waukee, Iowa
Mitchell, Mrs. James; Avon, Ill.
Reedy, Clyde; 5 Swallow Lane, St. Paul, Minn.
Samstag, Earl; 700 Plank Road, Naperville, Ill.
Shonkwiler, Boyd; R. 2, Sheldon, Ill.
Smith, Lloyd; Helenville, Wis.
Wade, Edward; Box 151, West Chicago, Ill.

Great Plains States:

Coulter, Eugene, 17645 West 44th Ave., Golden, Colo.
Edge, Joan; Evergreen, Colo.
Klein, Viggo; Laramie, Wyo.
Mullikin, David; Aspen, Colo.
Veach, Larry; R.D. 2, Derby, Kan.
Wilkey, Harry; Sterling, Kan.

Western States:

Buell, William; Box 134, Canoga Park, Calif.
Graves, Don; 4341 Sebastopol Road, Santa Rosa, Calif.
Knight, Beatrice; Gunther Road, Drain, Ore.
McCausland, William; 5920 Bernhard Ave., Richmond, Calif.
Wallbank, Paul; 1420 Willcrest Drive, Concord, Calif.

The above breeders list has been assembled from information given by secretaries of the national and area clubs. The editors have hoped to include those people who breed Saints on a more or less regular basis. Inevitably, the list will be incomplete, a fact for which the editors can only apologize.

The Saint in Canada:

An attempt to discuss the Saint Bernard in Canada could be the beginning of another book. The Saint is very much at home in Canada, not entirely because of climate, but because there is work to be done, and the Saint loves to work. There are Saints hard at work throughout the vast distances of Canada. It is difficult to report their exploits because Saint club organization in Canada is only just beginning.

A strong effort is being made to eliminate, as far as the Saint Bernard fancy is concerned, the geographically artificial border which separates the United States and Canada. The first barrier to crossing the border is lack of information. The first step in crossing the border is to get information.

The address of the Canadian Kennel Club is 667 Yonge Street, Toronto, Ont. The address of the American Kennel Club is 51 Madison Avenue, New York, N. Y. 10010. The postal rates are the same in either direction. The published regulations of these organizations are very similar in intent, though somewhat different in detail.

Anyone familiar with dog showing in the United States will find himself on easy and friendly ground in Canada, and vice versa. An inquiry addressed to either of the kennel clubs will bring information on shows, dates, procedures, customs regulations, and the name and address of the respective kennel club magazine.

Canada needs Saint Bernards, and Saint Bernards need Canada. That is why this chapter is entitled "The Saint Bernard in North America."

Editors' note: The foregoing lists of clubs and breeders were compiled in 1963. At that time we failed to predict how rapidly the Saint fancy would grow. Many new clubs and breeders deserve recognition, as well as new areas. The Saints have invaded Mexico, where the terrain is well suited to their use as working dogs. For the latest names and addresses which it has been possible to obtain, please refer to the Saint Fancier's Forum.

Head study of Canadian CH. KOBI VON STEINHERNHOF, owned by C. M. Cawker of Foxboro, Ontario. Kobi's breeder was Hans Zimmerli, of Langenthal, for many years president of the St. Bernard Breeders' Association of Switzerland. Mr. Cawker has done much to bring to the Canadian scene a St. Bernard which was truly a member of the working group.

Since this picture was taken, Kobi completed his AKC championship and became, it is believed, the first Canadian Saint ever to hold both titles. He was also busy at home, and at the latest count had sired 350 puppies.

In the top picture Gary Duyzer, kennel manager, has finished harness-
ing. In the lower picture the team is off for its daily five to eight mile
workout. Kobi is easy to identify in both. He's the big one.

Zwingo at four months, getting ready for 5 best in shows and 16 group firsts.

Frasie photo

CH. HARVEY'S ZWINGO BARRI VON BANZ, owner-handler Grace Harvey, and some of the tangible rewards for a best-in-show winner. Mrs. Harvey is more proud of Zwingo's success as a fine family dog than of his consistent win record.

On the bench at Chicago International, reading from left to right, are
ZWINGHOF JEANNEN VON XESBO, GEORGE M. HARVEY, II, and CH. ZWING-
HOF JUMBO VON XESBO. The scene is typical of the Saint Bernard benches
at a dog show, which seem to be occupied by almost as many children
as dogs.

Holding his ears in a typical pose of rapt attention is CH. ZWINGHOF TORO-ROCK VON ZWINGO, sired by Zwingo and bred by Grace Harvey, and owned by H. N. Pangle of Wapakoneta, Ohio.

140

Interpretation of the Standard

NOTHING in this chapter is intended as an objection to the official Saint Bernard standard, or an attempt to contradict or revise it. The wording of the standard can be changed only by action of the Saint Bernard Club of America, with approval of the American Kennel Club. The Saint Bernard Club of Switzerland would also be consulted.

The purpose of any breed standard is an attempt, and in no case can it be more than an attempt, to define perfection, in order to determine how fine or how faulty may be the dogs under consideration.

No apology need be made for offering an explanation of the written standard. Any document prepared by men, then read by other men, is subject to interpretation. This is why the Supreme Court of the United States sometimes reaches decisions by a vote of five to four.

The beginning fancier in any breed frequently asks why

141

there seems to be no way by which all dogs within that breed can be precisely evaluated. Since this chapter is addressed to beginners and not to experts, its first goal will be to answer that question.

The beginner frequently charges that the language of his breed standard is obscure. The second goal of this chapter will be to explain the reasons for that obscurity.

The third goal will be, not to revise, but to explain portions of the Saint Bernard standard in ways which may seem less obscure to the beginner.

The fourth goal will be to add some material not covered in the standard at all, in the hope of clarifying in the mind of the beginner what constitutes a good Saint Bernard.

General Analysis:

The language of any breed standard is more or less anthropomorphic, that is, the dogs are described in the same phrases which man uses to describe himself. This is flattering to dogs. The better man likes an animal, the more man-like become the phrases used to describe that animal.

Man finds it impossible to achieve perfection in himself. Assuming that the improbable goal of controlling every word and action could be achieved, perfection still can not be reached because society's definition of perfection includes many contradictions. A man is required to be at once aggressive and reserved, dignified and gay, possessed of initiative and patience.

Realizing the impossibility of human rightness, man hopes that his dog can achieve within canine limitations a degree of perfection which he himself cannot reach. This is why people have dogs.

When man attempts to describe perfection in his chosen breed of dog, he invariably transfers his own contradictions. He demands that the dog be aggressive and gentle, sturdy and graceful, friendly and firm. Man insists that his dog distinguish instantly between burglar and milkman, which is more than he can do himself. Man wants a dog that never starts a dog fight, but never loses one either.

Interest in obedience training is growing rapidly among Saint Bernard
fanciers. Here is CH. SANCTUARY WOODS GADABOUT, CDX (companion
dog extraordinary), one of the few Saints to achieve this obedience title.
Gadabout is owned by Mary Wade of West Chicago, Ill.

The surprising thing is that many dogs do approach success in meeting the compromises demanded of them.

With all dogs called on in some degree to carry this anthropomorphic burden, the Saint Bernard quite possibly carries the greatest burden of all, because man's approach to the Saint is closely linked to himself.

There are many reasons for this. The immediately obvious reason is that the Saint Bernard, among all breeds of dogs, has a forehead most closely resembling that of man. Admired along with the noble brow is the square jaw, the two together indicating, in man's own terms, the admired combination of intelligence and determination. Add to this the fact that the Saint Bernard is impressively big and impressively strong, yet his strength is in most cases easy to discipline and control. These are attributes sought in both guardian and servant.

Beyond all this, the Saint enjoys a well deserved reputation for life saving, to which task he applies intelligence and vigor plus sensory acuity beyond that of man. Putting life saving to one side, the Saint's status as a working dog is based on his use as a draft animal, to which task he applies docility, strength, and endurance. Being an effective guardian for small children, the Saint can, at the end of his day's work, fill in as your baby-sitter for the evening.

The intention here is not to establish that the Saint Bernard is the "finest dog of all." Since the preference for any one breed is entirely subjective, such a contention would give rise to endless and futile argument.

The intention is to point out that it is perhaps more difficult than with any other breed to avoid describing the Saint Bernard in terms of attributes which we like to believe are "human." In this respect, based on appearance if for no other reason, the Saint is the "ultimate dog."

This increases the difficulty of clarifying a breed standard. How can we clearly describe a dog who resembles a human being when we can't decide what a human being should be like?

Functional Analysis:

The problem can be approached in terms of function. The Saint Bernard is a working dog, and the function of his body

144

is to pull. In any evaluation of his body, it must be remembered that anything which contributes to his pulling ability is good; anything which detracts from it is not good.

The body of a good Saint Bernard bears a functional resemblance to the body of a good Percheron or Belgian horse, in that it looks able to pull. The requirements for straight and heavy-boned front legs, heavy-muscled and angulated back legs, in-line leg action, symmetrically massive and close-coupled legs and body, are all part of the specification which a mechanical engineer would write if he were asked to design a four-legged animal which could pull.

The head of a Saint Bernard has a different function, in this case entirely subjective. Having insisted that the good Saint be wise, gentle, kindly, determined, capable, and fearless, we expect him to look the part. The official standard attempts with considerable success to describe this anthropomorphic evaluation in terms of lines and measurements. We also insist, however, that the good Saint be "handsome." No description of parts can possibly define handsomeness, but we look for it all the same.

A third function of the Saint Bernard, this time for the satisfaction of his owners, is that he be recognizable as such. Because of the wide publicity which the breed has enjoyed, and because of his size and his very distinctive head markings, the Saint would probably win an identification contest conducted among non-fanciers.

The official standard is tolerant of variations in color and markings. By its omissions, it implies that handsomeness in a Saint may be reached in many different ways. To be recognized by a non-fancier, the Saint need be marked only in some combination of brown (meaning anything from orange through red to near-black) and white, with the absolute minimum of brown being the two ears, and the absolute minimum of white being the nose (hopefully with a trace of blaze), chest, four feet, and tip of tail. The point to describing these limits, broad as they are, is that outside them, the non-fancier is entitled to ask what kind of a dog it is.

The range of allowed markings is probably as great as that

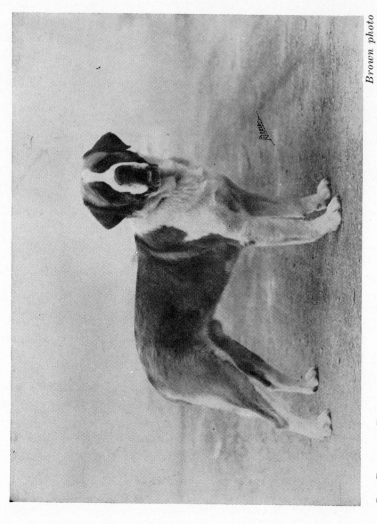

CH. BRYJONS DEMOSTHENES VON KRIS, bred by Dr. and Mrs. Breyfogle, of Massillon, Ohio. Owned by the Rev. Dominic Eagan, of Linden, N. J.

of any other breed standard, with the principal concern being a recognizable head. Beyond that, the emphasis lies essentially on soundness and strength.

Again by its omissions, the Saint Bernard standard shares with many other breeds an attempt to get away from the idea that there is a difference between a "show dog" and a "pet." To be sure, dog showing is a sport, and in any sport there is a tendency for the rules to become esoteric, but the strong, healthy, and good-natured pet of whom we can justifiably be proud will do his share of winning.

The show-winning Saint Bernard and the really fine working pet Saint Bernard are one and the same. Both the judge and the owner want the Saint to look pleasant enough to welcome a guest, big enough to scare off a burglar, strong enough to pull a wagon, smart enough to rescue a drowning man, and patient enough to look after the children.

Specific Analysis:

Breed standards are for the most part written by committees and modified by other committees, which fact tends to reduce the personal element but also tends to reduce clarity. The Saint Bernard standard, furthermore, is a direct translation from that adopted in 1887 at a congress in Zurich, Switzerland.

Any translator, no matter how skilled, has the problem of deciding between literal and conceptual accuracy. The presently approved translation, published in 1955 by the Saint Bernard Club of America, is reprinted in the next chapter.

In preparing, for the benefit of the beginner, a specific clarification of the standard, the editors have attempted to consult every Saint Bernard specialty judge in North America. Feeling, however, that the words of one man are inevitably clearer than the words of a committee, the editors present here without change a statement from Henry E. Wedig, Sr., M.D., of Cincinnati, Ohio. Dr. Wedig writes:

"Head structure is of prime importance as principal feature of breed identification. The skull should be massive, and the jaws equipped with teeth that are of even bite and strong

147

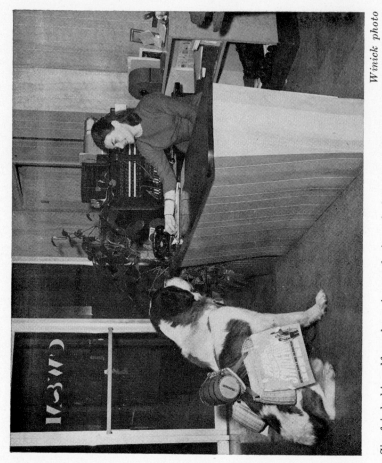

Siegfried, himself a champion and sire of champions, was not above working under contract to publicize a travel contest. Here he applies at the desk for his reservation.

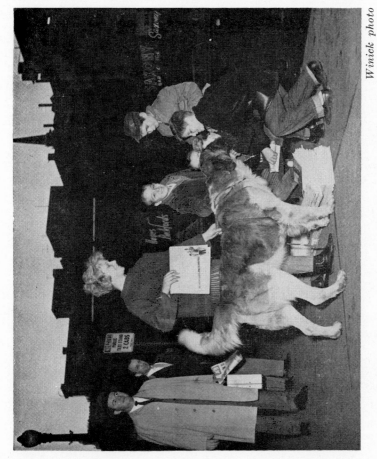

Winick photo

Also under contract for the same promotion was son Wunderbar. While waiting for his next office appointment, he pauses to chat with the newsboys.

development. The head must be wide, slightly arched, with the sides sloping gently into a curve that blends with strongly developed cheek bones. The occiput is only moderately developed. The supraorbital ridge is very strongly developed and forms nearly a right angle with the horizontal axis of the head.

"Deeply imbedded between the eyes and starting at the root of the muzzle, a furrow runs over the whole skull, strongly marked at the front section, and gradually disappearing at the base of the occiput. The lines at the sides of the head diverge from the outer corner of the eyes toward the back of the head. The skin of the forehead, above the eyes, forms rather noticeable wrinkles, more or less pronounced, which converge toward the furrow. When the dog is in action, these wrinkles are more prominent, without in the least giving the impression of morosity. These wrinkles must not be too strongly developed. (For definition of parts, see "Outline Chart"—Ed.)

"The slope of the skull to the muzzle is abrupt and rather steep. The muzzle is short, does not taper, and the vertical depth at the root of the muzzle must be greater than the length of the muzzle. The muzzle bridge is straight in most instances; however a slight break in this straight line is not seriously objectionable. A wide, well-marked shallow furrow runs from the root of the muzzle over the entire bridge to the nose.

"The flews of the upper jaw are strongly developed, and not sharply cut, but turning into a beautiful curve into the lower edge and slightly overhanging. The flews of the lower jaw must not be too pendant. The nose is very substantial, broad with wide open nostrils, and like the lips, always black.

"The ears are of medium size, rather high set, with a very strongly developed burr at the base. They stand slightly away from the head at the base, then drop with a sharp bend to the side and cling to the head without a turn. The flap is tender and forms a rounded triangle, slightly elongated toward the point, with the front edge lying firmly to the head, whereas the back edge stands away from the head somewhat, especially when the dog is at attention. A strongly developed ear gives

OUTLINE CHART OF A STANDARD-TYPE SAINT BERNARD

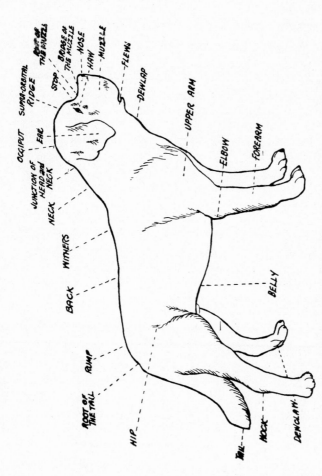

This drawing shows the anatomical parts of the dog as commonly used in descriptions and criticism of points.

Skeleton Diagram and External Outline of Standard Type St. Bernard Dog the skull a squarer, broader and more impressive appearance. (Dr. Wedig's excellent description of the ears neglects to mention that the ears, even more than the eyes, are the Saint Bernard's most expressive feature. In action and at attention, the Saint's ears are frequently though subtly changing their position.—Ed.)

"The eyes are set to the front, and are of medium size, dark brown, with intelligent, friendly expression, and set moderately deep. The lower eyelids, as a rule, do not close completely, and in these cases there is an angular wrinkle toward the inner corner of the eye. Eyelids must not be too pendant, or show a deep red haw.

"The neck is set high and is very strong. It must fully support the head in all angles of position and usage, and fully coordinate the muscular movements of the shoulders and foreback section, into which the neck blends.

"The back is strong, very broad, and straight as far as the haunches; from there gently sloping to the rump. A gentle, almost imperceptible merger into the root of the tail is mandatory. Strong, well developed chest structure is important, with a belly drawn up reasonably tight, and well set off from the loin section. The rib cage must be well developed for ample bellows action, but never to the point of being barrel chested.

"Front legs are to be very powerful, with forearms well developed muscularly, and are to be straight and strong. Legs should be sufficiently long to give a good working stride, with reasonable daylight underneath the dog, but without creating an impression of undue legginess. The shoulder is well muscled and placed in close apposition to the forward trunk section, with the shoulder blade ridge being well angulated in relation to the arms of the front leg.

"The hindquarters must be very strong, with impressively muscular legs, and there must be moderate angulation of the hocks. Dewclaws are permissible, so long as they do not interfere with the gait. Feet must be broad with strong toes, moderately closed, with rather high knuckles.

"Most important of all, there must be a well synchronized

"Beggar," from Sacramento, California, and three-year-old Bobby Mitchell both lived to have their picture taken because Beggar pulled Bobby out of the flooded American River in May of 1962. Beggar was judged "dog hero of the year" in a competition sponsored by a dog food company.

application of power transmission from the pads of the feet throughout the entire leg structure, fore and aft, to the muscles of the back and shoulders. This could be designated as the 'power drive factor,' and is a fundamental must for all properly constructed dogs. All dogs so possessed are able to move with a good springing step and a back movement that is completely smooth and free.

"The tail starts broad and powerful directly from the rump and is long, very heavy, ending in a powerful tip. In repose it hangs straight down, bending in the lower third only, with a slight turn to the side permissible. In action the tail is carried at or slightly above the level position, but may not be erect or rolled over the back.

"There are rough and smooth-coated Saint Bernards; both have identical body structure. Judges are to consider them of equal value. Any of the several distinguishing features between rough and smooth Saint Bernards must be considered a matter of personal choice as to which one may prefer to own.

"Body weights may vary greatly and are not taken into account in judging, except that it is considered favorable for a dog to be in good flesh, carrying its best weight, without the slightest suggestion of obesity.

"The official breed standard has been used extensively in composing this presentation. My own ideas have been interwoven as well, to amplify those points I have considered important beyond the scope of the standard.

"It would be entirely possible for any Saint Bernard owner to study the breed standard, to read over the various breed publications, to attend dog shows and evaluation events; and I am certain that it would be possible for that owner to evaluate his own stock as well as any of the licensed judges, providing that he is able to approach his task with an open mind, using the simple facts alone, and able to recognize the failings that may be present in the dog being evaluated. This need not in any sense detract from the value we place on the dog in terms of personal warmth and affection, which most of us have for these dogs that so easily become a part of our lives and our homes."

With the end of the quotation from Dr. Wedig, the editors are grateful to him for his analysis, in which he adheres to the standard in his capacity as a specialty judge, clarifies it in his capacity as a medical practitioner, and demonstrates warm affection in his capacity as a lover of Saint Bernards.

Additional Analysis:

The standard states in Paragraph 6 that "the neck in action is carried erect," a phrase which probably has suffered in translation of the words "in action." When posed or at attention, the Saint Bernard carries his head high, with his head and neck posture creating the impression that he is quite able to hold his own head up, without assistance, perhaps in order to get a better view.

When running free, without pulling, the head and neck are held approximately level, or raised slightly if a view of the ground ahead is required. When at work pulling a load, the Saint's head drops in proportion to his work effort, in exactly the same manner as a draft horse's head drops in order to get a better mechanical purchase on his load. When tracking, the Saint's head will fit the need, that is, raised for wind testing, then lowered for ground tracking.

The standard is silent on the subject of gait. To fill this gap, Dr. Wedig has supplied the phrase "power drive factor," and asks for "a good springing step."

On this point many members of the Saint Bernard fancy have expressed themselves. They wish to correct the often expressed notion that Saints, because strong and heavy, must therefore move ponderously and slowly. The fact is that a good Saint Bernard suits his gait to the occasion. If he is pulling, he digs in, straight and hard. In contrast, when running free the task of carrying himself is so easy he barely seems to touch the ground. The impression of light-footedness and of generally easy movement is very much to be desired.

Left to his own devices, the Saint will adjust the speed of his movement to the situation. If he has only a little way to go, he will walk. If a little farther, he will run slowly. In a

DANNY VON REGENSBERG, brought from the Sauliamt Kennels in Zurich by Edward Poor, secretary of the SBCA, stands in the Acton, Mass. snow.

The Edward Poor family calls this photogenic lady simply "The Moose."

In the same Acton yard, come summer, GLENMERE ALPINE HILDA looks out for an as yet un-named guest.

158

playful mood, he gallops. If in his mind an emergency has arisen, he can turn on as great a burst of speed as any racing dog.

Saint Bernard showmen complain that their dogs in competition are frequently assigned to small rings, under the impression that the Saint is a slow mover and therefore doesn't have to go very far. The fallacy here is that the good Saint by nature adjusts his gait to the distance he has to go. He can hardly be persuaded to move freely in a ring six times his own length, and somewhat smaller than his living room at home.

Freedom and ease of motion are as important to a Saint Bernard as to any other dog. The purpose of running is to get from here to there with a maximum of efficiency and a minimum of effort. The gait of a draft animal, however, will be different from that of a pure runner. It has been made clear that the draft animal's legs are most efficient when pulling straight into the load. When this same straight line action is accelerated, the animal's body, because of the necessary width between his legs, will roll slightly. The effect can be clearly observed when a good draft horse is asked to move rapidly. Excessive roll is undesirable, as indicating looseness, but no roll at all in a draft animal indicates too little freedom of movement.

Recent Developments:

Many Saint Bernard admirers, perhaps speaking from childhood memories, are fond of saying that Saints are not as big as they used to be. As a matter of fact, they are bigger. The desired shoulder height called for in the standard, of twenty-seven plus inches in the male and twenty-five plus inches in the female, would now be regarded as very small. On the other hand, breeders no longer work toward pure size or weight as ends in themselves.

Even though the average Saint is bigger than he used to be, there is a strong tendency to de-emphasize the importance of size in favor of good proportion, soundness, and freedom of movement. Having achieved pure size and strength, Saint

159

ED DODD

MARK TRAIL'S "ANDY"

Bernard breeders are now working toward the whole dog, an animal who is not only handsome in all his parts, but completely handsome in the entirety.

The Saint in Pictured Motion:

In conveying impressions of motion, the interpretation of a graphic artist is often more effective than photography. The editors close this chapter with a page of action sketches by Ed Dodd, author and artist of the nature serial strip "Mark Trail," whose Saint Bernard, "Andy" is one of the principal characters in the narrative, and thus easily the most widely seen and known Saint on this continent. Mr. Dodd writes, "I honestly believe people are as much concerned with Andy's welfare as they are with Mark Trail's." He adds that the original Andy, real-life model for these sketches, is now nine years old.

The group of sketches, printed here through the courtesy of Mr. Dodd and the Hall Syndicate, Inc., shows Andy in action, readiness for action, and attentive repose. Not only are the sketches correct on all details of movement, but they succeed in conveying the impression of strong and fluid grace which is characteristic of the well-constructed Saint Bernard.

A four-dog, tandem-hitched team waits in Alberta mountains for the call to bring up provisions. The lead dog in this team is ten months old. Jiggs, shown on page 163, is the wheel dog.

161

Forest ranger Elliott harnessed, loaded, and photographed in the dim northern light. Here the team takes off. You will notice that the three visible dogs are already trotting, and in perfect step.

Back-packers Buster and Dagwood are breaking trail. Between them is five-month-old Tannenbaum, carrying only a training pack. The photographer is standing on the following sled.

JIGGS OF THE HILLS demonstrates proper back pack. Owner J. Elliott, of the Upper Saskatchewan Ranger Station, Rocky Mountain House, Alberta, is a forest ranger covering wide reaches of wilderness both winter and summer.

When back-packing, three Saint Bernards are used, one loaded with food for man and dogs, the other two with camp gear and working or emergency equipment, such as for fire fighting. Seventy pounds is the usual back-pack load for a grown Saint.

When on predator control in the winter, Mr. Elliott harnesses his six-dog sled team all in tandem, because of the dense woods. He prefers three Samoyeds in front to break trail, and three Saints in back to do the heavy pulling.

Another chore performed is keeping the wolves away from night camp. On occasion, the Saints have been sent out alone to back-pack emergency food through otherwise inaccessible terrain.

163

****

A. The Short-Haired Saint Bernard Dog.

1. GENERAL: Powerful, proportionately tall figure, strong and muscular in every part, with powerful head and most intelligent expression. In dogs with a dark mask the expression appears more stern, but never ill-natured.

2. HEAD: Like the whole body, very powerful and imposing. The massive skull is wide, slightly arched and the sides slope in a gentle curve into the very strongly developed, high cheek bones. Occiput only moderately developed.

The supra-orbital ridge is very strongly developed and forms nearly a right angle with the horizontal axis of the head.

Deeply imbedded between the eyes and starting at the root of the muzzle, a furrow runs over the whole skull. It is strongly marked in the first half, gradually disappearing toward the base of the occiput. The lines at the sides of the head diverge considerably from the outer corner of the eyes toward the back of the head.

The skin of the forehead, above the eyes, forms rather noticeable wrinkles, more or less pronounced, which converge toward the furrow. Especially when the dog is in action, the wrinkles are more visible without in the least giving the impression of morosity. Too strongly developed wrinkles are not desired.

The slope from the skull to the muzzle is sudden and rather steep.

The muzzle is short, does not taper, and the vertical depth at the root of the muzzle must be greater than the length of the muzzle.

The bridge of the muzzle is not arched, but straight; in some dogs, occasionally, slightly broken.

A rather wide, well-marked, shallow furrow runs from the root of the muzzle over the entire bridge of the muzzle to the nose.

The flews of the upper jaw are strongly developed, not sharply cut, but turning in a beautiful curve into the lower edge, and slightly overhanging.

The flews of the lower jaw must not be deeply pendant.

The teeth should be sound and strong and should meet in either a scissors or an even bite: The scissors bite being preferable. The undershot bite although sometimes found with good specimens, is not desirable. The overshot bite is a fault.

A black roof of the mouth is desirable.

3. The nose (Schwamm) is very substantial, broad, with wide open nostrils, and, like the lips, always black.

4. The ears are of medium size, rather high set, with very strongly developed burr (Muschel) at the base. They stand slightly away from the head at the base, then drop with a sharp bend to the side and cling to the head without a turn. The flap is tender and forms a rounded triangle, slightly elongated toward the point, the front edge lying firmly to the head whereas the back edge may stand somewhat away from the head, especially when the dog is at attention. Lightly set ears, which at the base immediately cling to the head, give it an oval and too little marked exterior, whereas a strongly developed base gives the skull a squarer, broader and much more impressive appearance.

5. The eyes are set more to the front than the sides, are of medium size, dark brown, with intelligent, friendly expression, set moderately deep. The lower eyelids, as a rule, do not close completely and, if that is the case, form an angular wrinkle toward the inner corner of the eye. Eyelids which are too deeply pendant and show conspicuously the lachrymal glands, or a very red, thick haw, and eyes that are too light, are objectionable.

6. The neck is set high, very strong and in action is carried erect, otherwise horizontally or slightly downward. The junction of head and neck is distinctly marked by an indentation. The nape is very muscular and rounded at the sides which makes the neck appear rather short. The dewlap of throat and neck is well pronounced; too strong development, however, is not desirable.

7. The shoulders are sloping and broad, very muscular and powerful. The withers are strongly pronounced.

8. The chest is very well arched, moderately deep, not reaching below the elbows.

9. BACK: Very broad, perfectly straight as far as the haunches, from there gently sloping to the rump, and merging imperceptibly into the root of the tail.

10. HINDQUARTERS: Well developed. Legs very muscular.

11. BELLY: Distinctly set off from the powerful loin section, only little drawn up.

12. The tail starting broad and powerful directly from the rump is long, very heavy, ending in a powerful tip. In repose it hangs straight down, turning gently upward in the lower third only, which is not to be considered a fault. In a great many specimens the tail is carried with the end slightly bent and therefore hangs down in the shape of an f. In action all dogs carry the tail more or less turned upward. However it may not be carried too erect or by any means rolled over the back. A slight curling of the tip is sooner admissible.

13. FOREARM: Very powerful and extra-ordinarily muscular.

14. FORELEGS: Straight, strong.

15. HINDLEGS: Hocks of moderate angulation. Dewclaws are not desired; if present they must not obstruct the gait.

16. FEET: Broad, with strong toes, moderately closed, and with rather high knuckles. The so-called dewclaws which sometimes occur on the inside of the hindlegs are imperfectly developed toes. They are of no use to the dog and are not to be taken into consideration in judging. They may be removed by surgery.

17. The coat is very dense, shorthaired (stockhaarig), lying smooth, tough, without however feeling rough to the touch. The thighs are slightly bushy. The tail at the root has longer and denser hair which gradually becomes shorter toward the tip. The tail appears bushy, not forming a flag.

18.   COLOR : White with red or red with white, the red in its various shades; brindle patches with white markings. The colors red and brown-yellow are of entirely equal value. Necessary markings are: white chest, feet and tip of tail, nose band, collar or spot on the nape; the latter and blaze are very desirable. Never of one color or without white. Faulty are all other colors except the favorite dark shadings on the head (mask) and ears. One distinguishes between mantle dogs and splash-coated dogs.

19.   The height at the shoulder of the dog ought to be 70 centimeters (27.56 inches) minimum, of the bitch, 65 centimeters (25.59 inches). Female animals, thruout, are of a more delicate and finer build.

20.   Considered as faults are all deviations from the standard, as for instance a sway-back and a disproportionately long back, hocks too much bent, straight hindquarters, upward growing hair in spaces between the toes, out at elbows, cowhocks and weak pasterns.

B. The Long-Haired Saint Bernard Dog.

The long-haired variety completely resembles the short-haired variety except for the coat which is not short-haired (stockhaarig) but of medium length, plain to the wavy, never rolled or curly and not shaggy either. Usually, on the back, especially in the region of the haunches to the rump, the hair is more wavy, a condition, by the way, that is slightly indicated in the short-haired dogs.

The tail is bushy with dense hair of moderate length. Rolled or curly hair on the tail is not desirable. A tail with parted hair, or a flag tail, is faulty. Face and ears are covered with short and soft hair; longer, silky hair at the base of the ear is permissible. Forelegs only slightly feathered, thighs very bushy.

Special Problems of Giant Dogs

by Joe Stetson

A giant dog is one which is larger than nature meant the canine species to be. Man's stress on size in the selective breeding program which developed and typed the Saint Bernard breed, as well as other breeds almost as large, has resulted in the production of giants with the glandular characteristics of giantism or acromegaly. These by-products of the sought-after size were certainly not planned by the designers of the breed, but their manifestations must be recognized, and, if desirable dogs are to result, intelligent steps taken in the right direction.

The most important problem of the giant results from the dying of nerve cells in the anterior lobe of the lumbar region of the spine causing breaks in the nerve paths that stimulate muscle patterns in the hindquarters. This is called the "lethal neurone." The muscle patterns thereby unused, atrophy, and the dog is debilitated in accordance with which and how many of the cells die. Subsequent movement depends upon the remaining muscle patterns and the methods of locomotion substituted for normal gait by the dog, perhaps with the aid of exercise.

This phenomenon occurs in puppyhood and is usually observed at between six and twelve months of age. With no intention of libeling a fine breed, it may be readily observed in some Great Danes, where normal canine locomotion has been replaced by various substitutes, including straight stifled "high behinds," roached backs, dropped croups, or "hinge backs." Bulldogs, occasionally Bassets, Newfoundlands, and, of late years, Irish Wolfhounds demonstrate this characteristic. Improper hindquarter movement has long been a problem with the giant Saint Bernard.

In the last decade Newfoundland breeders have made great strides in eliminating this unsoundness from what they consider their superior individuals. More recently, Saint Bernards are improving in soundness, a trend which should become a mandate with the fancy. How is the problem solved? By considering soundness over size in judging and in selecting individuals for breeding. More than this; refuse to show or use for breeding any specimen, no matter how grand the size or head if it is a victim of the "lethal neurone." Recognize the limits nature has placed upon the species and respect them.

Lazy whelping is another problem confronting owners and breeders of dogs with the glandular idiosyncrasies of the giant. At birth puppies of average-sized dogs weigh from one twenty-fifth to one-fiftieth the weight of the dam. Toy pups may be as large as one-twentieth. Despite the fact that Saint puppies rarely weigh more than one-hundredth the weight of their mother, and therefore whelping should involve no mechanical difficulty, one or more pups may not be whelped. Should this occur, septicemia is likely to result. Care must be taken to assure the expelling of all puppies and preferably on schedule. X-ray can be used if a careful temperature check on the bitch has warned of trouble. In the meantime the veterinarian can administer drugs to stimulate whelping.

Intestinal torsion is another problem of the giant dog. When

KNABLAW'S EMO VON BARRE, bred by Paul Wallbank and owned by James Howlett, shares the soap with Kittie Howlett, who lives in Richmond, California. This bathtub scene got past the censors and was used to publicize an all-breed show in Oakland.

170

Once dried off, Emo worked with Alice in Wonderland (Beth Werschkul) to start a Children's Fairyland parade, also in Oakland.

171

stoppages occur with resulting bloat, time is of the essence in arresting the formation of gases and thus reducing the pressure, which may cause rupture of the stomach or intestines or death by pressure on the heart. Anti-ferments may be used and the veterinarian may find it necessary to tap the inflated area as is done to a horse suffering from colic.

Glandular imbalance in giants is probably also responsible for the irregular seasons and low percentage of conception which some breeders observe in their kennels.

There is some possibility that the quality of bone found in the giants may contribute to occurrence of rickets, a subject usually thought of only in terms of feeding. Some large, well-fed puppies develop bone poorly, while more nearly average-sized pups, even when poorly fed for perhaps economic reasons, are straight boned.

Some specimens of the giant breeds exhibit short life spans, with proneness to diabetes, heart conditions, and more than average distress from arthritis. This is yet another result of pushing the size factor beyond what was naturally evolved as the canine species.

These warnings do not, however, mean that size is in itself bad. All of these problems can be solved by not pushing nature's formula too far.

By virtue of their very size, Saint Bernards present other special problems not particularly medical in nature. For one thing, large dogs are just too big physically to breed small virgin bitches. The solution to this problem is either artificial insemination, which has as yet a rather low percentage of success, or using the larger stud only after breeding to one more nearly the bitch's size.

Anal glands require the periodic pressure of normal stools in order to function properly. It is often difficult to establish economically practical diets which maintain firm stools in large breeds. Anything less than a firm stool allows the contents of the anal glands to accumulate. When this condition becomes extreme, inflammation, tissue damage and infection ensue. Every practical means to maintain stools of adequate consistency is indicated, in lieu of which periodic manual pressure on the anal glands to approximate their normal secretion will avoid trouble.

The skin and coat covering the joints upon which large dogs must lie are often subject to harsh use, since Saints prefer to lie on cool concrete or stone surfaces, especially in warm weather. The heaviest coated dog can wear his coat thin on the elbows, hocks, and breastbone. When the skin becomes so calloused as to block the hair follicles, accumulation of fluid or infection sometimes follows. At best the calloused areas are unpleasing in appearance. One solution is to make a summer pad covered with oilcloth, plastic or other cool material and encourage the dog to use it. Should callouses develop, keep them lubricated with a light, clear oil.

The mechanics of breeding large dogs, where proportionate differences between the sexes are considerable and the dogs are too heavy to assist, can be aided by the preparation of a breeding platform. This consists of a number of boards covered with matting, which can be arranged as the circumstances require.

When not left free to take care of themselves, the large and especially the heavy-coated dogs are subject to heat exhaustion. Reasonable anticipation can prevent this by never confining a dog in automobile, room, or other sun exposure that can bring him to grief. If the accident occurs, however, the quickest way to reduce body temperature is to apply cool, wet compresses to the belly. Should cool water not be available, use cool metal or any good heat conductor at hand in order to draw heat from the large blood vessels lying close to the surface. Ice cubes wrapped in a cloth may save the day, but the best advice is not to leave your big dog in a closed car in the first place.

Hip dysplasia is a subject which continues to be controversial as to cause and possible prevention or remedy. We do know that dogs which are well developed muscularly and get plenty of exercise are rarely disturbed by it. There are many examples of dogs which have been apparently normal, then later lost their sockets when softened by lives of comfort and ease with new masters. Considering the size of Saint Ber-

Back-yard booty at the home of William Roberts in Tolland, Conn., showing, left to right: CH. FREIDA'S AL-VERDON FRAUSTY, CH. HIGH SHOT VON SHAGG-BARK, CH. MT. SNEFFELS KAMILLE, CH. GEO'S TAMRA OF SHAGG-BARK.

174

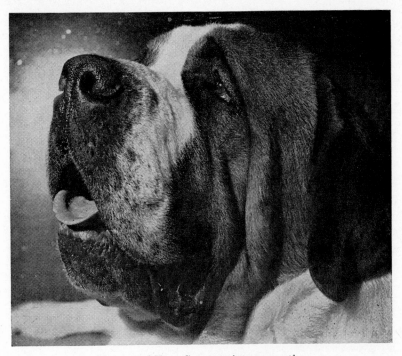

Close-up of HIGH SHOT at sixteen months.

CH. SHAGG-BARK'S MARKO CHOLLIE, bred by Norman Steadman and owned by Chauncy Simmons, of South Amherst, Mass. Counting back through four generations, a dog or a man has thirty ancestors. Eighteen of Chollie's were champions, including such famous names as Mighty Tiger, Mighty Moe, Frausty, Barri, Joggi, Sandman, Golden Gal, Minka, Faust, Chriss, and Freida.

Bob Streeter photo

175

nards and their rapid growth rate, which competes with exercise in the growing period of large breeds, every effort should be made to keep them in hard condition for their well being in general and the condition of their hip sockets in particular.

The Growth Pattern of a Giant Dog:

In the growth pattern of a puppy intended by nature to gain eighty to a hundred pounds in the first six months of his life, every day is important. It is not sufficient to say that because the puppy is apparently healthy and well nourished, he will get along all right. During his period of rapid growth, the giant puppy develops different parts at different times. To-morrow morning he will not even look the same as he did the night before. Therefore a health deficiency lasting only a few days in a giant puppy can leave a deficiency or impairment in the grown dog.

One of the requirements imposed upon the owner of a giant puppy is continuous attention to his health problems. The puppy is growing so fast in so many different places that a week of ill health can be disastrous to the perfection of his eventual development.

Scientific progress continuously improves techniques for the benefit of man and dog. At this writing, however, there are well developed means at hand for immunizing a high percentage of dogs against distemper, infectious hepatitis, rabies and leptospirosis. When used with care, these methods have proved successful. It may be surmised that these methods, though they may be slightly modified. will not be outmoded for years to come.

We now know that puppies normally acquire a blood level of antibodies from their mother both prenatally and by way of the colostrum in the milk of early nursing. This level is roughly dependent upon the mother's own antibody level and tapers off until, in puppies of a well immunized mother, it approaches insufficient protection from exposure to distemper and infectious hepatitis at from six to twelve weeks.

To afford maximum protection an injection of permanent vaccine at six weeks should be given. If antibody level is low enough for a puppy to be vulnerable at this time, the vaccine will be a challenge and immunity will be established. If the antibody level is high, the antibodies will prevent the modified virus in the vaccine from challenging successfully and no additional immunity will be produced. Such initially better protected puppies must then be vaccinated again at twelve weeks when the level of immunity is low enough for the vaccine to challenge successfully.

From this description it is obvious that one of the vaccinations will be wasted. Only one is necessary to give protection providing it is given at twelve weeks of age or later. This schedule can be used if it is considered safe to leave the puppies vulnerable until they are three months old. In this respect the location of the kennel, exposure to street virus, high level of immunity of the mother, and general health factors should be considered.

Such considerations should also affect the decision on whether or not to use serum in an immunizing program for a puppy. Serum can offer only very temporary protection, and yet permanent vaccine can not be administered successfully until the serum has become ineffective. In any case there must be a period of vulnerability before the vaccine can constitute a challenge. Granted a reasonable degree of protection from infection, many veterinarians have abandoned the use of serum in favor of permanent vaccine.

Leptospirosis and rabies, transferred by the urine and saliva, respectively, of infected animals, need not be guarded against where puppies are concerned until a later time when they may be exposed. Leptospirosis protection, when later required, must presently be periodically repeated. Modified-live-virus rabies vaccine provides lifetime immunity.

Body temperature, whether in a giant puppy or a grown dog, is the best indication of good health. The normal rectal temperature of a dog is 101.5 to 102 degrees Fahrenheit, with the higher limit more likely after meals, at the end of the day, or during excitement. A degree or more below or above the normal bracket is reason for concern and careful observation.

In this day of easy transportation, with qualified veterinarians usually available, there are still times when general recommendations can be helpful. A dog with abnormal temperature should be helped to a place where he can be observed and treated. Such a place should be dry, draft free, and reasonably warm. A dog with subnormal temperature, resulting from organic failure, loss of blood, exposure or poisoning, should be kept warm. A dog whose energies are being used to fight an invading disease will also be helped by warmth.

Diets will generally be prescribed in accordance with each situation. Frequent, small feedings are helpful. If the dog must be force fed, a simple method is to prepare food in liquid form and pour it slowly between the lips at one side of the mouth, while holding the dog's lips closed on the other side. The head need be tipped only slightly upward to facilitate swallowing.

One thing to remember in getting a dog to eat of his own initiative is that a dog associates food with scent. He is unlikely to want to eat what he can not smell. Cleaning the nostrils of a sick dog with a mild saline solution will often make the difference. If he can smell a piece of meat he will rarely refuse to eat it.

An attack of distemper suffered by a growing giant dog can seriously affect his later development. The distemper virus may take various forms. The virus is able to attack such tissue as is derived from the epithelium, that is, tissue which covers surfaces, forms glands and lines most cavities of the body, such as the lungs and intestines. When the virus is successfully attacking the lungs, the illness is respiratory, or intestinal when that area is the object of attack. When, usually after weakening the victim by successful invasion of lungs or intestines, the virus attacks the central nervous system, the illness becomes the nervous type, referred to at times as chorea or St. Vitus' Dance.

The nervous type, known as encephalitis, is usually delayed by some resistance to the virus getting through the so-called spinal barrier. When it does attack it destroys the nerve sheaths, leaving them exposed to stimuli. Thus exposed, the muscles which the nerve path would normally cause to contract

Bomars von Nell, according to owner W. E. Yoder, of Meyersdale, Pa., was very proud of the fawn which she raised.

Left, Sanctuary Woods Yes Indeed, bitch pup; right, Sanctuary Woods You Lucky Bum, dog pup; both at five months.

at the dog's volition are instead contracted spasmodically. When the nerve tissue damage is not too great, the dog often learns to compensate and seems quite normal until, in a period of stress or excitement, he suspends his effort to compensate. Then the uncontrolled stimuli take over and the dog jerks, or has convulsions or running fits. The debility caused by nerve tissue damage may be compensated for by the dog, but never repaired.

Obviously, the best cure for distemper is not to let your dog get it in the first place.

The same thought applies to heartworm, which is not an intestinal worm at all and thus not detectable through feces examination. Heartworm, until recently considered regional, has been spread country-wide as a result of transporting dogs great distances for benching, breeding, hunting, and field trials. A single dog, run or shown in heartworm territory, can return to infest an entire kennel or neighborhood.

Heartworm becomes a detriment to a dog when the adult worms lodge in large blood vessels or the chambers of the heart, reducing circulation efficiency chiefly because of the space they occupy. Once there they can be removed only with great difficulty, through the use of drugs, and some cases may be beyond treatment.

There is a prophylaxis, however, which will prevent adult worms from appearing. Since the microfilariae which become adult heartworms require about a hundred days to do so, quarterly administration of caricide in proper dosage kills the microfilariae and adults never reach the heart. In heartworm territory, this preventive measure has become essential to the success of bird dog activities, in which a debilitated dog is of little value. Any dog with a light infestation of adult worms can be kept from further damage by killing the microfilariae before they mature.

Periodic treatment with caricide for heartworm prevention will also rid the dog of any roundworms he may be carrying. This is especially important when dogs are with children, or defecate where children might make contact. The ingesting of embryonated roundworm eggs from either dog or cat, by humans, can cause considerable trouble. Canine roundworms, differing from the human roundworms, become aberrant in human beings. Instead of passing through the intestinal wall into the bloodstream, entering the lungs, being coughed up and swallowed to renew the cycle in the intestines, they circulate in the bloodstream. From there they may lodge in various parts of the body with varying results, including enlargement of the liver, a muscle pain similar to trichina, or a condition in the cornea of the eye which has been mistaken for carcinoma.

Roundworms are often ignored because adult dogs usually seem to tolerate them. A rapidly growing giant puppy, however, is a different story. Puppies can acquire them prenatally and thus be retarded or killed. Roundworms are easily eliminated, and in view of the danger both to puppies and to human beings, there seems no reason why roundworm infestation should be tolerated.

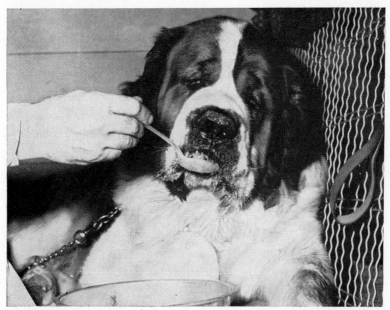

Howlett photo

CH. BARRE V STANISLAUS has a continent-wide pedigree. Sired by Ch. Helmar v Alpine Plateau, out of Delsa of Sunny Slopes, C.D., bred by Walter A. Schill and owned by Paul Wallbank, of Concord, California. The spoon feeding is a reward for best of breed at Oakland Kennel Club.

On Feb. 12, 1963, members of the Saint Bernard fancy held their breath until Mrs. William Long decided that a Saint brace handled by 15-year-old Jessica Roberts was best in the working group at the Westminster Kennel Club show. Photographers Brown and Shafer are at work on the dogs while Ruth Robbins shoots from the Madison Square Garden stands.

BEST BRACE IN SHOW

Shafer photo

Still breathless fanciers waited until late that night to watch judge Virgil Johnson agree with Mrs. Long's decision by awarding CH. HAAGEN VON NARBENHOLT and his younger full brother WUNDERBAR the title of best brace in show. This being an all-time first for Saints at Westminster, the New England St. Bernard Club promptly voted Jessica a lifetime membership.

183

184

A Week-End With the Saints

A broad look at the Saint Bernard was achieved during the long Memorial Day week-end of 1963. The three-day event, in quality, quantity, and comprehensive breed coverage, has been described as "once-in-a-lifetime." More important, the wide sampling permitted a definitive analysis of the present state of the breed.

The event attracted widespread attention from outside the fancy. Arithmetic-minded historians have discovered many world's records, at least one of which may stand for a long while; an all-time, all-breed record for pounds on the paw.

Program: Briefly, the week-end included:

Friday, May 31; Demonstration Day, an unofficial meeting for evaluation, discussion, handler training, and puppy competition, held on the grounds of the Stigmatine Fathers in Wellesley, Mass.

185

Saturday, June 1; the Saint Bernard Club of America specialty, a part of the Ladies' Dog Club all-breed show, was held on the same grounds, with 88 Saints accounting for 108 official entries. Then followed the first annual meeting of the newly reorganized SBCA.

Sunday, June 2; the New England Saint Bernard Club, Saturday's host club, held its own specialty at the Framingham (Mass.) District Kennel Club's all-breed show, with 81 Saints and 118 official entries.

Many members of the fancy came from a great distance, without dogs. All were accommodated at a nearby motel, where social events were held on Thursday, Friday, and Saturday evenings as a part of the breed discussion program.

Arithmetic: Breadth of coverage is illustrated by these figures:

Ninety-five owner-exhibitors participated. They came from twelve states. They represented seven of the twelve Saint Bernard clubs on this continent.

In the preceding chapter there is a list of 87 names, defined by their area clubs as "breeders." Of the 87 on this continent, 34 participated in the week-end, while many others contributed.

By the same definition, 61 non-breeders participated.

In the two formal American Kennel Club shows, 226 entries were made, including 132 by the "breeders" and 94 by the "non-breeders."

Nine of the twelve Saint Bernard clubs contributed to the trophy fund, as did 74 individuals, or 83 in all.

Eighteen American champions and one Canadian champion entered the specials ring at the SBCA show, no one of them without a string of best of breeds already to his credit. They were shown by nineteen different owners. All but one stayed to try again the next day. Perhaps most impressive of all; roughly two per cent of the registered Saint Bernards on this continent were participants.

What Does a Saint Bernard Weigh? The answer to this question has often been a blend of fancy, legend, childhood memory, and no doubt considerable prevarication. As part of the week-end's program, every participating Saint was weighed-in, registered, and photographed, thus providing broad information on what a well-conditioned Saint Bernard, 1963 style, weighs.

Heaviest dog was Ch. Powell's Triston of Riga, at 217 pounds. He was brought to the scales by the SBCA vice-president, Laurence Powell. A few others, looking equally heavy, were around the two hundred mark.

The weight spread between dogs, all of good quality, was wide. Adult males for the most part ran from 150 through 195. Adult females ranged evenly from 130 through 170, with the complete spread being from 120 to 186.

The average weight of all Saints which crossed the scales, including dogs, bitches, and puppies over six months, was 153 pounds, or about thirteen dogs to the ton. The accumulated weight of all entries came to just under seventeen tons.

Observation on Type: One conclusion to be drawn from the week-end's showing is that the emphasis on sheer bulk as a criterion of Saint Bernard quality has vanished. While remaining securely in first place with the heaviest of dogs, Saint breeders have abandoned bulk in favor of soundness, condition, and excellence of movement. The typical Saint now seems to have four good legs under him, not just the front two.

A Dedicated Fancy: The Saint Bernard is not a status symbol, he is a member of the family. The station wagons arriving for the week-end contained at least as many children as dogs. The breed is largely owner-trained and handled, with about ninety per cent of the owners handling their own dogs in the ring. No matter what the distance, once entered, the Saint Bernard family shows up. The number of absentees at the week-end was less than one-third that normally expected at a dog show.

Ch. Switzer of Shady Hollow, chosen by judge A. Alfred LePine as Best of Breed at the Saint Bernard Club of America specialty. Handler, Jane Kamp; owner, Phyllis Jackson of North Windham, Conn.

Mr. LePine's choice for Best of Opposite Sex, Ch. Gerda Christina of Skycroft. Handler, William Trainor; owner, Maritta Cox, of Seville, Ohio.

At the New England Saint Bernard Club specialty, judge Dorothy Breyfogle moved Gerda Christina to Best of Breed. Here she faces her full brother, CH. GERO CRISTOPHER OF SKYCROFT, who was judged Best of Opposite Sex.

CH. KOBI VON STEINERNHOF, whose owner, Charles Cawker, of Foxboro, Ontario, brought him to the United States for the first time, was handled by Jessica Roberts and judged Winners Dog and Best of Winners by both Mr. LePine and Mrs. Breyfogle for a history making ten-point week-end.

189

Ch. Siegfried von Alpenhof was weigh-in number
one to begin the week-end. Officials are Charles Sorenson, weighmaster, and Rex Roberts, week-end chairman.

A handler class, during Demonstration Day at the 1963 Saint Bernard
week-end, pauses to let television photographers get some cheesecake.
Embracing owner Al Saba is Ch. Queen of Sheba of Shady Hollow,
top-winning Saint bitch in 1961.

190

Mazanec photo

CH. AL-VER-DON FRAUSTY at the age of eight. Bred by Alfred Moulton, a Saint specialty judge, by Faust von Melina out of Frieda's Chrissty. Frausty sired some 450 Saints, which may put him close to the top in this regard. Already included in his progeny is a high percentage of champions.

Thom Loughman, who was then 15 years old, shows how some of the exhibitors got home.

Eighteen champions in one ring. Dog photographer Brown used his panoramic camera to get them all.

The Saint Fancier's Forum

IT is difficult not to notice a Saint Bernard, therefore owners get accustomed to answering questions. When Saint fanciers get together, they compare notes on how to answer. Here are some of their suggestions.

How Can I Find the Right Puppy?

The person who asks this question should be congratulated, and answered carefully, beginning with the counter-question, "What kind of puppy do you and your children want?" Children and puppies go together, but there are differences. The puppies grow up faster and cost less. In selecting a puppy, you can decide which one you want, rather than take pot-luck.

Any dog, and especially the Saint Bernard, becomes a working member of the family. When you acquire a dog, or a child, you acquire a responsibility and a delight. In either case, you will have to do some work and spend some money.

An average dog, over his average lifetime, will cost you a good deal more than his purchase price, but over the years it's a bargain-basement instalment plan with no interest charges, and perhaps twenty times less than the cost of raising an average child. Dogs have to be fed, but at bargain rates. They have to be housed and cared for, but most of them are adaptable and healthy. They need to be educated, but the tuition charge is low.

In any case, you will want to get as much reward as you can for your money. The most important step is to pick the right puppy. Here is how you go about it.

1. Inform yourself about the breed of your choice, which is probably a Saint Bernard, because otherwise you wouldn't be reading this book. There are books about every breed. Buy one, or several, and do your homework.

2. Inform yourself about nearby breeders. A good source of information is reached through breed clubs. Almost every breed has a national club, and area clubs. There may be an expert on your chosen breed who lives just around the corner. To find him, borrow a dog show catalog from anyone who shows dogs. Any such catalog will list dogs from a hundred or more different breeds, and the names and addresses of their owners. Select the name of the nearest owner and ask him for the name and address of the area club's secretary. Then ask the secretary for the names of the nearest breeders.

3. Attend a meeting of the breed club in your area, or better still, join the club. This is a quick way of getting acquainted with people who know more about the breed than you do. You'll also meet some good dogs. For further acquaintance, go to a dog show, or a session of the nearby obedience class.

4. By now you may have decided which breeder you prefer. From here on the puppies will speak for themselves. One of them will pick you out, and that's it. However, if your heart can be guided by your head, try to fall in love with the best pup in the litter. The breeder will have priced the litter members on his estimate of their quality. There won't be much difference in the prices, therefore the chances are that over

194

the life of the dog, the highest-priced pup will cost you less and satisfy you more.

What Does a Puppy Cost?

The first cost of a pup will be somewhere between three and ten per cent of his lifetime cost, but because it comes in one lump, puppy-pickers worry about it. Many of them, accustomed to buying commodities by the pound, assume that a large dog will naturally cost more than a small one. In fact, the cost of a purebred pup of any breed, quality for quality, will be about the same, whether the pup is a Chihuahua or a Saint Bernard.

There will be a wider price range between the good and poor specimens of any breed than among all breeds put together. The exception to this rule is that breed fashions change. There are always two or three breeds that are surging in popularity and become over-priced, then the cycle turns, supply exceeds demand, and the breeders can hardly give them away.

This phenomenon happened to the Saint Bernard in the late nineteenth century, when they became for a time the most numerous of all breeds, with the inevitable over-pricing and careless breeding. Fortunately this cycle happened long ago. The Saint's adaptability has made him a member of what society calls the "middle-class" family, of "medium" income, therefore the Saint Bernard pup is medium-priced and for the most part carefully bred, because the Saint-buying family wants to get its money's worth.

Obviously, if large pups and small pups sell for the same price, the Saint Bernard breeder is looking for love and exercise, not profit. As a practical matter, many of them defray the food bill by treating Saints as a hobby, then cut their dog-lover losses by raising a smaller breed as well.

What Does It Cost to Feed a Saint Bernard?

Whether you are sitting on the bench at a dog show, taking a walk in the woods, or dog-resting in your own living room, the first question asked of Saint fanciers is almost always,

"What does it cost to feed your dog?" The Saint owner attempts to shrug off this impolite question by replying jocosely, "Less than Junior, here," or "About the same as me," or "Roughly a hundred miles to the gallon of milk."

The serious and correct answer is, "Less per pound of dog than any other dog." The Saint's metabolic rate is low, that is, he uses his fuel with economy. He is surpassed in this respect by the confined, domestic rabbit, who converts four pounds of food into one pound of rabbit. Next comes the pastured steer, who can make a pound of beef out of five pounds of hay. Among canines, the Saint wins, being able to convert six pounds of food into one pound of dog. Smaller canines have less favorable conversion rates, ranging all the way up to thirty pounds of food per pound of dog.

Once the Saint has his growth, his poundage intake will be about the same as yours. His metabolism rate is about the same as yours, and on the average he outweighs you, but he worries less than you do and works fewer hours in the day, so you break even on food intake.

The Saint breeder is almost always asked, "How much will he eat?" At this point the breeder, torn between his desire to state the fact and his desire to see you get a good puppy, mumbles something like, "Not much." He seldom dares remind you that through a growing period of several months the Saint puppy's body is genetically conditioned to gain weight at the rate of a pound a day. If the conversion rate is six to one, the Saint puppy wants six pounds of food a day through this period, and from this food will produce the most dog for your money. Breeders ruefully point out that the ultimate bargain in dog-feeding, of course, is not to have a dog at all.

Will He Bite Me?

After, "How much does he eat?" the next question is usually, "Will he bite me?" The irresistible answer is, "Well, he's very fond of children." Other jocose answers run all the way from, "Probably not, sorry," through "Stick around and find out," to "Of course he will if you don't stop waving your fingers in his face."

Again the serious and correct answer is, "No, he won't, unless you give him a good reason." There are exceptions, but for the most part Saints are less inclined to violence than people.

Does He Have a Good Disposition?

The correct answer is, "Not always, but usually better than mine." In the close relationship between dogs and people, a process of natural selection sees to it that the larger the dog, the better his disposition will probably be. Dog-owners will tolerate bad disposition in a small dog because he is physically easy to control. A Saint Bernard, somewhat heavier and far stronger than you are, simply has to have a good disposition in order to be tolerated by humans.

A bad disposition can occur by accident, or it can be forced upon any animal if the owner tries hard enough. Most dogs try to behave themselves because it's easier to get along with their owners if they do. Most Saint Bernards have good dispositions for the unromantic but effective reason that if they don't, they are big enough to be intolerable and their owners remove them from the genetic process.

Is the Saint a Good Watchdog?

The answer is "No," if by "watchdog" the questioner means an animal that will attack anybody on sight. Most Saints have excellent hearing and very acute scent. They have good memory for both friend and foe. Their outstanding trait seems to be an instinct for the preservation of life. Physical violence offends them, whether it be a cat killing a mouse, a fox killing a cat, two men striking each other, or even a parent spanking the baby. Given a soft-voiced and gentle burglar, a Saint would probably show him where the family silver is stored. However, the burglars do not know this. The Saint's impressive mass, musculature, and deep bass voice persuade the burglar to go burgle somebody else.

The family-raised Saint, allowed to become acquainted with postmen, milkmen, breadmen and meter readers, acquires a discrimination which helps him to distinguish between right and wrong, most of the time. This qualifies him as a baby-sitter, although he cannot change diapers or answer the telephone. If you seek a watchdog with some ability to evaluate, the Saint is unsurpassed.

When Should Training Begin?

The answer is, "Right now." A dog's life span is one-seventh of ours, but his growth, learning, and maturity rate in the early weeks is perhaps twenty times as fast. He wants to learn, up to the limit of his capacity, and he regards you as his teacher. He can be trained at any age, but the sooner the better, because the puppy likes and respects authority.

The Saint Bernard cannot be controlled by muscle power. He has more than you. He is controlled by his desire to please you. Your requirements are conveyed to him by words, which if you use consistently he can understand, and by means of a leash and collar. The training collar, erroneously called a "choke" collar, is a device by which you signal your intentions to the dog. No cruelty is involved. The eight-weeks-old puppy quickly learns to read your signals. The leash becomes a symbol of attention and play. When it appears the puppy knows he is going to have a good time. If, however, the Saint first feels leash and collar when he is eight months old, he may not be sure whether they represent fun or punishment.

How Can I Keep Him Out of Trouble?

There is one right answer, "A fenced yard." It is not a favor to the dog to let him run free. The fence establishes his boundary and his home. When he leaves this sanctuary to explore the world, he does so with you. The fence also improves his chances of survival, keeps him from becoming a town bum, and betters your relations with the neighbors.

The puppy will enjoy his personal fence more if it is established early in life. An older dog, with long memories of having roamed his own way, may regard the fence as confinement rather than possession.

The worst thing you can do to your Saint is put him on collar and chain, then leave him alone. Without a fence around him he is both tethered and vulnerable. This tends to make any dog belligerent. Leash and collar, with you in command, represent fun. A sizable fenced yard represents freedom and safety. A chain, without a human hand at the other end of it, represents dangerous slavery.

This is not an advertisement for merry Oldsmobiles. Instead, it shows why no one steals your car if there is a Saint in it. Beau Chevals Trade-Mark and Beau Chevals El-Cid are owned by John Bean, of Newtown, Pennsylvania. El-Cid intends that his classically wrinkled brow should make him look wise, not threatening, but the potential car thief is unaware of his intentions.

199

Saint Bernard Organizations

Information, pictures, and opinions in this book are furnished entirely by members of the Saint Bernard fancy. Numerically, something over four thousand Saints a year are registered with the American Kennel Club, with many more in Canada and Mexico, and still more unregistered. The number of Saint-owning families on this continent can only be conjectured. An order-of-magnitude guess might be around fifty thousand, as the total membership of the fancy.

The only channel for soliciting information from all these people is through Saint Bernard organizations, especially their secretaries. It is then up to the editors to check information, choose between hundreds of pictures, and balance diverse opinions.

The Saint Bernard Club of America operates on a continent-wide basis, therefore almost entirely by mail. Its officers elected in 1966 were:

President, Laurence H. Powell
Vice-president, Earl Samstag
Secretary, Edward A. Poor, R.R. 1, Acton, Mass.
Treasurer, Howard Brown
Governors: Mrs. Fred Pyle and Mrs. Charles Rankin, Western Section
           Edward P. Wade, Jr. and Paul Cocanour, Central Section
           Rev. Dominic Eagan, Eastern Section

This organization is recognized by the American Kennel Club as the official spokesman for the breed. Its magazine, the *Saint Fancier*, publishes timely news from the area clubs, and most of its members also participate in their nearest area club.

From 1963 to 1966, seven new area clubs became active. As of this printing, and reading roughly from east to west across the continent, the list of area clubs and their secretaries is:

New England St. Bernard Club (Irene Mowry, 125 Arnold St., Attleboro, Mass.)

Long Island St. Bernard Club (Bernadette Rapali, 15 N. Clinton Ave., Bayshore, L. I., N. Y.)

New York St. Bernard Club (Gail Devine, 219 Atlantic Ave., Lynbrook, L. I., N. Y.)

St. Bernard Club of Northern New Jersey (Marian Sharp, Mine Hill, Dover, N. J.)

Eastern St. Bernard Association (Florence Anderson, Lake Tract, Woodbury, N. J.)

Middle Atlantic St. Bernard Club (Sarah Bussinger, 211 Ashland Ave., Belmont Hills, Philadelphia, Pa.)

St. Bernard Club of Ontario (Jean Cox, 11 Partridge Lane, Agincourt, Ontario)

Ohio St. Bernard Club (Mary Peabody, 744 Oliver St., Sheffield Lake, Ohio)

St. Bernard Club of Michigan (Penny Little, 23596 Candace, Rockwood, Mich.)

Central Indiana St. Bernard Club (Kaye Wessar, R.R. 3, Anderson, Indiana)

Northern Illinois St. Bernard Club (Pat Thibedeau, 41 S. Slusser, Grayslake, Ill.)

St. Bernard Club of Minnesota (Patricia Wiggins, 816 Sunkist Parkway, Minneapolis, Minn.)

St. Bernard Club of Greater St. Louis (Nancy Crane, 12144 Gravois Rd., St. Louis, Mo.)

St. Bernard Club of the Rockies (James Yost, 501 W. 70th Pl., Denver, Colo.)

St. Bernard Club of Southern California (Lillian Buell, 15995 Arminta, Van Nuys, Calif.)

Sacramento-Sierra St. Bernard Club (Anna Gainsley, 9012 Leedy Lane, Fair Oaks, Calif.)

St. Bernard Club of the Pacific Northwest (Janice Wick, 2125 El Capitan Way, Everett, Wash.)

St. Bernard Club of the Pacific Coast (Judy Harvey, 172 Ludell Dr., Walnut Creek, Calif.)

The area club secretaries change from year to year, as their task is transferred from one hand to another. All of the above secretaries have contributed to the compilation of this book,

201

and they will be able to help you find the present incumbents, if any change has been made.

The American Kennel Club licenses certain people to judge Saint Bernards, and Saints only, at dog shows. These people have made a profound study of the breed and are known as "specialty" judges, as distinguished from those who are licensed to judge many other breeds. Their opinions have been solicited for use in this book. As of this printing, the Saint specialty judges include Mrs. Dorothy Breyfogle, Howard E. Brown, Stanley Bussinger, H. Mercer Cresap, III, Arthur Hesser, Benjamin D. Hoyt, Norman Keller, Alfred Moulton, Laurence Powell, and John Stanek. The editors regret that Dr. Wedig, who contributed extensively to the standards chapter, has retired.

A famous brother and sister act, composed of Ch. Gerda Christina of Skycroft and Ch. Gero Christopher of Skycroft. In the inset puppy picture, taken in 1960 at the age of three weeks, Gero is at left and Gerda at right. In the adult picture, taken with Mr. and Mrs. John H. Cox, of Seville, Ohio, Gero is standing. Gerda became top winning bitch in 1963 and 1964, with Gero top dog in 1964. Gero's record at this time included 6 best in show, 22 group firsts, and 84 best of breeds.

Douglas and Karen Black, of Cambridge, Wisconsin, brought their show winning brace up by way of obedience training. Here are Black's Brandy, C.D., and Black's Boozer, C.D., as they were at 4 months and 15 months, respectively.

Widely-admired judge Alva Rosenberg decides that Brandy, Booze, and Mrs. Black should win. By this time the dogs had completed their obedience degrees, and went on to win best-brace-in-show at Chicago. *Ritter photo*

Booze, having by now scored his first best-in-show, is visited by an unidentified blond on his bench in Toronto at the Canadian National Exhibition. Photographer Turofsky couldn't resist this one.

203

Breeders:

The following list is intended to help the reader who wishes to find a nearby Saint breeder. It is compiled roughly by locality, rather than by area club membership. A breeder is defined as one who is continuously active in the fancy, and may be expected to have puppies more or less regularly for sale. The names are supplied by area club secretaries and by individuals. In a growing fancy, the list is not guaranteed to be complete, accurate, or up-to-date, but is based on the best information available. Each breeder is identified by one name only, omitting joint ownership and omitting kennel name. Since there are now scores of fine kennels, no attempt is made to compare one kennel with another.

Eastern Canada:

Willis, Cdr. Robert C.; Fathom Harbour, Halifax Co., N. S.

New England States:

Bedard, Carla; RFD 2, Skowhegan, Maine
Boynton, Aimee; Ashland, N. H.
Chudy, Tadeusz; Plainfield, Mass.
Cohn, Irwin; 746 West St., Leominster, Mass.
Crabb, Bruce; Baboosic Lake Road, Merrimac, N. H.
Dube, Donald; Hunts Bridge Road, N. Attleboro, Mass.
Holmes, Harold; 434 Elm St., Bridgewater, Mass.
Jackson, Richard; Back Road, RFD 2, Willimantic, Conn.
McKeever, Edward; Hampton Road, Exeter, N. H.
Myers, Margaret; RFD, N. Attleboro, Mass.
Natale, Benjamin; 835 Clintonville Road, Wallingford, Conn.
Ottum, Barbara; 77 Falmouth Road, Falmouth, Maine
Parker, Howard; Webbs Hill Road, Stamford, Conn.
Parsons, Robert; 353 Elm St., Bridgewater, Mass.
Poor, Edward A.; RFD 1, Acton, Mass.
Roberts, William; Baxter St., Tolland, Conn.
Saba, Alfred; Munsell Road, Belchertown, Mass.
Smith, Phyllis Jackson; North Windham, Conn.
Wagenknecht, Paul; RFD 2, Stafford Springs, Conn.

Middle Atlantic States:

Andersen, Fred; 269 Maple Road, Woodbury, N. J.
Anderson, Marlene; Old Anchor Road, Wycombe, Pa.
Black, Phyllis; Ryland Inn, Whitehouse, N. J.
Bos, Rudy; RFD 1, Englishtown, N. J.
Bowen, John; Box 163, North Wales, Pa.
Bussinger, Stanley; 211 Ashland Ave., Philadelphia, Pa.
Deitch, Harold; 290 E. Main St., Smithtown, L. I., N. Y.
Eagan, Rev. Dominic; 179 Hussa St., Linden, N. J.
Goldworm, Judith; 3333 Fischer Rd., Easton, Pa.
Gresham, Roy; 838 Lehigh Ave., Union, N. J.
Hauser, Dorothy; Box 462, Woodbridge, N. J.
Henry, Karl; Jenkins Road, Red Creek, N. Y.
Mallen, Louis; 46 Woodside Ave., Levittown, Pa.
McKeel, Robert; Box 143, Monaca, Pa.
Palmer, David G.; Union Springs, N. Y.
Powell, Laurence; Sutton Creek Road, Pittston, Pa.
Prodziewicz, Florence; 49 Hutchinson St., Clark, N. J.
Reeh, William; 2 Ryers Ave., Cheltenham, Pa.
Reiland, Mrs. Donald; 39 Briarcliff Road, Larchmont, N. Y.
Ridgeway, Ben; 72 E. Main St., Columbus, N. J.
Ritter, Joanna; Thorncrest Drive, Butler, Pa.
Rose, Joseph; Ridge Road, Highland Hills, N. Y.
Taylor, David; 121 E. Buffalo St., Churchville, N. Y.
Van Allen, Paul; 12 Seneca Turnpike, Clinton, N. Y.
Werner, Harry W.; 1112 Brookside Road, New Market, N. J.
Wilson, Robert; Pine Tree Lane, Old Westbury, L. I., N. Y.
Yoder, Walter; RFD 1, Meyersdale, Pa.

Central Canada:

Cawker, Charles; R.R. 1, Foxboro, Ont.
Cutting, Mae; Bowmanville, Ont.
Davis, Donald H.; R.R. 2, Claremont, Ont.
Seaman, Richard; R.R. 2, Markham, Ont.
Widdis, Ruby; R.R. 3, Brockville, Ont.
Wierzbicki, R.; Wyoming, Ont.

East Central States:

Bakas, Tom; 12150 Spencer Rd., Milford, Mich.
Becker, James; 25 White Oak Drive, Hubbard, Ohio
Beehler, Carl; 8033 Taylorsville Rd., Dayton, Ohio
Breyfogle, Dorothy; 1260 Taggart Ave., N. E., Massillon, Ohio
Burrows, Thelma; Greenfield, Ind.
Cloyd, Robert; RFD 2, Elida, Ohio
Cocanour, Paul; Box 33, Deerfield, Ohio
Cooley, William; 3556 Patton Dr., Indianapolis, Ind.
Cox, Shirlie; RD 1, Box 56, Seville, Ohio
Douglas, Dirk; 235 Kilgore Ave., Muncie, Ind.
Engler, Frank; 1384 Brimfield Dr., Kent, Ohio
Garton, Robert; RD 5, Box 286, Laporte, Ind.
Harvey, Grace; Syracuse, Ind.
House, Al; 9490 E. Clark Rd., East Lansing, Mich.
Irwin, Anne; 5136 Cascade Rd., Grand Rapids, Mich.
Irwin, Lee; 32414 River Rd., Rockwood, Mich.
King, Marilyn; RD 3, Sheridan, Ind.
Klever, Leo; 4620 N. Van Atta Rd., Okemos, Mich.
Laurie, Jack; RD 1, Reading, Mich.
Morgan, George; Chagrin Falls, Ohio
Peabody, Herman; 744 Oliver, Sheffield Lake, Ohio
Poling, Dorothy; RD 2, Elida, Ohio
Potts, Dr. Donald E.; RD 1, West Lafayette, Ohio
Randall, Morris; RD 1, Carmel, Ind.
Sickels, Earle; 6773 Big Creek, Middleburg Heights, Ohio
Thompson, Robert; RD 1, Albany, Ind.
Van Osch, Andre; RD 2; Lynn, Ind.
Vest, Gene; RD 4, Scottsburg, Ind.
Vigil, Bertha; 10580 Eighth Ave., Grand Rapids, Mich.
Wessar, George; RD 3, Box 389A, Anderson, Ind.
Worman, Charles; 122 Trailway Ave., Dayton, Ohio

West Central States:

Arland, Thomas; 3201 W. Owasso Blvd., St. Paul, Minn.
Bartell, Joseph; New Holstein, Wis.
Birkholz, Richard; RD 2, Box 172, Union Grove, Wis.

Crane, Jerry; RD 1, Box 426, Wilderness Lane, High Ridge, Mo.
Dabbs, Sam; Box 142, Edwardsville, Ill.
Elam, Leonard; 1120 May St., Joliet, Ill.
Hullah, Mrs. Stanley; RD 1, Lathers Rd., Beloit, Wis.
Jensen, Sally; RD 1, Box 169A1, Libertyville, Ill.
Justad, Mrs. M.; Cedar, Minn.
Koplin, E. D.; Litchfield, Minn.
Krook, James; 1065 Thomas Ave. South, Minneapolis, Minn.
Ledbetter, L.; RD 2, Box 583, Arnold, Mo.
Legg, Joy; RD 1, Box 268B, Colgate, Wis.
Llewellyn, Odessa; Waukee, Iowa
Martin, Winifred; RD 1, Roanoke, Ill.
Meier; RD 2, Monroe, Wis.
Mitchell, Mrs. James; Avon, Ill.
Montross, Harold; RD 2, Madison, Wis.
Paulik, Henry; RD 2, Box 298, Imperial, Mo.
Raulston, David; 504 Reynolds Rd., Marshalltown, Iowa
Reedy, Clyde; 5 Swallow Lane, St. Paul, Minn.
Samstag, Earl; 25 W 480 Plank Rd., Naperville, Ill.
Schlote, David; RD 1, Box 102, Catawissa, Mo.
Shull, Gerald; 780 Sanders, Deerfield, Ill.
Smith, Lloyd; Helenville, Wis.
Thibedeau, Norman; RD 2, Box 473A, Antioch, Ill.
Tynan, Richard; 504 E. Congress St., Elmhurst, Ill.
Wiggins, Richard; 816 Sunkist Parkway, Minneapolis, Minn.
Wilkus, Robert; Lakeville, Minn.

Great Plains States:

Cline, Norman; 139 S. Raleigh St., Denver, Colo.
Coulter, Eugene; 17645 West 44th Ave., Golden, Colo.
Gendell, Ernest; 7560 Lowell Blvd., Westminster, Colo.
Gingrich, Douglas; RD 1, Wray, Colo.
Klein, Viggo; Laramie, Wyo.
Mullikin, David; Aspen, Colo.
Munn, Joan; 520 University Blvd., Denver, Colo.
Veach, Larry; RD 2, Derby, Kan.
Wilkey, Harry; Sterling, Kan.

Western States:

Buell, William; 15995 Arminta, Van Nuys, Calif.
Gray, Jack; 3119 Greenwood Dr., Fremont, Calif.
Knight, Beatrice; Gunther Road, Drain, Ore.
McCausland, William; 975 Barrymore Dr., Concord, Calif.
Montgomery, John; 4111 Lovall Valley Rd., Sonoma, Calif.
Rankin, Eve; 1314 N E, Puyallup, Wash.
Smith, Neil; RD 1, Chewelah, Wash.
Wallbank, Paul; 1420 Willcrest Drive, Concord, Calif.

Western Canada:

Elliott, J.; Upper Saskatchewan Ranger Station, Rocky Mountain House, Alberta

AKC and CKC CH. KOBI VON STEINERNHOF, is not averse to socializing with a girl-child. This 12-weeks-old female was bred by Irwin Cohn, of Leominster, Mass. A Saint Bernard's ears are his most expressive feature. Three attitudes of listening are expressed here by Kobi, aged nine, in the center, flanked by his year-old sons, Charlinore's Grand Brandy and Grand Winston, both of whom already outweighed their father. Kobi's get by this time numbered over 350. Two of them were photographed here to demonstrate family solidarity.

Riley photos

Junior handler and owner Jack Vest, of Scottsburg, Indiana, who showed CH. BROWSER L'OURS ALPIN all the way to his title, demonstrates his method of bathing a Saint. First the garden hose, then the soap. Cooperation from Browser is a must. (The photographs are by C. Thomas Hardin, courtesy of *Courier-Journal* and *Louisville Times*.)

Careful around the head, because Saints don't like soap in their eyes any more than you do. In these pictures, Ch. Browser is 18 months old, and Jack is 13 years.

Here is a lot of action, although no one is going anywhere. Only the camera can remember what a wet Saint does when he decides to shake. Jack is now as wet as Browser.

To complicate matters, TEDDI V SCHWARZWALD HOF, owned by Jack's father, Gene Vest, has gone for a swim in the pond. Toweling a Saint is a little like painting a barn, except that Jack uses both hands.

The Saint In Action

THE Saint Bernard suffers from his own reputation. He is expected to be a draft animal, a house pet, a plaything and a workhorse. Pound for pound, he is presumed to be able to outpull any draft animal living, yet he is asked to run freely and gracefully when not under load. This is like asking a Percheron to dance the polka. The test of a good Saint is how well he can meet these varying demands.

In the following group of pictures you will observe a variety of gaits. Artists and photographers have done much work on the complexities of four-legged motion. Perhaps the earliest motion pictures were invented at the behest of a millionaire who wanted to prove that at certain moments a trotting horse has all four feet off the ground. A two-legged mammal is easy to observe. He has only two gaits, walk and run, the difference being that when he walks one foot is always on the ground. Four-legged mammals have a variety of gaits, among which the most common are called walk, trot, gallop, and pace.

The walk rhythm is "ca-lump ca-lump," with the left hind foot hitting the ground just before the right front foot, and just before the left front foot lifts off. When walking, a dog always has three feet on the ground at any given instant.

Walk becomes trot when the rhythm is hastened, with the sequence of leg movements remaining the same. The sound now becomes "clump clump," because two feet are coming down and the other two lifting off at almost, though not quite, the same time. This is the action customarily referred to by dog fanciers as "gaiting."

A gallop is entirely different. The sound becomes "too-too-bum too-too-bum." With all four feet off the ground, the front two then strike in sequence, followed by the power stroke of the back two hitting the ground almost together. Puppies gallop before they trot, presumably because the coordination of the hind legs is not yet well developed. Almost any dog, in the excitement of play, will gallop to get from here to there.

Instead of trotting, some four-footed mammals prefer to pace. In this action the two right and two left legs work together. As in a trot, the sound is "clump clump," but made by two on a side rather than two on opposite sides. The feet cannot interfere with each other, therefore the animal does not have to move slightly sideways in order to keep from stepping on his own feet. However, the animal cannot pace slowly, because he depends on inertia to keep from falling over. Many dog show judges will reject a pacer as not "gaiting" properly, even though the pace at proper speed is the smoothest of all possible gaits, and allows the dog to run in a straight line.

The Saint Bernard when used as a draft animal always walks or trots. His best gait is exhibited when he is at work, whether pulling, hill-climbing, or plowing through snow. Under load, his hindquarters drop down, his angulation increases, his back straightens, and his head drops as he gets his front shoulders into the work. As you will see, the purpose of his front legs is to hold him up, and the purpose of his back legs is to pull.

At a leisurely crossover from walk to trot, a Saint will go into a gait which horse fanciers call "singlefoot." In this gait two feet will be on the ground, one on each side and on the diagonal to each other. What happens next depends on how fast he wants to go, and how much load he is pulling. He will either drop back to a walk, with three feet on the ground, or move up to a trot, with one foot on the ground. No four-footed mammal will attempt to gallop under load unless he is unduly excited.

This four-dog, double-harnessed team is practicing in a Colorado snowstorm for the winter's races held by the Rocky Mountain Sled Dog Club, where they were to compete with Huskies, Malemutes, and Samoyeds.

Left lead: Ch. Terry's Copper King, dog, 4 years old. Right lead: Adrian v.d. Eichmatt, dog pup, 10 months. Left wheel: Duchanz v. Katrina, bitch, 6 years. Right wheel: Alpi v.d. Eichmatt, dog pup, 10 months.

A good sled dog is where you find him. These four dogs have four different owners. Adrian and Alpi are litter brothers imported from Eichmatt, Switzerland. Their instructor, King, held the Rocky Mountain Regional single-dog weight pulling record at 1050 pounds. (King, the left lead, is at your right in the picture.)

You will notice that the dogs are pulling in their favorite way, in step with each other and on opposite sides. Even the ears are waving in unison. The almost invisible driver is Don Johnson, of Denver. Picture is by Robert Hurley.

212

Little's Swiss Miss, aged 3, and Princess Margaret, aged 1, are headed
north at a brisk trot. Owner Donald C. Little, of Rockwood, Michigan,
is not pushing. He's trying to get aboard for the ride.

The master of ceremonies, Roy Taylor, of Flint, Mich., introduces his two end-women. On his right is Heidi's Spice v. Schwarzwald Hof. On his left is Sugar Plum v. Schwarzwald Hof, both owned by Walter Taylor, of Caro, Mich.

To begin the show, Heidi's Spice exhibits a slow trot, with two opposite feet firmly on the ground, and the other two coming forward. At this mid-point in gait, the back lifts in the middle.

This is a rare exhibition of pace, shown by the slightly older and heavier Sugar Plum. The two far legs have just come down, and the near two are just lifting off. At full stretch in gait, the back lowers in the middle.

The last act is devoted to good music, with Heidi's Spice about to break into song.

The dogs have just started a medium load, and are accelerating from walk into trot. Only the camera could detect that they are reaching almost, but not quite, in step.

Breaking into full working trot under light load, with the near back legs doing all the work at this instant. When the load is light, the dogs sometimes step off in parallel, rather than with opposite action.

Jarvis Hunt photos

A puppy and an adult, close relatives, and both walking. The puppy seems to be down in his pasterns, but in a few months' time he will have the same graceful movement as the adult. Photo study is by courtesy of Phyllis Jackson Smith, North Windham, Conn.

217

A Puppy Comes Home

Just over nine weeks
old, and on my way.

Here we are.

First I gallop while
chasing my elders.

Then learn to trot on
my way to breakfast.

I can even stand
still to be combed.

But I'd rather be out-
doors than in the studio.
Jarvis Hunt photos

Out of Action

AKC and CKC Ch. Bowser Waller was not in action at the time. He was resting after his sixtieth best of breed and fortieth group place. Bowser, owned by William Roberts of Tolland, Conn., was sired by Ch. Frausty out of Ch. Tolly, and the rest of his pedigree is almost a directory of recently memorable names, including Faust, Sandman, Golden Gal, Minka, Chriss, Frieda, Gerd, Felix, Rasrakko, Kurt, and Carmen Promise.

The Saint Puppy and His Parent

Ch. Sanctuary Woods Vanity, a daughter of two champions, bred by Beatrice Knight and owned by Davy Hug, of Enterprise, Oregon. Here are four of her puppies, smooth and rough in the same litter. Left to right are Hugme's Fortune Cookie, smooth bitch, Friendly Nature and Final Touch, rough dogs, and Flare for Luck, smooth dog. They were sired by Ch. Sanctuary Woods You Lucky Boy. The width of a blaze does not ordinarily increase in proportion with head growth, therefore a puppy will seem to have a narrower blaze when he grows up.

At left, Ch. Bomars Pride, affectionately known to the fancy as Atlas, guards one of his offspring. Atlas was bred by Walter Yoder, owned and shown by Marlene Anderson, of Wycombe, Pa., then showed them how to sire Saints in Missouri. Atlas, above, with Mrs. Anderson, watches over representatives of five different litters at feeding time.

Photos by Walter Klages

James Howlett, of Richmond, California, is a Saint fancier and talented amateur photographer, with a large collection of Saint Bernard pictures of his own making. At the editors' request he assembled a family story. The cast of characters includes: Sire, CH. KNABLAW'S EMO VON BARRE, bred by Paul Wallbank and owned by the Howletts; Dam, CH. KNABLAW'S GAY GIDGET VON ESBO, bred and owned by the Wallbanks; Get, a litter of ten pups, whelped in 1963 and photographed for two years thereafter. Three males appear in this series of pictures: Jimbo, Jericho, and Joshua von Emo. Jimbo's adventures appear in some detail.

First to appear is the sire, Ch. Emo, photographed at the age of eight.

Introducing the dam, Ch. Gidget, and whelp.

Knablaw's Jimbo von Emo, one day old.

Jimbo (left) and Jaguar, one week old. Jimbo's eyes are beginning to open.

Emo and Jimbo, with parental discipline saying that there will be no rough stuff in the house.

Jericho (left) and Joshua (right) are both trotting to greet brother Jimbo who has come to visit. Jimbo's gait can only be described as undecided.

Jimbo, having survived both parental discipline and sibling play, looked like this at the age of two.

Part II

GENERAL CARE AND TRAINING OF YOUR DOG

by

Elsworth S. Howell
Milo G. Denlinger
A. C. Merrick, D.V.M.

Introduction

THE normal care and training of dogs involve no great mysteries. The application of common sense and good judgment is required, however. The pages that follow distill the combined experience and knowledge of three authorities who have devoted most of their lives to dogs.

Milo Denlinger wrote many books out of his rich and varied experience as a breeder, exhibitor and owner of a commercial kennel. Elsworth Howell has been a fancier since young boyhood and claims intimate knowledge of 25 different breeds; he is an American Kennel Club delegate and judge of the sporting breeds. Dr. A. C. Merrick is a leading veterinarian with a wide practice.

The chapter on "Training and Simple Obedience" covers the basic behavior and performance every dog should have to be accepted by your friends, relatives, neighbors and strangers. The good manners and exercises described will avoid costly bills for damage to the owner's or neighbor's property and will prevent heartbreaking accidents to the dog and to the people he meets. The instructions are given in simple, clear language so that a child may easily follow them.

"The Exhibition of Dogs" describes the kinds of dog shows, their classes and how an owner may enter his dog and show it. If one practices good sportsmanship, shows can be enjoyable.

The chapter on feeding offers sound advice on feeding puppies,

3

adult dogs, the stud dog and the brood bitch. The values of proteins, carbohydrates, fats, minerals and vitamins in the dog's diet are thoroughly covered. Specific diets and quantities are not given because of the many variations among dogs, even of the same breed or size, in their individual needs, likes, dislikes, allergies, etc.

"The Breeding of Dogs" contains the fundamental precepts everyone who wishes to raise puppies should know. Suggestions for choosing a stud dog are given. The differences among outcrossing, inbreeding and line breeding are clearly explained. Care tips for the pregnant and whelping bitch will be found most helpful.

The material on "External Vermin and Parasites" gives specific treatments for removing and preventing fleas, lice, ticks and flies. With today's wonder insecticides and with proper management there is no excuse for a dog to be infested with any of these pests which often cause secondary problems.

"Intestinal Parasites and Their Control" supplies the knowledge dog owners must have of the kinds of worms that invade dogs and the symptoms they cause. While drugs used for the removal of these debilitating dog enemies are discussed, dosages are not given because it is the authors' and publisher's belief that such treatment is best left in the hands of the veterinarian. These drugs are powerful and dangerous in inexperienced hands.

The chapter on "Skin Troubles" supplies the information and treatments needed to recognize and cure these diseases. The hints appearing on coat care will do much to prevent skin problems.

One of the most valuable sections in this book is the "instant" advice on "FIRST AID" appearing on pages 95-98. The publisher strongly urges the reader to commit this section to memory. It may save a pet's life.

The information on diseases will help the dog owner to diagnose symptoms. Some dog owners rush their dogs to the veterinarian for the slightest, transitory upsets.

Finally, the chapters on "Housing for Dogs" and "Care of the Old Dog" round out this highly useful guide for all dog lovers.

Training and
Simple Obedience

E VERY DOG that is mentally and physically sound can be taught good manners and simple obedience by any normal man, woman, or child over eight years old.

Certain requirements must be met by the dog, trainer and the environment if the training is to be enjoyable and effective. The dog must be rested and calm. The trainer must be rested, calm, gentle, firm, patient and persistent. The training site should be dry, comfortable and, except for certain exercises, devoid of distractions.

Proper techniques can achieve quick and sure results. Always use short, strong words for commands and always use the *same* word or words for the same command. Speak with authority; never scream or yell. Teach one command or exercise at a time and make sure the dog understands it and performs it perfectly before you proceed to the next step. Demand the dog's undivided attention; if he wavers or wanders, speak his name or pat him smartly or jerk his leash. Use pats and praise plentifully; avoid tidbit training if at all possible because tidbits may not always be available in an emergency and the dog will learn better without them. Keep lessons short; when the dog begins to show boredom, stop and do not resume in less than two hours. One or two ten-minute lessons a day should be ample, especially for a young puppy. Dogs have their good and bad days; if your well dog seems unduly lazy, tired, bored or off-color, put off the lesson until tomorrow. Try to make lessons a joy, a happy time both for you and the dog, but do demand and get the desired action. Whenever correction or punishment is needed, use ways and devices that the dog does not connect with you; some of these means are given in the following instructions. Use painful punishment only as a last resort.

"NO!"

The most useful and easily understood command is "NO!" spoken in a sharp, disapproving tone and accompanied with a shaking finger. At first, speak the dog's name following with "NO!" until the meaning of the word—your displeasure—is clear.

"COME!"

Indoors or out, let the dog go ten or more feet away from you. Speak his name following at once with "COME!" Crouch, clap your hands, pick up a stick, throw a ball up and catch it, or create any other diversion which will lure the dog to you. When he comes, praise and pat effusively. As with all commands and exercises repeat the lesson, until the dog *always* comes to you.

THE FIRST NIGHTS

Puppies left alone will bark, moan and whine. If your dog is not to have the run of the house, put him in a room where he can do the least damage. Give him a Nylabone and a strip of beef hide (both available in supermarkets or pet shops and excellent as teething pacifiers). A very young puppy may appreciate a loud-ticking clock which, some dog trainers say, simulates the heart-beat of his former litter mates. Beyond providing these diversions, grit your teeth and steel your heart. If in pity you go to the howling puppy, he will howl every time you leave him. Suffer one night, two nights or possibly three, and you'll have it made.

The greatest boon to dog training and management is the wooden or wire crate. Any two-handed man can make a ⅜" plywood crate. It needs only four sides, a top, a bottom, a door on hinges and

6

with a strong hasp, and a fitting burlap bag stuffed with shredded newspaper, cedar shavings or 2″ foam rubber. Feed dealers or seed stores should give you burlap bags; be sure to wash them thoroughly to remove any chemical or allergy-causing material. The crate should be as long, as high and three times as wide as the dog will be full grown. The crate will become as much a sanctuary to your dog as a cave was to his prehistoric ancestor; it will also help immeasurably in housebreaking.

HOUSEBREAKING

The secret to housebreaking a healthy normal dog is simple: take him out every hour if he is from two to six months old when you get him; or the first thing in the morning, immediately after every meal, and the last thing at night if he is over six months.

For very young puppies, the paper break is indicated. Lay eight or ten layers of newspapers in a room corner most remote from the puppy's bed. By four months of age or after two weeks in a new home if older, a healthy puppy should not need the paper *IF* it is exercised outdoors often and *IF* no liquid (including milk) is given after 5 P.M. and *IF* it is taken out not earlier than 10 P.M. at night and not later than 7 A.M. the next morning.

When the dog does what it should when and where it should, praise, praise and praise some more. Be patient outdoors: keep the dog out until action occurs. Take the dog to the same general area always; its own traces and those of other dogs thus drawn to the spot will help to inspire the desired action.

In extreme cases where frequent exercising outdoors fails, try to catch the dog in the act and throw a chain or a closed tin can with pebbles in it near the dog but not on him; say "NO!" loudly as the chain or can lands. In the most extreme case, a full 30-second spanking with a light strap may be indicated but be sure you catch the miscreant *in the act.* Dog memories are short.

Remember the crate discussed under "THE FIRST NIGHTS." If you give the dog a fair chance, he will NOT soil his crate.

Do not rub his nose in "it." Dogs have dignity and pride. It is permissible to lead him to his error as soon as he commits it and to remonstrate forcefully with "NO!"

7

COLLAR AND LEASH TRAINING

Put on a collar tight enough not to slip over the head. Leave it on for lengthening periods from a few minutes to a few hours over several days. A flat collar for shorthaired breeds; a round or rolled collar for longhairs. For collar breaking, do NOT use a choke collar; it may catch on a branch or other jutting object and strangle the dog.

After a few days' lessons with the collar, attach a heavy cord or rope to it without a loop or knot at the end (to avoid snagging or catching on a stump or other object). Allow the dog to run free with collar and cord attached a few moments at a time for several days. Do not allow dog to chew cord!

When the dog appears to be accustomed to the free-riding cord, pick up end of the cord, loop it around your hand and take your dog for a walk (not the other way around!). DON'T STOP WALKING if the dog pulls, balks or screams bloody murder. Keep going and make encouraging noises. If dog leaps ahead of you, turn sharply left or right whichever is *away* from dog's direction— AND KEEP MOVING! The biggest mistake in leash training is stopping when the dog stops, or going the way the dog goes when the dog goes wrong. You're the leader; make the dog aware of it. This is one lesson you should continue until the dog realizes who is boss. If the dog gets the upper leg now, you will find it difficult to resume your rightful position as master. Brutality, no; firmness, yes!

If the dog pulls ahead, jerk the cord—or by now, the leash— backward. Do not pull. Jerk or snap the leash only!

JUMPING ON PEOPLE

Nip this annoying habit at once by bumping the dog with your knee on his chest or stepping with authority on his rear feet. A sharp "NO!" at the same time helps. Don't permit this action when you're in your work clothes and ban it only when dressed in glad rags. The dog is not Beau Brummel, and it is cruel to expect him to distinguish between denim and silk.

8

THE "PROBLEM" DOG

The following corrections are indicated when softer methods fail. Remember that it's better to rehabilitate than to destroy.

Biting. For the puppy habit of mouthing or teething on the owner's hand, a sharp rap with a folded newspaper on the nose, or snapping the middle finger off the thumb against the dog's nose, will usually discourage nibbling tactics. For the biter that means it, truly drastic corrections may be preferable to destroying the dog. If your dog is approaching one year of age and is biting in earnest, take him to a professional dog trainer and don't quibble with his methods unless you would rather see the dog dead.

Chewing. For teething puppies, provide a Nylabone (trade mark) and beef hide strips (see "THE FIRST NIGHTS" above). Every time the puppy attacks a chair, a rug, your hand, or any other chewable object, snap your finger or rap a newspaper on his nose, or throw the chain or a covered pebble-laden tin can near him, say "NO!" and hand him the bone or beef hide. If he persists, put him in his crate with the bone and hide. For incorrigible chewers, check diet for deficiencies first. William Koehler, trainer of many movie dogs including *The Thin Man's* Asta, recommends in his book, *The Koehler Method of Dog Training,* that the chewed object or part of it be taped crosswise in the dog's mouth until he develops a hearty distaste for it.

Digging. While he is in the act, throw the chain or noisy tin can and call out "NO!" For the real delinquent Koehler recommends filling the dug hole with water, forcing the dog's nose into it until the dog thinks he's drowning—and he'll never dig again. Drastic perhaps, but better than the bullet from an angry neighbor's gun, or a surreptitious poisoning.

The Runaway. If your dog wanders while walking with you, throw the chain or tin can and call "COME!" to him. If he persists, have a friend or neighbor cooperate in chasing him home. A very long line, perhaps 25 feet or more, can be effective if you permit the dog to run its length and then snap it sharply to remind him not to get too far from you.

9

Car Chasing. Your dog will certainly live longer if you make him car-wise; in fact, deathly afraid of anything on wheels. Ask a friend or neighbor to drive you in *his* car. Lie below the windows and as your dog chases the car throw the chain or tin can while your neighbor or friend says "GO HOME!" sharply. Another method is to shoot a water pistol filled with highly diluted ammonia at the dog. If your dog runs after children on bicycles, the latter device is especially effective but may turn the dog against children.

The Possessive Dog. If a dog displays overly protective habits, berate him in no uncertain terms. The chain, the noisy can, the rolled newspaper, or light strap sharply applied, may convince him that, while he loves you, there's no percentage in overdoing it.

The Cat Chaser. Again, the chain, the can, the newspaper, the strap—or the cat's claws if all else fails, but only as the last resort.

The Defiant, or Revengeful, Wetter. Some dogs seem to resent being left alone. Some are jealous when their owners play with another dog or animal. Get a friend or neighbor in this case to heave the chain or noisy tin can when the dog relieves himself in sheer spite.

For other canine delinquencies, you will find *The Koehler Method of Dog Training* effective. William Koehler's techniques have been certified as extremely successful by directors of motion pictures featuring dogs and by officers of dog obedience clubs.

OBEDIENCE EXERCISES

A well-mannered dog saves its owner money, embarrassment and possible heartbreak. The destruction of property by canine delinquents, avoidable accidents to dogs and children, and other unnecessary disadvantages to dog ownership can be eliminated by simple obedience training. The elementary exercises of heeling, sitting, staying and lying down can keep the dog out of trouble in most situations.

The only tools needed for basic obedience training are a slip collar made of chain link, leather or nylon and a strong six-foot leather leash with a good spring snap. Reviewing the requirements and basic techniques given earlier, let's proceed with the dog's schooling.

Heeling. Keep your dog on your left side, with the leash in your left hand. Start straight ahead in a brisk walk. If your dog pulls ahead, jerk (do not pull) the leash and say "Heel" firmly. If the dog persists in pulling ahead, stop, turn right or left and go on for several yards, saying "Heel" each time you change direction.

If your dog balks, fix leash *under* his throat and coax him forward by repeating his name and tapping your hip.

Whatever you do, don't stop walking! If the dog jumps up or "fights" the leash, just keep moving briskly. Sooner than later he will catch on and with the repetition of "Heel" on every correction, you will have him trotting by your side with style and respect.

Sit. Keeping your dog on leash, hold his neck up and push his rump down while repeating "Sit." If he resists, "spank" him lightly several times on his rump. Be firm, but not cruel. Repeat this lesson often until it is learned perfectly. When the dog knows the command, test him at a distance without the leash. Return to him every time he fails to sit and repeat the exercise.

Stay. If you have properly trained your dog to "Sit," the "Stay" is simple. Take his leash off and repeat "Stay" holding your hand up, palm toward dog, and move away. If dog moves toward you, you must repeat the "sit" lesson until properly learned. After your

11

dog "stays" while you are in sight, move out of his sight and keep repeating "Stay." Once he has learned to "stay" even while you are out of his sight, you can test him under various conditions, such as when another dog is near, a child is playing close to him, or a car appears on the road. (Warning: do not tax your dog's patience on the "stay" until he has learned the performance perfectly.)

Down. For this lesson, keep your dog on leash. First tell him to "sit." When he has sat for a minute, place your shoe over his leash between the heel and sole. Slowly pull on the leash and repeat "Down" while you push his head down with your other hand. Do this exercise very quietly so that dog does not become excited and uncontrollable. In fact, this performance is best trained when the dog is rather quiet. Later, after the dog has learned the voice signal perfectly, you can command the "Down" with a hand signal, sweeping your hand from an upright position to a downward motion with your palm toward the dog. Be sure to say "Down" with the hand signal.

For more advanced obedience the following guides by Blanche Saunders are recommended:
The Complete Novice Obedience Course
The Complete Open Obedience Course
The Complete Utility Obedience Course (with Tracking)
Dog Training for Boys and Girls (includes simple tricks.)
All are published by Howell Book House at $3.00 each.

OBEDIENCE TRIALS

Booklets covering the rules and regulations of Obedience Trials may be obtained from The American Kennel Club, 51 Madison Avenue, New York, N.Y. 10010. In Canada, write The Canadian Kennel Club, 667 Yonge Street, Toronto, Ontario.

Both these national clubs can give you the names and locations of local and regional dog clubs that conduct training classes in obedience and run Obedience Trials in which trained dogs compete for degrees as follow: CD (Companion Dog), CDX (Companion Dog Excellent), UD (Utility Dog), TD (Tracking Dog) and UDT (Utility Dog, Tracking.)

The Exhibition
of Dogs

NOBODY should exhibit a dog in the shows unless he can win without gloating and can lose without rancor. The showing of dogs is first of all a sport, and it is to be approached in a sportsmanlike spirit. It is not always so approached. That there are so many wretched losers and so many supercilious winners among the exhibitors in dog shows is the reason for this warning.

The confidence that one's dog is of exhibition excellence is all that prompts one to enter him in the show, but, if he fails in comparison with his competitors, nobody is harmed. It is no personal disgrace to have a dog beaten. It may be due to the dog's fundamental faults, to its condition, or to inexpert handling. One way to avoid such hazards is to turn the dog over to a good professional handler. Such a man with a flourishing established business will not accept an inferior dog, one that is not worth exhibiting. He will put the dog in the best possible condition before he goes into the ring with him, and he knows all the tricks of getting out of a dog all he has to give. Good handlers come high, however. Fees for taking a dog into the ring will range from ten to twenty-five dollars, plus any cash prizes the dog may win, and plus a bonus for wins made in the group.

Handlers do not win all the prizes, despite the gossip that they do, but good handlers choose only good dogs and they usually finish at or near the top of their classes. It is a mistake to assume that this is due to any favoritism or any connivance with the judges; the handlers have simply chosen the best dogs, conditioned them well, and so maneuvered them in the ring as to bring out their best points.

The services of a professional handler are not essential, however. Many an amateur shows his dogs as well, but the exhibitor without previous experience is ordinarily at something of a disadvantage. If the dog is good enough, he may be expected to win.

The premium list of the show, setting forth the prizes to be offered, giving the names of the judges, containing the entry form, and describing the conditions under which the show is to be held, are usually mailed out to prospective exhibitors about a month before the show is scheduled to be held. Any show superintendent is glad to add names of interested persons to the mailing list.

Entries for a Licensed show close at a stated date, usually about two weeks before the show opens, and under the rules no entry my be accepted after the advertised date of closing. It behooves the exhibitor to make his entries promptly. The exhibitor is responsible for all errors he may make on the entry form of his dog; such errors cannot be rectified and may result in the disqualification of the exhibit. It therefore is wise for the owner to double check all data submitted with an entry. The cost of making an entry, which is stated in the premium list, is usually from six to eight dollars. An unregistered dog may be shown at three shows, after which he must be registered or a statement must be made to the American Kennel Club that he is ineligible for registry and why, with a request for permission to continue to exhibit the dog. Such permission is seldom denied. The listing fee for an unregistered dog is twenty-five cents, which must be added to the entry fee.

Match or Sanctioned shows are excellent training and experience for regular bench shows. Entry fees are low, usually ranging from fifty cents to a dollar, and are made at the show instead of in advance. Sanctioned shows are unbenched, informal affairs where the puppy may follow his owner about on the leash and become accustomed to strange dogs, to behaving himself in the ring, and to being handled by a judge. For the novice exhibitor, too, Sanctioned shows will provide valuable experience, for ring procedure is similar to that at regular bench shows.

14

The classes open at most shows and usually divided by sex are as follows: Puppy Class (often Junior Puppy for dogs 6 to 9 months old, and Senior Puppy for dogs 9 to 12 months); Novice Class, for dogs that have never won first in any except the Puppy Class; Bred-by-Exhibitor Class, for dogs of which the breeder and owner are the same person or persons; the American-bred Class, for dogs whose parents were mated in America; and the Open Class, which is open to all comers. The respective first prize winners of these various classes compete in what is known as the Winners Class for points toward championship. No entry can be made in the Winners Class, which is open without additional charge to the winners of the earlier classes, all of which are obligated to compete.

A dog eligible to more than one class can be entered in each of them, but it is usually wiser to enter him in only one. A puppy should, unless unusually precocious and mature, be placed in the Puppy Class, and it is unfair to so young a dog to expect him to defeat older dogs, although an exceptional puppy may receive an award in the Winners Class. The exhibitor who is satisfied merely that his dog may win the class in which he is entered is advised to place him in the lowest class to which he is eligible, but the exhibitor with confidence in his dog and shooting for high honors should enter the dog in the Open Class, where the competition is usually the toughest. The winner of the Open Class usually (but by no means always) is also the top of the Winners Class; the runner-up to this dog is named Reserve Winners.

The winner of the Winners Class for dogs competes with the Winners Bitch for Best of Winners, which in turn competes for Best of Breed or Best of Variety with any Champions of Record which may be entered for Specials Only. In the closing hours of the show, the Best of Breed or Best of Variety is eligible to compete in the respective Variety Group to which his breed belongs. And if, perchance, he should win his Variety Group, he is obligated to compete for Best Dog in Show. This is a major honor which few inexperienced exhibitors attain and to which they seldom aspire.

Duly entered, the dog should be brought into the best possible condition for his exhibition in the show and taught to move and to pose at his best. He should be equipped with a neat, strong collar without ornaments or spikes, a show lead of the proper length, width and material for his size and coat, and a nickel bench chain of strong links with which to fasten him to his bench. Food such as the dog is used to, a bottle of the water he is accustomed to drink, and all grooming equipment should be assembled in a bag the night before departure for the show. The exhibitor's pass, on which the dog is assigned a stall number, is sent by mail by the show superintendent and should not be left behind, since it is difficult to have the pass duplicated and it enables the dog's caretaker to leave and return to the show at will.

The time of the opening of the show is stated in the premium list, and it is wise to have one's dog at the show promptly. Late arrivals are subject to disqualification if they are protested.

Sometimes examination is made by the veterinarian at the entrance of the show, and healthy dogs are quickly passed along. Once admitted to the show, if it is a "benched" show, it is wise to find one's bench, the number of which is on the exhibitor's ticket, to affix one's dog to the bench, and not to remove him from it except for exercising or until he is to be taken into the ring to be judged. A familiar blanket or cushion for the bench makes a dog feel at home there. It is contrary to the rules to remove dogs from their benches and to keep them in crates during show hours, and these rules are strictly enforced. Many outdoor shows are not "benched," and you provide your own crate or place for your dog.

At bench shows some exhibitors choose to sit by their dog's bench, but if he is securely chained he is likely to be safe in his owner's absence. Dogs have been stolen from their benches and others allegedly poisoned in the shows, but such incidents are rare indeed. The greater danger is that the dog may grow nervous and insecure, and it is best that the owner return now and again to the bench to reassure the dog of his security.

The advertised program of the show permits exhibitors to know the approximate hour of the judging of their respective breeds. Although that time may be somewhat delayed, it may be depended upon that judging will not begin before the stated hour. The dog should have been groomed and made ready for his appearance in the show ring. When his class is called the dog should be taken unhurriedly to the entrance of the ring, where the handler will receive an arm band with the dog's number.

When the class is assembled and the judge asks that the dogs be paraded before him, the handler should fall into the counter-clock-wise line and walk his dog until the signal to stop is given. In moving in a circle, the dog should be kept on the inside so that he may be readily seen by the judge, who stands in the center of the ring. In stopping the line, there is no advantage to be gained in maneuvering one's dog to the premier position, since the judge will change the position of the dogs as he sees fit.

Keep the dog alert and facing toward the judge at all times. When summoned to the center of the ring for examination, go briskly but not brashly. It is unwise to enter into conversation with the judge, except briefly to reply to any questions he may ask. Do not call his attention to any excellences the dog may possess or excuse any shortcomings; the judge is presumed to evaluate the exhibit's merits as he sees them.

If asked to move the dog, he should be led directly away from the judge and again toward the judge. A brisk but not too rapid trot is the gait the judge wishes to see, unless he declares otherwise. He may ask that the movement be repeated, with which request the handler should respond with alacrity. It is best not to choke a dog in moving him, but rather to move him on a loose lead. The judge will assign or signal a dog to his position, which should be assumed without quibble.

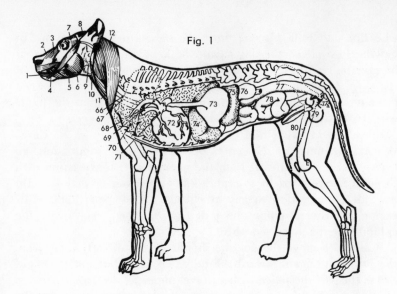

Fig. 1

Fig. 2

Fig. 1

1 Orbicularis oris.
2 Levator nasolabialis.
3 Levator labii superioris proprius (levator of upper lip).
4 Dilator naris lateralis.
5 Zygomaticus.
6 Masseter (large and well developed in the dog).
7 Scutularis.
8 Parotid Gland.
9 Submaxillary Gland.
10 Parotido-auricularis.
11 Sterno-hyoideus.
12 Brachio-cephalicus.

(Between figures 8 and 12 on top the Elevator and Depressor muscles of the ear are to be seen.)

66 Œsophagus (gullet).
67 Trachea (wind pipe).
68 Left Carotid Artery.
69 Anterior Aorta.
70 Lungs.
71 Posterior Aorta.
72 Heart.
73 Stomach.

74 Liver. (The line in front of Liver shows the Diaphragm separating Thoracic from Abdominal cavity.)
75 Spleen.
76 Kidney (left).
77 Rectum.
77A Anal Glands (position) just inside rectum.
78 Intestine.
79 Testicle.
80 Penis.
(Midway between 76 and 79 is the seat of the Bladder and behind this the seat of the Prostate gland in males, uterus in females.)

Fig. 2

Section of Head and Neck.
1 Nasal septum.
2 Tongue.
3 Cerebrum.
4 Cerebellum.
5 Medulla oblongata.
6 Spinal Cord.
7 Œsophagus (gullet).
8 Trachea (wind pipe).
9 Hard palate.
10 Soft palate.
11 Larynx, containing vocal cords.

18

The Feeding of Dogs,
Constitutional Vigor

I N selecting a new dog, it is quite as essential that he shall be of sound constitution as that he shall be of the correct type of his own particular breed. The animal that is thoroughly typical of his breed is likely to be vigorous, with a will and a body to surmount diseases and ill treatment, but the converse of this statement is not always true. A dog may have constitutional vigor without breed type. We want both.

Half of the care and effort of rearing a dog is saved by choosing at the outset a puppy of sound constitution, one with a will and an ability to survive and flourish in spite of such adversity and neglect as he may encounter in life. This does not mean that the reader has any intention of obtaining a healthy dog and ill treating it, trusting its good constitution to bring it through whatever crises may beset it. It only means that he will save himself work, expense, and disappointment if only he will exercise care in the first place to obtain a healthy dog, one bred from sound and vigorous parents and one which has received adequate care and good food.

The first warning is not to economize too much in buying a dog. Never accept a cull of the litter at any price. The difference in first cost between a fragile, ill nourished, weedy, and unhealthy puppy and a sound, vigorous one, with adequate substance and the will to survive, may be ten dollars or it may be fifty dollars. But whatever it may be, it is worthwhile. A dog is an investment and it

19

is not the cost but the upkeep that makes the difference. We may save fifty dollars on the first price of a dog, only to lay out twice or five times that sum for veterinary fees over and above what it would cost to rear a dog of sound fundamental constitution and structure.

The vital, desirable dog, the one that is easy to rear and worth the care bestowed upon him, is active, inquisitive, and happy. He is sleek, his eyes free from pus or tears, his coat shining and alive, his flesh adequate and firm. He is not necessarily fat, but a small amount of surplus flesh, especially in puppyhood, is not undesirable. He is free from rachitic knobs on his joints or from crooked bones resultant from rickets. His teeth are firm and white and even. His breath is sweet to the smell. Above all, he is playful and responsive. Puppies, like babies, are much given to sleep, but when they are awake the sturdy ones do not mope lethargically around.

An adult dog that is too thin may often be fattened; if he is too fat he may be reduced. But it is essential that he shall be sound and healthy with a good normal appetite and that he be active and full of the joy of being alive. He must have had the benefit of a good heredity and a good start in life.

A dog without a fundamental inheritance of good vitality, or one that has been neglected throughout his growing period is seldom worth his feed. We must face these facts at the very beginning. Buy only from an owner who is willing to guarantee the soundness of his stock, and before consummating the purchase, have the dog, whether puppy or adult, examined by a veterinarian in order to determine the state of the dog's health.

If the dog to be cared for has been already acquired, there is nothing to do but to make the best of whatever weaknesses or frailties he may possess. But, when it is decided to replace him with another, let us make sure that he has constitutional vigor.

20

THE FEEDING AND NUTRITION OF
THE ADULT DOG

The dog is a carnivore, an eater of meat. This is a truism that cannot be repeated too often. Dog keepers know it but are prone to disregard it, although they do so at their peril and the peril of their dogs. Despite all the old-wives' tales to the contrary, meat does not cause a dog to be vicious, it does not give him worms nor cause him to have fits. It is his food. This is by no means all that is needed to know about food for the dog, but it is the essential knowledge. Give a dog enough sound meat and he will not be ill fed.

The dog is believed to have been the first of the animals that was brought under domestication. In his feral state he was almost exclusively an eater of meat. In his long association with man, however, his metabolism has adjusted itself somewhat to the consumption of human diet until he now can eat, even if he cannot flourish upon, whatever his master chooses to share with him, be it caviar or corn pone. It is not to be denied that a mature dog can survive without ill effects upon an exclusive diet of rice for a considerable period, but it is not to be recommended that he should be forced to do so.

Even if we had no empirical evidence that dogs thrive best upon foods of animal origin, and we possess conclusive proof of that fact, the anatomy and physiology of the dog would convince us of it. An observation of the structure of the dog's alimentary canal, superimposed upon many trial and error methods of feeding, leads us to the conclusion that a diet with meat predominating is the best food we can give a dog.

To begin with, the dental formation of the dog is typical of the carnivores. His teeth are designed for tearing rather than for mastication. He bolts his food and swallows it with a minimum of chewing. It is harmless that he should do this. No digestion takes place in the dog's mouth.

The capacity of the dog's stomach is great in comparison with the size of his body and with the capacity of his intestines. The amounts of carbohydrates and of fats digested in the stomach are minimal. The chief function of the dog's stomach is the digestion of proteins. In the dog as in the other carnivores, carbohydrates and fats are digested for the most part in the small intestine, and absorption of food materials is largely from the small intestine. The enzymes necessary for the completion of the digestion of proteins which have not been fully digested in the stomach and for the digestion of sugars, starches, and fats are present in the pancreatic and intestinal juices. The capacity of the small intestine in the dog is not great and for that reason digestion that takes place there must be rapid.

The so-called large intestine (although in the dog it is really not "large" at all) is short and of small capacity in comparison with that of animals adapted by nature to subsist wholly or largely upon plant foods. In the dog, the large gut is designed to serve chiefly for storage of a limited and compact bulk of waste materials, which are later to be discharged as feces. Some absorption of water occurs there, but there is little if any absorption there of the products of digestion.

It will be readily seen that the short digestive tract of the dog is best adapted to a concentrated diet, which can be quickly digested and which leaves a small residue. Foods of animal origin (flesh, fish, milk, and eggs) are therefore suited to the digestive physiology of the dog because of the ease and completeness with which they are digested as compared with plant foods, which contain considerable amounts of indigestible structural material. The dog is best fed with a concentrated diet with a minimum of roughage.

This means meat. Flesh, milk, and eggs are, in effect, vegetation partly predigested. The steer or horse eats grain and herbage, from which its long digestive tract enables it to extract the food value and eliminate the indigestible material. The carnivore eats the flesh of the herbivore, thus obtaining his grain and grass in a concentrated form suitable for digestion in his short alimentary tract. Thus it is seen that meat is the ideal as a chief ingredient of the dog's ration.

Like that of all other animals, the dog's diet must be made up of proteins, carbohydrates, fats, minerals, vitamins, and water. None of these substances may be excluded if the dog is to survive. If he fails to obtain any of them from one source, it must come from another. It may be argued that before minerals were artificially supplied in the dog's diet and before we were aware of the existence of the various vitamins, we had dogs and they (some of them) appeared to thrive. However, they obtained such substances in their foods, although we were not aware of it. It is very likely that few dogs obtained much more than their very minimum of requirements of the minerals and vitamins. It is known that rickets were more prevalent before we learned to supply our dogs with ample calcium, and black tongue, now almost unknown, was a common canine disease before we supplied in the dog's diet that fraction of the vitamin B complex known as nicotinic acid. There is no way for us to know how large a portion of our dogs died for want of some particular food element before we learned to supply all the necessary ones. The dogs that survived received somewhere in their diet some of all of these compounds.

PROTEIN

The various proteins are the nitrogenous part of the food. They are composed of the amino acids, singly or in combination. There are at least twenty-two of these amino acids known to the nutritional scientists, ten of which are regarded as dietary essentials, the others of which, if not supplied in the diet, can be compounded in the body, which requires an adequate supply of all twenty-two. When any one of the essential ten amino acids is withdrawn from the diet of any animal, growth ceases or is greatly retarded. Thus, a high protein content in any food is not an assurance of its food value if taken alone; it may be lacking in one or more of the essential ten amino acids. When the absent essential amino acids are added to it in sufficient quantities or included separately in the diet, the protein may be complete and fully assimilated.

Proteins, as such, are ingested and in the digestive tract are broken down into the separate amino acids of which they are composed. These amino acids have been likened to building stones, since they are taken up by the blood stream and conveyed to the various parts of the animal as they may be required, where they are deposited and re-united with other complementary amino acids again to form bone and muscles in the resumed form of protein.

To correct amino acid deficiencies in the diet, it is not necessary to add the required units in pure form. The same object may be accomplished more efficiently by employing proteins which contain the required amino acids.

Foods of animal origin—meat, fish, eggs, and milk—supply proteins of high nutritive value, both from the standpoint of digestibility and amino acid content. Gelatin is an exception to that statement, since gelatin is very incomplete.

Even foods of animal origin vary among themselves in their protein content and amino acid balance. The protein of muscle meat does not rank quite as high as that of eggs or milk. The glandular tissues—such as liver, kidneys, sweetbreads or pancreas—contain proteins of exceptionally high nutritive value, and these organs should be added to the dog's diet whenever it is possible to do so. Each pint of milk contains two-thirds of an ounce (dry weight) of particularly high class protein, in addition to minerals, vitamins, carbohydrates, and fats. (The only dietary necessity absent

24

from milk is iron.) Animal proteins have a high content of dietary-essential amino acids, which makes them very effective in supplementing many proteins of vegetable origin. The whites of eggs, while somewhat inferior to the yolks, contain excellent proteins. The lysine of milk can be destroyed by excessive heat and the growth promoting value of its protein so destroyed. Evaporated tinned milk has not been subjected to enough heat to injure its proteins.

Thus we can readily see why meat with its concentrated, balanced, and easily assimilated proteins should form the major part of dry weight of a dog's ration.

It has never been determined how much protein the dog requires in his diet. It may be assumed to vary as to the size, age, and breed of the dog under consideration; as to the individual dog, some assimilating protein better, or utilizing more of it than others; as to the activity or inactivity of the subject; and as to the amino acid content of the protein employed. When wheat protein gliadin is fed as the sole protein, three times as much of it is required as of the milk protein, lactalbumin. It has been estimated that approximately twenty to twenty-five percent of animal protein (dry weight) in a dog's diet is adequate for maintenance in good health, although no final conclusion has been reached and probably never can be.

Our purpose, however, is not to feed the dog the minimum ration with which he can survive or even the minimum ration with which he can flourish. It is rather to give him the maximum food in quantity and balance which he can digest and enjoy without developing a paunch. Who wants to live on the minimum diet necessary for adequate sustenance? We all enjoy a full belly of good food, and so do our dogs.

Roy G. Daggs found from experimentation that milk production in the dog was influenced by the different kinds of proteins fed to it. He has pointed out that relatively high protein diets stimulate lactation and that, in the bitch, animal proteins are better suited to the synthesis of milk than plant proteins. He concluded that liver was a better source of protein for lactation than eggs or round steak.

THE CARBOHYDRATES

The carbohydrates include all the starches, the sugars, and the cellulose and hemicellulose, which last two, known as fiber, are the chief constituents of wood, of the stalks and leaves of plants, and of the coverings of seeds. There remains considerable controversy as to the amount of carbohydrates required or desirable in canine nutrition. It has been shown experimentally that the dog is able to digest large quantities of cornstarch, either raw or cooked. Rice fed to mature dogs in amounts sufficient to satisfy total energy requirements has been found to be 95 percent digested. We know that the various commercial biscuits and meals which are marketed as food for dogs are well tolerated, especially if they are supplemented by the addition of fresh meat. There seems to be no reason why they should not be included in the dog's ration.

Carbohydrates are a cheap source of energy for the dog, both in their initial cost and in the work required of the organism for their metabolism. Since there exists ample evidence that the dog has no difficulty in digesting and utilizing considerable amounts of starches and sugars for the production of energy, there is no reason why they should be excluded from his diet. Some carbohydrate is necessary for the metabolism of fats. The only danger from the employment of carbohydrates is that, being cheap, they may be employed to the exclusion of proteins and other essential elements of the dog's diet. It should be noted that meat and milk contain a measure of carbohydrates as well as of proteins.

Thoroughly cooked rice or oatmeal in moderate quantities may well be used to supplement and cheapen a meat diet for a dog without harm to him, as may crushed dog biscuit or shredded wheat waste or the waste from manufacture of other cereal foods. They are not required but may be used without harm.

Sugar and candy, of which dogs are inordinately fond, used also to be *verboten*. They are an excellent source of energy—and harmless. They should be fed in only moderate quantities.

FATS

In the dog as in man, body fat is found in largest amounts under the skin, between the muscles and around the internal organs. The fat so stored serves as a reserve source of heat and energy when the caloric value of the food is insufficient, or for temporary periods when no food is eaten. The accumulation of a certain amount of fat around vital organs provides considerable protection against cold and injury.

Before fats can be carried to the body cells by means of the circulating blood, it is necessary for them to be digested in the intestines with the aid of enzymes. Fats require a longer time for digestion than carbohydrates or proteins. For this reason, they are of special importance in delaying the sensations of hunger. This property of fats is frequently referred to as "staying power."

It is easily possible for some dogs to accumulate too much fat, making them unattractive, ungainly, and vaguely uncomfortable. This should be avoided by withholding an excess of fats and carbohydrates from the diets of such dogs whenever obesity threatens them. There is greater danger, however, that dogs may through inadequacy of their diets be permitted to become too thin.

Carbohydrates can in part be transformed to fats within the animal body. The ratio between fats and carbohydrates can therefore be varied within wide limits in the dog's ration so long as the requirements for proteins, vitamins, and minerals are adequately met. Some dogs have been known to tolerate as much as forty percent of fat in their diets over prolonged periods, but so much is not to be recommended as a general practice. Perhaps fifteen to twenty percent of fat is adequate without being too much.

Fat is a heat producing food, and the amount given a dog should be stepped up in the colder parts of the year and reduced in the summer months. In a ration low in fat it is particularly important that a good source of the fat-soluble vitamins be included or that such vitamins be artificially supplied. Weight for weight, fat has more than twice the food value of the other organic food groups—carbohydrates and proteins. The use of fat tends to decrease the amount of food required to supply caloric needs. The fats offer a means of increasing or decreasing the total sum of energy in the diet with the least change in the volume of food intake.

It is far less important that the dog receive more than a minimum amount of fats, however, than that his ration contain an adequate amount and quality balance of proteins. Lean meat in adequate quantities will provide him with such proteins, and fats may be added to it in the form of fat meat, suet, or lard. Small quantities of dog biscuits, cooked rice, or other cereals in the diet will supply the needed carbohydrates. However, cellulose or other roughage is not required in the diet of the carnivore. It serves only to engorge the dog's colon, which is not capacious, and to increase the volume of feces, which is supererogatory.

MINERALS

At least eleven minerals are present in the normal dog, and there are probably others occurring in quantities so minute that they have not as yet been discovered. The eleven are as follows: Calcium (lime), sodium chloride (table salt), copper, iron, magnesium, manganese, phosphorus, zinc, potassium, and iodine.

Of many of these only a trace in the daily ration is required and that trace is adequately found in meat or in almost any other normal diet. There are a few that we should be at pains to add to the diet. The others we shall ignore.

Sodium chloride (salt) is present in sufficient quantities in most meats, although, more to improve the flavor of the food than to contribute to the animal's nutrition, a small amount of salt may be added to the ration. The exact amount makes no material difference, since the unutilized portions are eliminated, largely in the urine. If the brand of salt used is iodized, it will meet the iodine requirements, which are very small. Iodine deficiency in dogs is rare, but food crops and meats grown in certain areas contain little or no iodine, and it is well to be safe by using iodized salt.

Sufficient iron is usually found in meat and milk, but if the dog appears anemic or listless the trace of iron needed can be supplied with one of the iron salts—ferric sulphate, or oxide, or ferrous gluconate. Iron is utilized in the bone marrow in the synthesis of hemoglobin in the blood corpuscles. It is used over and over; when a corpuscle is worn out and is to be replaced, it surrenders its iron before being eliminated.

When more iron is ingested than can be utilized, some is stored in the liver, after which further surplus is excreted. The liver of the newborn puppy contains enough iron to supply the organism up until weaning time. No iron is present in milk, which otherwise provides a completely balanced ration.

A diet with a reasonable content of red meat, especially of liver or kidney, is likely to be adequate in respect to its iron. However, bitches in whelp require more iron than a dog on mere maintenance. It is recommended that the liver content of bitches' diets be increased for the duration of pregnancy.

Iron requires the presence of a minute trace of copper for its utilization, but there is enough copper in well nigh any diet to supply the requirements.

Calcium and phosphorous are the only minerals of which an insufficiency is a warranted source of anxiety. This statement may not be true of adult dogs not employed for breeding purposes, but it does apply to brood bitches and to growing puppies. The entire skeleton and teeth are made largely from calcium and phosphorus, and it is essential that the organism have enough of those minerals.

If additional calcium is not supplied to a bitch in her diet, her own bone structure is depleted to provide her puppies with their share of calcium. Moreover, in giving birth to her puppies or shortly afterward she is likely to go into eclampsia as a result of calcium depletion.

The situation, however, is easily avoided. The addition of a small amount of calcium phosphate diabasic to the ration precludes any possible calcium deficiency. Calcium phosphate diabasic is an inexpensive substance and quite tasteless. It may be sprinkled in or over the food, especially that given to brood bitches and puppies. It is the source of strong bones and vigorous teeth of ivory whiteness.

But it must be mentioned that calcium cannot be assimilated into the bone structure, no matter how much of it is fed or otherwise administered, except in the presence of vitamin D. That is D's function, to facilitate the absorption of calcium and phosphorus. This will be elaborated upon in the following discussion of the vitamins and their functions.

VITAMINS

Vitamins have in the past been largely described by diseases resulting from their absence. It is recognized more and more that many of the subacute symptoms of general unfitness of dogs may be attributable to an inadequate supply in the diet of one or more of these essential food factors. It is to be emphasized that vitamins are to be considered a part of the dog's food, essential to his health and well being. They are not to be considered as medication. Often the morbid conditions resultant from their absence in the diet may be remedied by the addition of the particular needed vitamin.

The requirements of vitamins, as food, not as medication, in the diet cannot be too strongly emphasized. These vitamins may be in the food itself, or they may better be added to it as a supplement to insure an adequate supply. Except for vitamin D, of which it is remotely possible (though unlikely) to supply too much, a surplus of the vitamin substances in the ration is harmless. They are somewhat expensive and we have no disposition to waste them, but if too much of them are fed they are simply eliminated with no subsequent ill effect.

It must be realized that vitamins are various substances, each of which has a separate function. It is definitely not safe to add to a dog's (or a child's) diet something out of a bottle or box indefinitely labeled "Vitamins," as is the practice of so many persons. We must know which vitamins we are giving, what purpose each is designed to serve, and the potency of the preparation of the brand of each one we are using.

Any one of the "shotgun" vitamin preparations is probably adequate if administered in large enough dosages. Such a method may be wasteful, however; to be sure of enough of one substance, the surplus of the others is wasted. It is much better to buy a product that contains an adequate amount of each of the needed vitamins and a wasteful surplus of none. Such a procedure is cheaper in the long run.

There follows a brief description of each of the various vitamins so far discovered and a statement of what purpose in the diet they are respectively intended to serve:

Vitamin A—This vitamin in some form is an absolute requisite for good health, even for enduring life itself. Symptoms of ad-

31

vanced deficiency of vitamin A in dogs are an eye disease with resulting impaired vision, inflammation of the conjunctiva or mucous membranes which line the eyelid, and injury to the mucous membranes of the body. Less easily recognized symptoms are an apparent lowered resistance to bacterial infection, especially of the upper respiratory tract, retarded growth, and loss of weight. Diseases due to vitamin A deficiency may be well established while the dog is still gaining in weight. Lack of muscular coordination and paralysis have been observed in dogs and degeneration of the nervous system. Some young dogs deprived of vitamin A become wholly or partially deaf.

The potency of vitamin A is usually calculated in International Units, of which it has been estimated that the dog requires about 35 per day for each pound of his body weight. Such parts as are not utilized are not lost, but are stored in the liver for future use in time of shortage. A dog well fortified with this particular vitamin can well go a month or more without harm with none of it in his diet. At such times he draws upon his liver for its surplus.

It is for its content of vitamins A and D that cod-liver oil (and the oils from the livers of other fish) is fed to puppies and growing children. Fish liver oils are an excellent source of vitamin A, and if a small amount of them is included in the diet no anxiety about deficiency of vitamin A need be entertained. In buying cod-liver oil, it pays to obtain the best grade. The number of International Units it contains per teaspoonful is stated on most labels. The vitamin content of cod-liver oil is impaired by exposure to heat, light, and air. It should be kept in a dark, cool place and the bottle should be firmly stopped.

Another source of vitamin A is found in carrots but it is almost impossible to get enough carrots in a dog to do him any good. It is better and easier to use a preparation known as carotene, three drops of which contains almost the vitamin A in a bushel of carrots.

Other natural sources of vitamin A are liver, kidney, heart, cheese, egg yolks, butter and milk. If these foods, or any one of them, are generously included in the adult dog's maintenance ration, all other sources of vitamin A may be dispensed with. The ration for all puppies, however, and for pregnant and lactating bitches should be copiously fortified either with fish liver oil or with tablets containing vitamin A.

Vitamin B. What was formerly known as a single vitamin B has now been found to be a complex of many different factors. Some of them are, in minute quantities, very important parts of the diets of any kind of animals. The various factors of this complex, each a separate vitamin, are designated by the letter B followed by an inferior number, as B_1, B_2, or B_6.

The absence or insufficiency in the diet of Vitamin B_1, otherwise known as thiamin, has been blamed for retarded growth, loss of weight, decreased fertility, loss of appetite, and impaired digestion. A prolonged shortage of B_1 may result in paralysis, the accumulation of fluid in the tissues, and finally in death, apparently from heart failure.

It is not easy to estimate just how much B_1 a dog requires per pound of body weight, since dogs as individuals vary in their needs, and the activity of an animal rapidly depletes the thiamin in his body. The feeding of 50 International Units per day per pound of body weight is probably wasteful but harmless. That is at least enough.

Thiamin is not stored in the system for any length of time and requires a daily dosage. It is destroyed in part by heat above the boiling point. It is found in yeast (especially in brewer's yeast), liver, wheat germ, milk, eggs, and in the coloring matter of vegetables. However, few dogs or persons obtain an optimum supply of B_1 from their daily diet, and it is recommended that it be supplied to the dog daily.

Brewer's yeast, either in powdered or tablet form affords a cheap and rather efficient way to supply the average daily requirements. An overdose of yeast is likely to cause gas in the dog's stomach.

Another factor of the vitamin B complex, riboflavin, affects particularly the skin and hair. Animals fed a diet in which it is deficient are prone to develop a scruffy dryness of the skin, especially about the eyes and mouth, and the hair becomes dull and dry, finally falling out, leaving the skin rough and dry. In experiments with rats deprived of riboflavin the toes have fallen off.

Riboflavin is present in minute quantities in so many foods that a serious shortage in any well balanced diet is unlikely. It is especially to be found in whey, which is the explanation of the smooth skin and lively hair of so many dogs whose ration contains cottage cheese.

33

While few dogs manifest any positive shortage of riboflavin, experiments on various animals have shown that successively more liberal amounts of it in their diets, up to about four times as much as is needed to prevent the first signs of deficiency, result in increased positive health.

Riboflavin deteriorates with exposure to heat and light. Most vitamin products contain it in ample measure.

Dogs were immediately responsible for the discovery of the existence of vitamin B_2, or nicotinic acid, formerly known as vitamin G. The canine disease of black tongue is analogous with the human disease called pellagra, both of which are prevented and cured by sufficient amounts of nicotinic acid in the diet. Black tongue is not a threat for any dog that eats a diet which contains even a reasonable quantity of lean meat, but it used to be prevalent among dogs fed exclusively upon corn bread or corn-meal mush, as many were.

No definite optimum dosage has been established. However, many cases of vaguely irritated skin, deadness of coat, and soft, spongy, or bleeding gums have been reported to be remedied by administration of nicotinic acid.

It has been demonstrated that niacin is essential if a good sound healthy appetite is to be maintained. Pantothenic acid is essential to good nerve health. Pyridoxin influences proper gastro-intestinal functions. Vitamin B_{12}, the "animal protein factor," is essential for proper growth and health in early life. And the water soluble B factor affects the production of milk.

Vitamin C, the so-called anti-scorbutic vitamin, is presumed to be synthesized by the dog in his own body. The dog is believed not to be subject to true scurvy. Vitamin C, then, can well be ignored as pertains to the dog. It is the most expensive of the vitamins, and, its presence in the vitamin mixture for the dog will probably do no good.

Vitamin D, the anti-rachitic vitamin, is necessary to promote the assimilation of calcium and phosphorus into the skeletal structure. One may feed all of those minerals one will, but without vitamin D they will pass out of the system unused. It is impossible to develop sound bones and teeth without its presence. Exposure to sunshine unimpeded by glass enables the animal to manufacture vitamin D in his system, but sunshine is not to be depended upon for an entire supply.

Vitamin D is abundant in cod-liver oil and in the liver oils of some other fish, or it may be obtained in a dry form in combination with other vitamins. One International Unit per pound of body weight per day is sufficient to protect a dog from rickets. From a teaspoonful to a tablespoonful of cod-liver oil a day will serve well instead for any dog.

This is the only one of the vitamins with which overdosage is possible and harmful. While a dog will not suffer from several times the amount stated and an excess dosage is unlikely, it is only fair to warn the reader that it is at least theoretically possible.

Vitamin E is the so-called fertility vitamin. Whether it is required for dogs has not as yet been determined. Rats fed upon a ration from which vitamin E was wholly excluded became permanently sterile, but the finding is not believed to pertain to all animals. Some dog keepers, however, declare that the feeding of wheat germ oil, the most abundant source of vitamin E, has prevented early abortions of their bitches, has resulted in larger and more vigorous litters of puppies, has increased the fertility of stud dogs, has improved the coats of their dogs and furthered the betterment of their general health. Whether vitamin E or some other factor or factors in the wheat germ oil is responsible for these alleged benefits is impossible to say.

Vitamin E is so widely found in small quantities in well nigh all foods that the hazard of its omission from any normal diet is small.

Numerous other vitamins have been discovered and isolated in recent years, and there are suspected to be still others as yet unknown. The ones here discussed are the only ones that warrant the use of care to include them in the dog's daily ration. It is well to reiterate that vitamins are not medicine, but are food, a required part of the diet. Any person interested in the complete nutrition of his dog will not neglect them.

It should go without saying that a dog should have access to clean, fresh, pure drinking water at all times, of which he should be permitted to drink as much or as little as he chooses. The demands of his system for drinking water will depend in part upon the moisture content of his food. Fed upon dry dog biscuits, he will probably drink considerable water to moisten it; with a diet which contains much milk or soup, he will need little additional water.

That he chooses to drink water immediately after a meal is harmless. The only times his water should be limited (but not entirely withheld from him) is after violent exercise or excitement, at which times his thirst should be satisfied only gradually.

The quantities of food required daily by dogs are influenced and determined by a number of factors: the age, size, individuality, and physical condition of the animal; the kind, quality, character, and proportions of the various foods in the ration; the climate, environment and methods of management; and the type and amount of work done, or the degree of exercise. Of these considerations, the age and size of the dog and the kind and amount of work are particularly important in determining food requirements. During early puppyhood a dog may require two or three (or even more) times as much food per pound of body weight as the same dog will require at maturity.

Any statement we should make here about the food requirements of a dog as to weight or volume would be subject to modification. Dogs vary in their metabolism. One dog might stay fat and sleek on a given amount of a given ration, whereas his litter brother in an adjoining kennel might require twice or only half as much of the same ration to maintain him in the same state of flesh.

The only sound determiners of how much to feed a dog are his appetite and his condition. As a general rule, a dog should have as much food for maintenance as he will readily clean up in five or ten minutes, unless he tends to lay on unwanted fat, in which case his intake of food should be reduced, especially its content of fats and carbohydrates. A thin dog should have his ration increased and be urged to eat it. The fats in his ration should be increased, and he may be fattened with a dessert of candy, sugar, or sweet cake following his main meal. These should never be used before a meal, lest they impair the appetite, and they should not be given to a fat dog at all. Rightly employed, they are useful and harmless, contrary to the prevalent belief.

Growing puppies require frequent meals, as will be discussed later. Pregnant and lactating bitches and frequently used stud dogs should have at least two meals, and better three, each day. For the mere maintenance of healthy adult dogs, one large meal a day appears to suffice as well as more smaller ones. Many tenderhearted dog keepers choose to divide the ration into two parts and to feed their dogs twice each day. There can be no objection offered to such a program except that it involves additional work for the keeper. Whether one meal or two, they should be given at regular hours, to which dogs soon adjust and expect their dinner at a given time.

It is better to determine upon an adequate ration, with plenty of meat in it, and feed it day after day, than to vary the diet in the assumption that a dog tires of eating the same thing. There is no evidence that he does, and it is a burden upon his carnivorous digestion to be making constant adjustments and readjustments to a new diet.

Today there are available for dogs many brands of canned foods, some good and others not so good. But it is safe to feed your dog exclusively—if you do not object to the cost—a canned dog food which has been produced by a reliable concern. Many of the producers of canned dog foods are subject to Federal inspection because they also process meat and meat products for human consumption. The Federal regulations prohibit the use of diseased or unsuitable by-products in the preparation of dog food. Some of the canned dog foods on the market are mostly cereal. A glance at the analysis chart on the label will tell you whether a particular product is a good food for your dog.

If fish is fed, it should be boned—thoroughly. The same is true of fowl and rabbit meats. Small bones may be caught in the dog's throat or may puncture the stomach or intestines. Large, raw shank bones of beef may be given to the dog with impunity, but they should be renewed at frequent intervals before they spoil. A dog obtains much amusement from gnawing a raw bone, and some nutrition. Harm does not accrue from his swallowing of bone fragments, which are dissolved by the hydrochloric acid in his stomach. If the dog is fed an excessive amount of bones, constipation may result. When this occurs, the best way to relieve the condition is by the use of the enema bag. Medicinal purges of laxatives given at this time may cause irreparable damage.

Meat for dogs may be fed raw, or may be roasted, broiled, or boiled. It is not advisable to feed fried foods to dogs. All soups, gravies and juices from cooked meat must be conserved and included in the food, since they contain some of the minerals and vitamins extracted from the meat.

A well-known German physician selected a medium sized, strong, healthy bitch, and after she had been mated, he fed her on chopped horse meat from which the salts were to a large extent extracted by boiling for two hours in distilled water. In addition to this she was given each day a certain quantity of fried fat. As drink she had only distilled water. She gave birth to six healthy puppies, one of which was killed immediately, and its bones found to be strong and well built and free from abnormalities. The other puppies did not thrive, but remained weak, and could scarcely walk at the end of a month, when four died from excessive feebleness. And the sixth was killed two weeks later. The mother in the meantime had become very lean but was tolerably lively and had a fair appetite. She was killed one hundred and twenty-six days after the beginning of the experiment, and it was then found that the bones of her spine and pelvis were softened—a condition known to physicians as osteomalacia.

The results of this experiment are highly interesting and instructive, showing clearly as they do that the nursing mother sends out to her young, in her milk, a part of her store of lime, which is absolutely essential to their welfare. They show also that if proper food is denied her, when in whelp and when nursing, not only her puppies but she as well must suffer greatly in consequence. And in the light of these facts is uncovered one of the most potential causes of rickets, so common among large breeds.

It may therefore be accepted that bitches in whelp must have goodly quantities of meat; moreover, that while cooking may be the rule if the broth is utilized, it is a wise plan to give the food occasionally in the raw state.

There is little choice among the varieties of meat, except that pork is seldom relished by dogs, usually contains too much fat, and should be cooked to improve its digestibility when it is used at all. Beef, mutton, lamb, goat, and horse flesh are equally valuable. The choice should be made upon the basis of their comparative cost and their availability in the particular community. A dog suddenly changed from another diet to horse flesh may develop a harmless and temporary diarrhea, which can be ignored. Horse flesh is likely to be deficient in fats, which may be added in the form of suet, lard or pure corn oil.

The particular cuts of whatever meat is used is of little consequence. Liver and kidney are especially valuable and when it is possible they should be included as part of the meat used. As the only meat in the ration, liver and kidney tend to loosen the bowels. It is better to include them as a part of each day's ration than to permit them to serve as the sole meat content one or two days a week.

It makes no difference whether meat is ground or is fed to the dog in large or medium sized pieces. He is able to digest pieces of meat as large as he can swallow. The advantage of grinding meat is that it can be better mixed with whatever else it is wished to include in the ration, the dog being unable to pick out the meat and reject the rest. There is little harm in his doing so, except for the waste, since it is the meat upon which we must depend for the most part for his nutrition.

Fresh ground meat can be kept four or five days under ordinary refrigeration without spoiling. It may be kept indefinitely if solidly frozen. Frozen ground horse meat for dogs is available in many markets, is low in price, and is entirely satisfactory for the purpose intended.

A suggested ration is made as follows: Two-thirds to three-quarters by weight of ground meat including ten to twenty percent of fat and a portion of liver or kidney, with the remainder thoroughly cooked rice or oatmeal, or shredded wheat, or dog biscuit, or wheat germ, with a sprinkling of calcium phosphate diabasic. Vitamins may be added, or given separately.

If it is desired to offer the dog a second meal, it may be of shredded wheat or other breakfast cereal with plenty of milk, with or without one or more soft boiled eggs. Evaporated canned milk or powdered milk is just as good food for the dog as fresh milk. Cottage cheese is excellent for this second meal.

These are not the only possible rations for the dog, but they will prove adequate. Leavings from the owner's table can be added to either ration, but can hardly be depended upon for the entire nourishment of the dog.

The dog's food should be at approximately body heat, tepid but never hot.

Little consideration is here given to the costs of the various foods. Economies in rations and feeding practices are admittedly desirable, but not if they are made at the expense of the dog's health.

SOME BRIEF PRECEPTS ABOUT FEEDING

Many dogs are overfed. Others do not receive adequate rations. Both extremes should be avoided, but particularly overfeeding of grown dogs. Coupled with lack of exercise, overfeeding usually produces excessive body weight and laziness, and it may result in illness and sterility. Prolonged undernourishment causes loss of weight, listlessness, dull coats, sickness, and death.

An adequate ration will keep most mature dogs at a uniform body weight and in a thrifty, moderately lean condition. Observation of condition is the best guide in determining the correct amount of food.

The axiom, "One man's meat is another man's poison," is applicable to dogs also. Foods that are not tolerated by the dog or those that cause digestive and other disturbances should be discontinued. The use of moldy, spoiled, or rotten food is never good practice. Food should be protected from fouling by rats or mice, especially because rats are vectors of leptospirosis. The excessive use of food of low energy content and low biological values will often result in poor condition and may cause loss of weight and paunchiness.

All feeding and drinking utensils must be kept scrupulously clean. They should be washed after each using.

It is usually desirable to reduce the food allotment somewhat during hot weather. Dogs should be fed at regular intervals, and the best results may be expected when regular feeding is accompanied by regular, but not exhausting, exercise.

Most dogs do not thrive on a ration containing large amounts of sloppy foods, and excessive bulk is to be avoided especially for hardworking dogs, puppies, and pregnant or lactating bitches. If the ration is known to be adequate and the dog is losing weight or is not in good condition, the presence of intestinal parasites is to be suspected. However, dogs sometimes go "off feed" for a day or two. This is cause for no immediate anxiety, but if it lasts more than two or three days, a veterinarian should be consulted.

FOOD FOR THE STUD DOG

The stud dog that is used for breeding only at infrequent intervals requires only the food needed for his maintenance in good health, as set forth in the foregoing pages. He should be well fed with ample meat in his diet, moderately exercised to keep his flesh firm and hard, and not permitted to become too thin or too fat.

More care is required for the adequate nutrition of the dog offered at public stud and frequently employed for breeding. A vigorous stud dog may very handily serve two bitches a week over a long period without a serious tax upon his health and strength if he is fully nourished and adequately but not excessively exercised. Such a dog should have at least two meals a day, and they should consist of even more meat, milk (canned is as good as fresh), eggs, cottage cheese, and other foods of animal origin than is used in most maintenance rations. Liver and some fat should be included, and the vitamins especially are not to be forgotten. In volume this will be only a little more than the basic maintenance diet, the difference being in its richness and concentration.

An interval of an hour or two should intervene between a dog's meal and his employment for breeding. He may be fed, but only lightly, immediately after he has been used for breeding.

The immediate reason that a stud dog should be adequately fed and exercised is the maintenance of his strength and virility. The secondary reason is that a popular stud dog is on exhibition at all times, between the shows as well as at the shows. Clients with bitches to be bred appear without notice to examine a dog at public stud, and the dog should be presented to them in the best possible condition—clean, hard, in exactly the most becoming state of flesh, and with a gleaming, lively coat. These all depend largely upon the highly nutritious diet the dog receives.

FOOD FOR THE BROOD BITCH

Often a well fed bitch comes through the ordeal of rearing a large litter of puppies without any impairment of her vitality and flesh. In such case she may be returned to a good maintenance ration until she is ready to be bred again. About the time she weans her puppies her coat will be dead and ready to drop out, but if she is healthy and well fed a new and vigorous coat will grow in, and she will be no worse off for her maternal ordeal. Some bitches, either from a deficient nutrition or a constitutional disposition to contribute too much of their own strength and substance to the nutrition of the puppies, are thin and exhausted at the time of weaning. Such a bitch needs the continuance of at least two good and especially nutritious meals a day for a month or more until her flesh and strength are restored before she is returned to her routine maintenance ration, upon which she may be kept until time comes to breed her again.

At breeding time a bitch's flesh should be hard, and she should be on the lean side rather than too fat. No change in her regular maintenance diet need be made until about the fourth or fifth week of her pregnancy. The growth of the fetus is small up until the middle of the pregnancy, after which it becomes rapid.

The bitch usually begins to "show in whelp" in four to six weeks after breeding, and her food consumption should be then gradually stepped up. If she has been having only one meal a day, she should be given two; if she has had two, both should be larger. Henceforth until her puppies are weaned, she must eat not merely for two, as is said of the pregnant woman, but for four or five, possibly for ten or twelve. She is not to be encouraged to grow fat. Especial emphasis should be laid upon her ration's content of meat, including liver, milk, calcium phosphate, and vitamins A and D, both of which are found in cod-liver oil.

Some breeders destroy all but a limited number of puppies in a litter in the belief that a bitch will be unable adequately to nourish all the puppies she has whelped. In some extreme cases it may be necessary to do this or to obtain a foster mother or wet nurse to share the burden of rearing the puppies. However, the healthy bitch with normal metabolism can usually generate enough milk to feed adequately all the puppies she has produced, provided she is well enough fed and provided the puppies are fed additionally as soon as they are able to eat.

After whelping until the puppies are weaned, throughout the lactating period, the bitch should have all the nourishing food she can be induced to eat—up to four or five meals a day. These should consist largely of meat and liver, some fat, a small amount of cereals, milk, eggs, cottage cheese, calcium phosphate, and vitamins, with especial reference to vitamins A and D. At that time it is hardly possible to feed a bitch too much or to keep her too fat. The growth of the puppies is much more rapid after they are born than was their growth in the dam's uterus, and the large amount of food needed to maintain that rapid growth must pass through the bitch and be transformed to milk, while at the same time she must maintain her own body.

THE FEEDING OF PUPPIES

If the number of puppies in a litter is small, if the mother is vigorous, healthy, and a good milker, the youngsters up until their weaning time may require no additional food over and above the milk they suck from their dam's breasts. If the puppies are numerous or if the dam's milk is deficient in quality or quantity, it is wise to begin feeding the puppies artificially as soon as they are able and willing to accept food. This is earlier than used to be realized.

It is for the sake of the puppies' vigor rather than for the sake of their ultimate size that their growth is to be promoted as rapidly as possible. Vigorous and healthy puppies attain early maturity if they are given the right amounts of the right quality of food. The ultimate size of the dog at maturity is laid down in his germ plasm, and he can be stunted or dwarfed, if at all, only at the expense of his type. If one tries to prevent the full growth of a dog by withholding from him the food he needs, one will wind up with a rachitic, cowhocked dog, one with a delicate digestive apparatus, a sterile one, one with all of these shortcomings combined, or even a dead dog.

Growth may be slowed with improper food, sometimes without serious harm, but the dog is in all ways better off if he is forced along with the best food and encouraged to attain his full size at an early age. Dogs of the smaller breeds usually reach their full maturity several months earlier than those of the larger breeds. A well grown dog reaches his sexual maturity and can be safely used for limited breeding at one year of age.

As soon as teeth can be felt with the finger in a puppy's mouth, which is usually at about seventeen or eighteen days of age, it is safe to begin to feed him. His first food (except for his mother's milk) should be of scraped raw beef at body temperature. The first day he may have $1/4$ to 2 teaspoonfuls, according to size. He will not need to learn to eat this meat; he will seize upon it avidly and lick his chops for more. The second day he may have $1/3$ to 3 teaspoonfuls, according to size, with two feedings 12 hours apart. Thereafter, the amount and frequency of this feeding may be rapidly increased. By the twenty-fifth day the meat need not be scraped, but only finely ground. This process of the early feeding of raw meat to puppies not only gives them a good start in life, but it also relieves their mother of a part of her burden of providing milk for them.

At about the fourth week, some cereal (thoroughly cooked oatmeal, shredded wheat, or dried bread) may be either moistened and mixed with the meat or be served to the puppies with milk, fresh or canned. It may be necessary to immerse their noses into such a mixture to teach them to eat it. Calcium phosphate and a small amount of cod-liver oil should be added to such a mixture, both of which substances the puppies should have every day until their maturity. At the fourth week, while they are still at the dam's breast, they may be fed three or four times a day upon this extra ration, or something similar, such as cottage cheese or soft boiled egg. By the sixth week their dam will be trying to wean them, and they may have four or five meals daily. One of these may be finely broken dog biscuit thoroughly soaked in milk. One or two of the meals should consist largely or entirely of meat with liver.

The old advice about feeding puppies "little and often" should be altered to "much and often." Each puppy at each meal should have all the food he will readily clean up. Food should not be left in front of the puppies. They should be fed and after two or three minutes the receptacle should be taken away. Young puppies should be roly-poly fat, and kept so up to at least five or six months of age. Thereafter they should be slightly on the fat side, but not pudgy, until maturity.

The varied diet of six-week-old puppies may be continued, but at eight or nine weeks the number of meals may be reduced to four, and at three months, to three large rations per day. After six months the meals may be safely reduced again to two a day, but they must be generous meals with meat, liver, milk, cod-liver oil, and calcium phosphate. At full maturity, one meal a day suffices, or two may be continued.

The secret of turning good puppies into fine, vigorous dogs is to keep them growing through the entire period of their maturation. The most important item in the rearing of puppies is adequate and frequent meals of highly nourishing foods. Growth requires two or three times as much food as maintenance. Time between meals should be allowed for digestion, but puppies should never be permitted to become really hungry. Water in a shallow dish should be available to puppies at all times after they are able to walk.

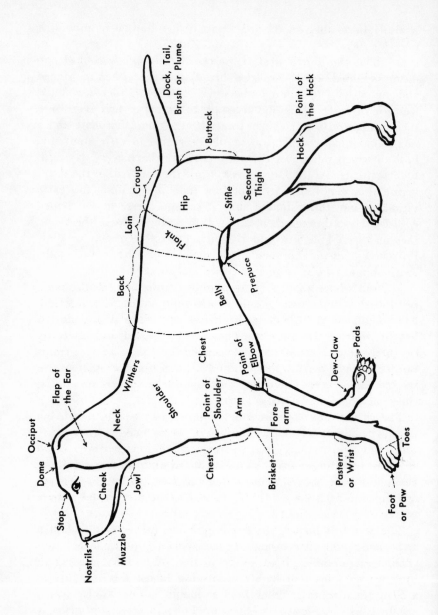

46

The Breeding
of Dogs

H ERE, if anywhere in the entire process of the care
and management of dogs, the exercise of good judgment is involved.
Upon the choice of the two dogs, male and female, to be mated
together depends the future success or failure of one's dogs. If the
two to be mated are ill chosen, either individually or as pertains
to their fitness as mates, one to the other, all the painstaking care
to feed and rear the resultant puppies correctly is wasted. The
mating together of two dogs is the drafting of the blueprints and
the writing of the specifications of what the puppies are to be
like. The plans, it is true, require to be executed; the puppies,
when they arrive, must be adequately fed and cared for in order
to develop them into the kinds of dogs they are in their germ plasm
designed to become. However, if the plans as determined in the
mating are defective, just so will the puppies that result from them
be defective, in spite of all the good raising one can give them.

The element of luck in the breeding of dogs cannot be discounted,
for it exists. The mating which on paper appears to be the best
possible may result in puppies that are poor and untypical of
their breed. Even less frequently, a good puppy may result from
a chance mating together of two ill chosen parents. These results
are fortuitous and unusual, however. The best dogs as a lot come
from parents carefully chosen as to their individual excellences and
as to their suitability as mates for each other. It is as unwise as

it is unnecessary to trust to luck in the breeding of dogs. Careful planning pays off in the long run, and few truly excellent dogs are produced without it.

Some breeders without any knowledge of genetics have been successful, without knowing exactly why they succeeded. Some of them have adhered to beliefs in old wives' tales and to traditional concepts that science has long since exploded and abandoned. Such as have succeeded have done so in spite of their lack of knowledge and not because of it.

There is insufficient space at our disposal in this book to discuss in detail the science of genetics and the application of that science to the breeding of dogs. Whole books have been written about the subject. One of the best, clearest, and easiest for the layman to understand is *The New Art of Breeding Better Dogs,* by Philip Onstott, which may be obtained from Howell Book House, the publisher. In it and in other books upon the subject of genetics will be found more data about the practical application of science to the breeding of livestock than can be included here.

The most that can be done here is to offer some advice soundly based upon the genetic laws. Every feature a dog may or can possess is determined by the genes carried in the two reproductive cells, one from each parent, from the union of which he was developed. There are thousands of pairs of these determiners in the life plan of every puppy, and often a complex of many genes is required to produce a single recognizable attribute of the dog.

These genes function in pairs, one member of each pair being contributed by the father and the other member of the pair coming from the mother. The parents obtained these genes they hand on from their parents, and it is merely fortuitous which half of any pair of genes present in a dog's or a bitch's germ plasm may be passed on to any one of the progeny. Of any pair of its own genes, a dog or a bitch may contribute one member to one puppy and the other member to another puppy in the same litter or in different litters. The unknown number of pairs of genes is so great that there is an infinite number of combinations of them, which accounts for the differences we find between two full brothers or two full sisters. In fact, it depends upon the genes received whether a dog be a male or a female.

We know that the male dog contributes one and the bitch the

other of every pair of genes that unite to determine what the puppy will be like and what he will grow into. Thus, the parents make exactly equal contributions to the germ plasm or zygote from which every puppy is developed. It was long believed that the male dog was so much more important than the bitch in any mating that the excellence or shortcomings of the bitch might be disregarded. This theory was subsequently reversed and breeders considered the bitch to be more important than the dog. We now know that their contribution in every mating and in every individual puppy is exactly equal, and neither is to be considered more than the other.

There are two kinds of genes—the recessive genes and the dominant. And there are three kinds of pairs of genes: a recessive from the sire plus a recessive from the dam; a dominant from the sire plus a dominant from the dam; and a dominant from one parent plus a recessive from the other. It is the last combination that is the source of our trouble in breeding. When both members of a pair of genes are recessive, the result is a recessive attribute in the animal that carries them; when both members of the pair are dominant, the result is a pure dominant attribute; but when one member of the pair is recessive and the other member dominant, the result will be a wholly or only partially dominant attribute, which will breed true only half of the time. This explains why a dog or a bitch may fail to produce progeny that looks at all like itself.

If all the pairs of a dog's genes were purely dominant, we could expect him to produce puppies that resembled himself in all particulars, no matter what kind of mate he was bred to. Or if all his genes were recessive and he were mated to a bitch with all recessive genes, the puppies might be expected to look quite like the parents. However, a dog with mixed pairs of genes bred to a bitch with mixed pairs of genes may produce anything at all, puppies that bear no resemblance to either parent.

Long before the Mendelian laws were discovered, some dogs were known to be "prepotent" to produce certain characters, that is the characters would show up in their puppies irrespective of what their mates might be like. For instance, some dogs, themselves with dark eyes, might be depended upon never to produce a puppy with light eyes, no matter how light eyed the mate to which he was

49

bred. This was true despite the fact that the dog's litter brother which had equally dark eyes, when bred to a light eyed bitch might produce a large percentage of puppies with light eyes.

Before it is decided to breed a bitch, it is well to consider whether she is worth breeding, whether she is good enough as an individual and whether she came from a good enough family to warrant the expectations that she will produce puppies worth the expense and trouble of raising. It is to be remembered that the bitch contributes exactly half the genes to each of her puppies; if she has not good genes to contribute, the time and money involved in breeding her and rearing her puppies will be wasted.

It is conceded that a bad or mediocre bitch when bred to an excellent dog will probably produce puppies better than herself. But while one is "grading up" from mediocre stock, other breeders are also grading upward from better stock and they will keep just so far ahead of one's efforts that one can never catch up with them. A merely pretty good bitch is no good at all for breeding. It is better to dispose of a mediocre bitch or to relegate her to the position of a family pet than to breed from her. It is difficult enough, with all the care and judgment one is able to muster, to obtain superlative puppies even from a fine bitch, without cluttering the earth with inferior puppies from just any old bitch.

If one will go into the market and buy the best possible bitch from the best possible family one's purse can afford and breed her sensibly to the best and most suitable stud dog one can find, success is reasonably sure. Even if for economy's sake, the bitch is but a promising puppy backed up by the best possible pedigree, it will require only a few months until she is old enough to be bred. From such a bitch, one may expect first-rate puppies at the first try, whereas in starting with an inferior bitch one is merely lucky if in two or three generations he obtains a semblance of the kind of dog he is trying to produce.

Assuming it is decided that the bitch is adequate to serve as a brood bitch, it becomes necessary to choose for her a mate in collaboration with which she may realize the ultimate of her possibilities. It is never wise to utilize for stud the family pet or the neighbor's pet just because he happens to be registered in the studbook or because his service costs nothing. Any dog short of the best and most suitable (wherever he may be and whoever may own him) is an extravagance. If the bitch is worth breeding at all, she is worth shipping clear across the continent, if need be, to obtain for her a mate to enable her to realize her possibilities. Stud fees may range from fifty to one hundred dollars or even more. The average value of each puppy, if well reared, should at the time of weaning approximate the legitimate stud fee of its sire. With a good bitch it is therefore profitable to lay out as much as may be required to obtain the services of the best and most suitable stud dog—always assuming that he is worth the price asked. However, it is never wise to choose an inferior or unsuitable dog just because he is well ballyhooed and commands an exorbitant stud fee.

There are three considerations by which to evaluate the merits of a stud dog—his outstanding excellence as an individual, his pedigree and the family from which he derived, and the excellence or inferiority of the progeny he is known to have produced.

As an individual a good stud dog may be expected to be bold and aggressive (not vicious) and structurally typical of his breed, but without any freakish exaggerations of type. He must be sound, a free and true mover, possess fineness and quality, and be a gentleman of his own breed. Accidentally acquired scars or injuries such as broken legs should not be held against him, because he can transmit only his genes to his puppies and no such accidents impair his genes.

A dog's pedigree may mean much or little. One of two litter brothers, with pedigrees exactly alike, may prove to be a superlative show and stud dog, and the other worth exactly nothing for either purpose. The pedigree especially is not to be judged on its length, since three generations is at most all that is required, although further extension of the pedigree may prove interesting to a curious owner. No matter how well-bred his pedigree may show a dog to be, if he is not a good dog the ink required to write the pedigree was wasted.

The chief value of a pedigree is to enable us to know from which of a dog's parents, grandparents, or great-grandparents, he derived his merits, and from which his faults. In choosing a mate for him (or for her, as the case may be) one seeks to reinforce the one and to avoid the other. Let us assume that one of the grandmothers was upright in shoulder, whereas the shoulder should be well laid back; we can avoid as a mate for such a dog one with any

51

tendency to straight shoulders or one from straight shouldered ancestry. The same principle would apply to an uneven mouth, a light eye, a soft back, splayed feet, cowhocks, or to any other inherited fault. Suppose, on the other hand, that the dog himself, the parents, and all the grandparents are particularly nice in regard to their fronts; in a mate for such a dog, one desires as good a front as is obtainable, but if she, or some of her ancestors are not too good in respect to their fronts, one may take a chance anyway and trust to the good fronted dog with his good fronted ancestry to correct the fault. That then is the purpose of the pedigree as a guide to breeding.

A stud dog can best be judged, however, by the excellence of the progeny he is known to have produced, if it is possible to obtain all the data to enable the breeder to evaluate that record. A complete comparative evaluation is perhaps impossible to make, but one close enough to justify conclusions is available. Not only the number but the quality of the bitches to which the dog has been bred must enter into the consideration. A young dog may not have had the opportunity to prove his prowess in the stud. He may have been bred to few bitches and those few of indifferent merits, or his get may not be old enough as yet to hit the shows and establish a record for themselves or for their sire. Allowance may be made for such a dog.

On the other hand, a dog may have proved himself to be phenomenal in the show ring, or may have been made to seem phenomenal by means of the owner's ballyhoo and exploitation. Half of the top bitches in the entire country may have been bred to him upon the strength of his winning record. Merely from the laws of probability such a dog, if he is not too bad, will produce some creditable progeny. It is necessary to take into consideration the opportunities a dog has had in relation to the fine progeny he has produced.

That, however, is the chief criterion by which a good stud dog may be recognized. A dog which can sire two or three excellent puppies in every litter from a reasonably good bitch may be considered as an acceptable stud. If he has in his lifetime sired one or two champions each year, and especially if one or two of the lot are superlative champions, top members of their breed, he is a great stud dog. Ordinarily and without other considerations, such a dog is to be preferred to one of his unproved sons, even though the son be as good or better an individual. In this way one employs genes one knows to produce what one wants. The son may be only hybrid dominant for his excellent qualities.

In the choice of a stud dog no attention whatever need be paid to claims that he sires numerically big litters. Unless the sire is deficient in sperm, the number of puppies in the litter, provided there are any puppies at all, depends entirely upon the bitch. At one service, a dog deposits enough spermatozoa to produce a million puppies, if there were so many ova to be fertilized. In any event, the major purpose should be to obtain good puppies, not large numbers of them.

There are three methods of breeding employed by experienced breeders—outcrossing, inbreeding, and line breeding. By outcrossing is meant the breeding together of mates of which no blood relationship can be traced. It is much favored by novice breeders, who feel that the breeding together of blood relatives is likely to result in imbecility, constitutional weakness, or some other kind of degeneration. Inbreeding is the mating together of closely related animals—father to daughter, mother to son, brother to sister, half brother to half sister. Some of the best animals ever produced have been bred from some such incestuous mating, and the danger from such practices, if they are carried out by persons who know what they are about, is minimal. Line breeding is the mating together of animals related one to another, but less closely—such as first cousins, grandsire to granddaughter, granddam to grandson, uncle to niece, or aunt to nephew.

Absolute outcrossing is usually impossible, since all the good dogs in any breed are more or less related—descended from some common ancestor in the fifth or sixth or seventh generation of their pedigrees. In any event, it is seldom to be recommended, since the results from it in the first generation of progeny are usually not satisfactory. It may be undertaken by some far-sighted and experienced breeder for the purpose of bringing into his strain some particular merit lacking in it and present in the strain of the unrelated dog. While dogs so bred may obtain an added vigor from what is known in genetics as *heterosis*, they are likely to manifest a coarseness and a lack of uniformity in the litter which is not to be found in more closely bred puppies. Good breeders never outcross if it is possible to obtain the virtues they want by sticking to their own strain. And when they do outcross, it is for the purpose of utilizing the outcrossed product for further breeding. It is not an end in itself.

Inbreeding (or incest breeding, as it is sometimes called) involves no such hazards as are and in the past have been attributed to it. It produces some very excellent dogs when correctly employed, some very bad ones even when correctly employed, and all bad ones when carelessly used. All the standard breeds of dogs were established as uniform breeds through intense inbreeding and culling over many generations. Inbreeding brings into manifestation undesirable recessive genes, the bearers of which can be discarded and the strain can thus be purged of its bad recessives.

Dogs of great soundness and excellence, from excellent parents and grandparents, all of them much alike, may be safely mated together, no matter how closely they may be related, with reasonable hope that most of the progeny will be sound and typical with a close resemblance to all the members of their ancestry. However, two such superlative and well-bred dogs are seldom to be found. It is the way to make progress rapidly and to establish a strain of dogs much alike and which breeds true. The amateur with the boldness and courage to try such a mating in the belief that his dogs are good enough for it is not to be discouraged. But if his judgment is not justified by the results, let him not complain that he has not been warned.

Line breeding is the safest course between the Scylla of outcrossing and the Charybdis of inbreeding for the inexperienced navigator in the sea of breeding. It, too, is to be used with care, because when it succeeds it partakes much of the nature of inbreeding. At any rate, its purpose is the pairing of like genes.

Here the pedigrees come into use. We examine the pedigree of the bitch to be bred. We hope that all the dogs named in it are magnificent dogs, but we look them over and choose the best of the four grandparents. We check this grandparent's breeding and find it good, as it probably is if it is itself a dog or bitch of great excellence. We shall assume that this best dog in the bitch's pedigree is the maternal grandsire. Then our bitch may be bred back to this particular grandsire, to his full brother if he has one of equal excellence, to his best son or best grandson. In such a fashion we compound the genes of this grandsire, and hope to obtain some puppies with his excellences intensified.

The best name in the pedigree may be some other dog or bitch, in which case it is his or her germ plasm that is to be doubled to serve for the foundation of the pedigrees of the puppies of the projected litter.

In making a mating, it is never wise to employ two dogs with the same positive fault. It is wise to use two dogs with as many of the same positive virtues as it is possible to obtain. Neither should faults balance each other, as one with a front too wide, the other with a front too narrow; one with a sway back, the other roach backed. Rather, one member of the mating should be right where the other is wrong. We cannot trust to obtain the intermediate, if we overcompensate the fault of one mate with a fault of the other.

NEGOTIATIONS TO USE THE STUD DOG

Plans to use a stud dog should be laid far enough in advance to enable one to make sure that the services of the dog will be available when they are required. Most men with a dog at public stud publish "stud cards," on which are printed the dog's pedigree and pertinent data pertaining to its record. These should be requested for all the dogs one contemplates using. Most such owners reserve the right to refuse to breed their dogs to bitches they deem unsuitable for them; they wish to safeguard their dog's reputation as a producer of superior puppies, by choosing the bitches to which he shall be bred. Therefore, it is advisable to submit a description of the bitch, with or without a picture of her, and her pedigree to the stud dog's owner at the time the application to use him is made.

Notification should be sent to the owner of the dog as soon as the bitch begins to show in heat, and she should be taken or sent by air or by railway express to the dog's owner about the time she is first recognized to be in full heat and ready to breed. The stud dog's owner should be advised by telegram or telephone just how she has been sent and just when she may be expected, and instruction should be given about how she is to be returned.

Extreme care should be used in securely crating a bitch for shipment when she is in heat. Such bitches are prone to chew their way out of insecure boxes and escape to be bred by some vagrant mongrel. A card containing a statement of the bitch's condition should be attached to the crate as a warning to the carrier to assure her greater security.

MATING

The only time the bitch may become pregnant is during her period of oestruation, a time also variously referred to as the "oestrus," "the season," and as being in "heat." A bitch's first season usually occurs when she is between six and nine months of age, with the average age being eight months. In rare instances it may occur as early as five months or as late as thirteen months of age. After the first season, oestrus usually recurs at intervals of approximately six months, though this too is subject to variation. Also, the bitch's cycle may be influenced by factors such as a change of environment or a change of climate, and her cycle will, of course, be changed if it is interrupted by pregnancy. Most bitches again come in season four to six months after whelping.

There is a decided controversy among breeders as to the wisdom of breeding a bitch during her first season. Some believe a really fine bitch should be bred during her first season in order that she may produce as many puppies as possible during the fertile years of her life span. Others feel that definite physical harm results from breeding a bitch at her first season. Since a normal healthy bitch can safely produce puppies until she is about nine years old, she can comfortably yield eight to ten litters with rests between them in her life. Any breeder should be satisfied with this production from one animal. It seems wiser, therefore, to avoid the risk of any harm and pass her first season. Bitches vary in temperament and in the ages at which they reach sufficient maturity for motherhood and its responsibilities. As with the human animal, stability comes with age and a dam is much more likely to be a good mother if she is out of the puppy phase herself. If the bitch is of show quality, she might become a champion between her first and second heats if not bred.

Usually, oestruation continues for a period of approximately three weeks, but this too is subject to variation. Prior to the beginning of the oestrus, there may be changes in the bitch's actions and demeanor; she may appear restless, or she may become increasingly affectionate. Often there is increased frequency of urination and the bitch may be inclined to lick her external parts. The breeder should be alert for any signs of the approach of oestrus since the bitch must be confined and protected at this time in order to preclude the

57

possibility of the occurrence of a mating with any but the selected stud.

The first physical sign of oestrus is a bloody discharge of watery consistency. The mucous membrane lining the vulva becomes congested, enlarged, and reddened, and the external parts become puffy and swollen. The color of the discharge gradually deepens during the first day or two until it is a rich red color; then it gradually becomes lighter until by the tenth to twelfth day it has only a slightly reddish, or straw-colored, tinge. During the next day or so it becomes almost clear. During this same period, the swelling and hardness of the external parts gradually subside, and by the time the discharge has lost most of its color, the parts are softened and spongy. It is at this time that ovulation, the production of ripened ova (or eggs), takes place, although physical manifestations of oestrus may continue for another week.

A normal bitch has two ovaries which contain her ova. All the eggs she will produce during her lifetime are present in the ovaries at birth. Ordinarily, some of the ova ripen each time the bitch comes in season. Should a bitch fail to ovulate (produce ripened ova), she cannot, of course, become pregnant. Actually, only one ovary is necessary for ovulation, and loss of or damage to one ovary without impairment of the other will not prevent the bitch from producing puppies.

If fertilization does not occur, the ova (and this is also true of the sperm of the male) live only a short time—probably a couple of days at the most. Therefore, if mating takes place too long before or after ovulation, a bitch will not conceive, and the unfertilized ova will pass through the uterus into the vagina. Eventually they will either be absorbed or will pass out through the vulva by the same opening through which urination takes place. If fertilization does occur, the fertilized eggs become implanted on the inner surface of the uterus and grow to maturity.

Obviously, the breeder must exercise great care in determining when the dog and the bitch should be put together. Because the length of time between the beginning of the oestrus and the time of ovulation varies in different bitches, no hard and fast rule can be established, although the twelfth to fourteenth day is in most cases the correct time. The wise breeder will keep a daily record of the changes in the bitch's condition and will arrange to put the bitch

58

and dog together when the discharge has become almost clear and the external parts are softened and spongy. If the bitch refuses the advances of the dog, it is preferable to separate the two, wait a day, then again permit the dog to approach the bitch.

Ordinarily, if the bitch is willing to accept the dog, fertilization of the ovum will take place. Usually one good service is sufficient, although two at intervals of twenty-four to forty-eight hours are often allowed.

Male dogs have glands on the penis which swell after passing the sphincter muscle of the vagina and "tie" the two animals together. The time may last for a period of a few minutes, a half hour, or occasionally up to an hour or more, but will end naturally when the locking glands have deflated the needful amount. While tying may increase the probability of success, in many cases no tie occurs, yet the bitches become pregnant.

Sperm are produced in the dog's testicles and are stored in the epididymis, a twisting tube at the side of the testicle. The occasional male dog whose testicles are not descended (a cryptorchid) is generally conceded to be sterile, although in a few instances it has been asserted that cryptorchids were capable of begetting progeny. The sterility in cryptorchids is believed to be due to the fact that the sperm are destroyed if the testicle remains within the abdominal cavity because the temperature is much higher there than in the normally descended testicle. Thus all sperm produced by the dog may be destroyed if both testicles are undescended. A monorchid (a dog with one testicle descended, the other undescended) may be fertile. Nevertheless, it is unwise to use a monorchid for stud purposes, because monorchidism is believed to be a heritable trait, and the monorchid, as well as the cryptorchid, is ineligible for the show ring.

After breeding, a bitch should be confined for a week to ten days to avoid mismating with another dog.

WHELPING CALENDAR

Find the month and date on which your bitch was bred in one of the left-hand columns. Directly opposite that date, in the right-hand column, is her expected date of whelping, bearing in mind that 61 days is as common as 63.

Date bred: January	Date due: March	Date bred: February	Date due: April	Date bred: March	Date due: May	Date bred: April	Date due: June	Date bred: May	Date due: July	Date bred: June	Date due: August	Date bred: July	Date due: September	Date bred: August	Date due: October	Date bred: September	Date due: November	Date bred: October	Date due: December	Date bred: November	Date due: January	Date bred: December
1	5	1	5	1	3	1	3	1	3	1	3	1	2	1	3	1	3	1	3	1	3	1
2	6	2	6	2	4	2	4	2	4	2	4	2	3	2	4	2	4	2	4	2	4	2
3	7	3	7	3	5	3	5	3	5	3	5	3	4	3	5	3	5	3	5	3	5	3
4	8	4	8	4	6	4	6	4	6	4	6	4	5	4	6	4	6	4	6	4	6	4
5	9	5	9	5	7	5	7	5	7	5	7	5	6	5	7	5	7	5	7	5	7	5
6	10	6	10	6	8	6	8	6	8	6	8	6	7	6	8	6	8	6	8	6	8	6
7	11	7	11	7	9	7	9	7	9	7	9	7	8	7	9	7	9	7	9	7	9	7
8	12	8	12	8	10	8	10	8	10	8	10	8	9	8	10	8	10	8	10	8	10	8
9	13	9	13	9	11	9	11	9	11	9	11	9	10	9	11	9	11	9	11	9	11	9
10	14	10	14	10	12	10	12	10	12	10	12	10	11	10	12	10	12	10	12	10	12	10
11	15	11	15	11	13	11	13	11	13	11	13	11	12	11	13	11	13	11	13	11	13	11
12	16	12	16	12	14	12	14	12	14	12	14	12	13	12	14	12	14	12	14	12	14	12
13	17	13	17	13	15	13	15	13	15	13	15	13	14	13	15	13	15	13	15	13	15	13
14	18	14	18	14	16	14	16	14	16	14	16	14	15	14	16	14	16	14	16	14	16	14
15	19	15	19	15	17	15	17	15	17	15	17	15	16	15	17	15	17	15	17	15	17	15
16	20	16	20	16	18	16	18	16	18	16	18	16	17	16	18	16	18	16	18	16	18	16
17	21	17	21	17	19	17	19	17	19	17	19	17	18	17	19	17	19	17	19	17	19	17
18	22	18	22	18	20	18	20	18	20	18	20	18	19	18	20	18	20	18	20	18	20	18
19	23	19	23	19	21	19	21	19	21	19	21	19	20	19	21	19	21	19	21	19	21	19
20	24	20	24	20	22	20	22	20	22	20	22	20	21	20	22	20	22	20	22	20	22	20
21	25	21	25	21	23	21	23	21	23	21	23	21	22	21	23	21	23	21	23	21	23	21
22	26	22	26	22	24	22	24	22	24	22	24	22	23	22	24	22	24	22	24	22	24	22
23	27	23	27	23	25	23	25	23	25	23	25	23	24	23	25	23	25	23	25	23	25	23
24	28	24	28	24	26	24	26	24	26	24	26	24	25	24	26	24	26	24	26	24	26	24
25	29	25	29	25	27	25	27	25	27	25	27	25	26	25	27	25	27	25	27	25	27	25
26	30	26	30	26	28	26	28	26	28	26	28	26	27	26	28	26	28	26	28	26	28	26
27	31	27	1 (May)	27	29	27	29	27	29	27	29	27	28	27	29	27	29	27	29	27	29	27
28	1 (Apr.)	28	2	28	30	28	30 (July)	28	30	28	30	28	29	28	30	28	30 (Dec.)	28	30	28	30	28
29	2			29	31	29	1	29	31	29	31	29	30	29	31	29	1	29	31	29	31	29
30	3			30	1 (June)	30	2	30	1 (Aug.)	30	1 (Sep.)	30	1 (Oct.)	30	1 (Nov.)	30	2	30	1 (Jan.)	30	1 (Feb.)	30
31	4			31	2			31	2			31	2	31	2			31	2			31

THE PREGNANCY AND WHELPING
OF THE BITCH

The "period of gestation" of the bitch, by which is meant the duration of her pregnancy, is usually estimated at sixty-three days. Many bitches, especially young ones, have their puppies as early as sixty days after they are bred. Cases have occurred in which strong puppies were born after only fifty-seven days, and there have been cases that required as many as sixty-six days. However, if puppies do not arrive by the sixty-fourth day, it is time to consult a veterinarian.

For the first five to six weeks of her pregnancy, the bitch requires no more than normal good care and unrestricted exercise. For that period, she needs no additional quantity of food, although her diet must contain sufficient amounts of all the food factors, as is stated in the division of this book that pertains to food. After the fifth to sixth week, the ration must be increased and the violence of exercise restricted. Normal running and walking are likely to be better for the pregnant bitch than a sedentary existence but she should not be permitted to jump, hunt, or fight during the latter half of her gestation. Violent activity may cause her to abort her puppies.

About a week before she is due to whelp, a bed should be prepared for her and she be persuaded to use it for sleeping. This bed may be a box of generous size, big enough to accommodate her with room for activity. It should be high enough to permit her to stand upright, and is better for having a hinged cover. An opening in one side will afford her ingress and egress. This box should be placed in a secluded location, away from any possible molestation by other dogs, animals, or children. The bitch must be made confident of her security in her box.

A few hours, or perhaps a day or two, before her whelping, the bitch will probably begin arranging the bedding of the box to suit herself, tearing blankets or cushions and nosing the parts into the corners. Before the whelping actually starts, however, it is best to substitute burlap sacking, securely tacked to the floor of the box. This is to provide traction for the puppies to reach the dam's breast.

The whelping may take place at night without any assistance from the owner. The box may be opened in the morning to reveal the happy bitch nursing a litter of complacent puppies. But she may need some assistance in her parturition. If whelping is recognized to be in process, it is best to help the bitch.

As the puppies arrive, one by one, the enveloping membranes should be removed as quickly as possible, lest the puppies suffocate. Having removed the membrane, the umbilical cord should be severed with clean scissors some three or four inches from the puppy's belly. (The part of the cord attached to the belly will dry up and drop off in a few days.) There is no need for any medicament or dressing of the cord after it is cut.

The bitch should be permitted to eat the afterbirth if she so desires, and she normally does. If she has no assistance, she will probably remove the membrane and sever the cord with her teeth. The only dangers are that she may delay too long or may bite the cord too short. Some bitches, few of them, eat their newborn puppies (especially bitches not adequately fed during pregnancy). This unlikelihood should be guarded against.

As they arrive, it is wise to remove all the puppies except one, placing them in a box or basket lined and covered by a woolen cloth, somewhere aside or away from the whelping bed, until all have come and the bitch's activity has ceased. The purpose of this is to prevent her from walking or lying on the whelps, and to keep her from being disturbed by the puppies' whining. A single puppy should be left with the bitch to ease her anxiety.

It is best that the "midwife" be somebody with whom the bitch is on intimate terms and in whom she has confidence. Some bitches exhibit a jealous fear and even viciousness while they are whelping. Such animals are few, and most appear grateful for gentle assistance through their ordeal.

The puppies arrive at intervals of a few minutes to an hour until all are delivered. It is wise to call a veterinarian if the interval is greater than one hour. Though such service is seldom needed, an experienced veterinarian can usually be depended upon to withdraw with obstetrical forceps an abnormally presented puppy. It is possible, but unlikely, that the veterinarian will recommend a Caesarian section. This surgery in the dog is not very grave, but it should be performed only by an expert veterinarian. It is unnecessary to describe the process here, or the subsequent management of the patient, since, if a Caesarian section should be necessary, the veterinarian will provide all the needed instructions.

Some bitches, at or immediately after their whelping period, go into a convulsive paralysis, which is called *eclampsia*. This is unlikely if the bitch throughout her pregnancy has had an adequate measure of calcium in her rations. The remedy for eclampsia is the intravenous or intramuscular administration of parenteral calcium. The bitch suspected of having eclampsia should be attended by a veterinarian.

Assuming that the whelping has been normal and without untoward incident, all of the puppies are returned to the bitch, and put, one by one, to the breast, which strong puppies will accept with alacrity. The less handling of puppies for the first four or five hours of their lives, the better. However, the litter should be looked over carefully for possible defectives and discards, which should be destroyed as soon as possible. There is no virtue in rearing hare-lipped, crippled, or mismarked puppies.

It is usually unwise to destroy sound, healthy puppies just to reduce the number in the litter, since it is impossible to sort young puppies for excellence and one may be destroying the best member of the litter, a future champion. Unless a litter is extraordinarily numerous, the dam, if well fed, can probably suckle them all. If it is found that her milk is insufficient, the litter may be artificially fed or may be divided, and the surplus placed on a foster mother if it is possible to obtain one. The foster mother need not be of the same breed as the puppies, a mongrel being as good as any. She should be approximately the same size as the actual mother of the puppies, clean, healthy, and her other puppies should be of as nearly the same age as the ones she is to take over as possible. She should be removed from her own puppies (which may well be destroyed) and her breasts be permitted to fill with milk until she is somewhat uncomfortable, at which time her foster puppies can be put to her breasts and will usually be accepted without difficulty. Unless the services of the foster mother are really required, it is better not to use her.

The whelping bitch may be grateful for a warm meal even between the arrivals of her puppies. As soon as her chore is over, she should be offered food in her box. This should be of cereal and milk or of meat and broth, something sloppy. She will probably not leave her puppies to eat and her meals must be brought to her.

63

It is wise to give a mild laxative for her bowels, also milk of magnesia. She will be reluctant to get out of her box even to relieve herself for about two days, but she should be urged, even forced, to do so regularly. A sensible bitch will soon settle down to care for her brood and will seldom give further trouble. She should be fed often and well, all that she can be induced to eat during her entire lactation.

As a preventive for infections sometimes occurring after whelping, some experienced breeders and veterinarians recommend injecting the bitch with penicillin or another antibiotic immediately following the birth of the last puppy. Oral doses of the same drug may be given daily thereafter for the first week. It is best to consult your veterinarian about this treatment.

ACID MILK

Occasionally a bitch produces early milk (colostrum) so acid that it disagrees with, sometimes kills, her puppies. The symptoms of the puppies are whining, disquiet, frequently refusal to nurse, frailty, and death. It is true that all milk is slightly acid, and it should be, turning blue litmus paper immersed in it a very light pink. However, milk harmfully on the acid side will readily turn litmus paper a vivid red. It seems that only the first two or three days milk is so affected. Milk problems come also from mastitis and other infections in the bitch.

This is not likely to occur with a bitch that throughout her pregnancy has received an adequate supply of calcium phosphate regularly in her daily ration. That is the best way to deal with the situation—to see to the bitch's correct nutrition in advance of her whelping. The owner has only himself to blame for the bitch's too acid milk, since adequate calcium in advance would have neutralized the acid.

If it is found too late that her milk is too acid, the puppies must be taken from her breast and either given to a foster mother or artificially fed from bottle or by medicine dropper. Artificial feeding of very young puppies seldom is successful. Sometimes the acidity of the dam's milk can be neutralized by giving her large doses of bicarbonate of soda (baking soda), but the puppies should not be restored to her breasts until her milk ceases to turn litmus paper red.

If it is necessary to feed the puppies artificially, "Esbilac," a commercial product, or the following orphan puppy formula, may be used.

7 oz. whole milk
1 oz. cream (top milk)
1 egg yolk
2 tbsp. corn syrup
2 tbsp. lime water

REARING THE PUPPIES

Puppies are born blind and open their eyes at approximately the ninth day thereafter. If they were whelped earlier than the full sixty-three days after the breeding from which they resulted, the difference should be added to the nine days of anticipated blindness. The early eye color of young puppies is no criterion of the color to which the eyes are likely to change, and the breeder's anxiety about his puppies' having light eyes is premature.

In breeds that require the docking of the tail, this should be done on the third day and is a surgical job for the veterinarian. Many a dog has had his tail cut off by an inexperienced person, ruining his good looks and his possibility for a win in the show ring. Dew claws should be removed at the same time. There is little else to do with normal puppies except to let them alone and permit them to grow. The most important thing about their management is their nutrition, which is discussed in another chapter. The first two or three weeks, they will thrive and grow rapidly on their mother's milk, after which they should have additional food as described.

Puppies sleep much of the time, as do other babies, and they should not be frequently awakened to be played with. They grow more and more playful as they mature.

After the second week their nails begin to grow long and sharp. The mother will be grateful if the puppies' nails are blunted with scissors from time to time so that in their pawing of the breast they do not lacerate it. Sharp nails tend to prompt the mother to wean the whelps early, and she should be encouraged to keep them with her as long as she will tolerate them. Even the small amount of milk they can drain from her after the weaning process is begun is the best food they can obtain. It supplements and makes digestible the remainder of their ration.

Many bitches, after their puppies are about four weeks of age, eat and regurgitate food, which is eaten by the puppies. This food is warmed and partly digested in the bitch's stomach. This practice, while it may appear digusting to the novice keeper of dogs, is perfectly normal and should not be discouraged. However, it renders it all the more necessary that the food of the bitch be sound, clean, and nutritious.

It is all but impossible to rear a litter of puppies without their becoming infested with roundworms. Of course, the bitch should be wormed, if she harbors such parasites, before she is bred, and her teats should be thoroughly washed with mild soap just before she whelps to free them from the eggs of roundworms. Every precaution must be taken to reduce the infestation of the puppies to a minimum. But, in spite of all it is possible to do, puppies will have roundworms. These pests hamper growth, reduce the puppies' normal resistance to disease, and may kill them outright unless the worms are eliminated. The worming of puppies is discussed in the chapter entitled "Intestinal Parasites and Their Control."

External Vermin
and Parasites

UNDER this heading the most common external parasites will be given consideration. Fleas, lice, ticks, and flies are those most commonly encountered and causing the most concern. The external parasite does not pose the problem that it used to before we had the new "miracle" insecticides. Today, with DDT, lindane, and chlordane, the course of extermination and prevention is much easier to follow. Many of the insecticide sprays have a four to six weeks residual effect. Thus the premises can be sprayed and the insect pests can be quite readily controlled.

FLEAS

Neglected dogs are too often beset by hundreds of blood-thirsty fleas, which do not always confine their attacks to the dogs but also sometimes feast upon their masters. Unchecked, they overrun kennels, homes, and playgrounds. Moreover, they are the intermediate hosts for the development of the kind of tapeworm most frequently found in dogs, as will be more fully discussed under the subject of *Intestinal Parasites*. Fleas are all-round bad actors and nuisances. Although it need hardly concern us in America, where the disease is not known to exist, fleas are the recognized and only vectors of bubonic plague.

There are numerous kinds and varieties of fleas, of which we shall discuss here only the three species often found on dogs. These are the human flea (*Pulex irritans*), the dog flea (*Ctenocephalides canis*), and the so-called chicken flea or sticktight flea (*Echidnophaga gallinacea*).

Of these the human flea prefers the blood of man to that of the dog, and unless humans are also bothered, are not likely to be found on the dog. They are small, nearly black insects, and occur mostly in the Mississippi Valley and in California. Their control is the same as for the dog flea.

The dog flea is much larger than his human counterpart, is dark brown in color and seldom bites mankind. On an infested dog these dog fleas may be found buried in the coat of any part of the anatomy, but their choicest habitat is the area of the back just forward from the tail and over the loins. On that part of a badly neglected dog, especially in summer, fleas by the hundreds will be found intermixed with their dung and with dried blood. They may cause the dog some discomfort or none. It must not be credited that because a dog is not kept in a constant or frequent agitation of scratching that he harbors no fleas. The coats of pet animals are soiled and roughened by the fleas and torn by the scratching that they sometimes induce. Fleas also appear to be connected with summer eczema of dogs; at least the diseased condition of the skin often clears up after fleas are eradicated.

Although the adults seldom remain long away from the dog's body, fleas do not reproduce themselves on the dog. Rather, their breeding haunts are the debris, dust, and sand of the kennel floor, and especially the accumulations of dropped hair, sand, and loose soil of unclean sleeping boxes. Nooks and cracks and crannies of the kennel may harbor the eggs or maggot-like larvae of immature fleas.

This debris and accumulation must be eliminated—preferably by incineration—after which all possible breeding areas should be thoroughly sprayed with a residual effect spray.

The adult dog may be combed well, then bathed in a detergent solution, rinsed thoroughly in warm water, and allowed to drip fairly dry. A solution of Pine Oil (1 oz. to a quart of water) is then used as a final rinse. This method of ridding the dog of its fleas is ideal in warm weather. The Pine Oil imparts a pleasant odor to the dog's coat and the animal will enjoy being bathed and groomed.

The same procedure may be followed for young puppies except that the Pine Oil solution should be rinsed off. When bathing is not feasible, then a good flea powder—one containing lindane—should be used.

Sticktight fleas are minute, but are to be found, if at all, in patches on the dog's head and especially on the ears. They remain quiescent and do not jump, as the dog fleas and human fleas do. Their tiny heads are buried in the dog's flesh. To force them loose from the area decapitates them and the heads remain in the skin which is prone to fester from the irritation. They may be dislodged by placing a cotton pad or thick cloth well soaked in ether or alcohol over the flea patch, which causes them immediately to relinquish their hold, after which they can be easily combed loose and destroyed.

These sticktights abound in neglected, dirty, and abandoned chicken houses, which, if the dogs have access to them, should be cleaned out thoroughly and sprayed with DDT.

Fleas, while a nuisance, are only a minor problem. They should be eliminated not only from the dog but from all the premises he inhabits. Dogs frequently are reinfested with fleas from other dogs with which they play or come in contact. Every dog should be occasionally inspected for the presence of fleas, and, if any are found, immediate means should be taken to eradicate them.

LICE

There are even more kinds of lice than of fleas, although as they pertain to dogs there is no reason to differentiate them. They do not infest dogs, except in the events of gross neglect or of unforeseen accident. Lice reproduce themselves on the body of the dog. To rid him of the adult lice is easy. The standard Pine Oil solution used to kill fleas will also kill lice. However, the eggs or "nits" are harder to remove. Weather permitting, it is sometimes best to have the dog clipped of all its hair. In heavily infested dogs this is the only sure way to cope with the situation. When the hair is clipped, most of the "nits" are removed automatically. A good commercial flea and louse powder applied to the skin will then keep the situation under control.

Rare as the occurrence of lice upon dogs may be, they must be promptly treated and eradicated. Having a dog with lice can prove to be embarrassing, for people just do not like to be around anything lousy. Furthermore, the louse may serve as the intermediate host of the tapeworm in dogs.

The dog's quarters should be thoroughly sprayed with a residual spray of the same type recommended for use in the control of fleas. The problem of disinfecting kennel and quarters is not as great as it is in the case of fleas, for the louse tends to stay on its host, not leaving the dog as the flea does.

TICKS

The terms "wood ticks" and "dog ticks," as usually employed, refer to at least eight different species, whose appearances and habits are so similar that none but entomologists are likely to know them apart. It is useless to attempt to differentiate between these various species here, except to warn the reader that the Rocky Mountain spotted fever tick (*Dermacentor andersoni*) is a vector of the human disease for which it is named, as well as of rabbit fever (tularemia), and care must be employed in removing it from dogs lest the hands be infected. Some one or more of these numerous species are to be found in well nigh every state in the Union, although there exist wide areas where wood ticks are seldom seen and are not a menace to dogs.

All the ticks must feed on blood in order to reproduce themselves. The eggs are always deposited on the ground or elsewhere after the female, engorged with blood, has dropped from the dog or other animal upon which she has fed. The eggs are laid in masses in protected places on the ground, particularly in thick clumps of grass. Each female lays only one such mass, which contains 2500 to 5000 eggs. The development of the American dog tick embraces four stages: the egg, the larva or seed tick, the nymph, and the adult. The two intermediate stages in the growth of the tick are spent on rodents, and only in the adult stage does it attach itself to the dog. Both sexes affix themselves to dogs and to other animals and feed on their blood; the males do not increase in size, although the female is tremendously enlarged as she gorges. Mating occurs while the female is feeding. After some five to thirteen days, she drops from her host, lays her eggs and dies. At no time do ticks feed on anything except the blood of animals.

The longevity and hardihood of the tick are amazing. The larvae and nymphs may live for a full year without feeding, and the adults survive for more than two years if they fail to encounter a host to which they may attach. In the Northern United States the adults are most active in the spring and summer, few being found after July. But in the warmer Southern states they may be active the year around.

Although most of the tick species require a vegetative cover and wild animal hosts to complete their development, at least one species, the brown tick (*Rhipicephalus sanguinius*), is adapted to life in the dryer environment of kennels, sheds, and houses, with the dog as its only necessary host. This tick is the vector of canine piroplasmosis, although this disease is at this time almot negligible in the United States.

This brown dog tick often infests houses in large numbers, both immature and adult ticks lurking around baseboards, window casings, furniture, the folds of curtains, and elsewhere. Thus, even dogs kept in houses are sometimes infested with hundreds of larvae, nymphs, and adults of this tick. Because of its ability to live in heated buildings, the species has become established in many Northern areas. Unlike the other tick species, the adult of the brown dog tick does not bite human beings. However, also unlike the other ticks, it is necessary not only to rid the dogs of this particular tick but also to eliminate the pests from their habitat, especially the dogs' beds and sleeping boxes. A spray with a 10% solution of DDT suffices for this purpose. Fumigation of premises seldom suffices, since not only are brown dog ticks very resistant to mere fumigation, but the ticks are prone to lurk around entry ways, porches and outbuildings, where they cannot be reached with a fumigant. The spraying with DDT may not penetrate to spots where some ticks are in hiding, and it must be repeated at intervals until all the pests are believed to be completely eradicated.

Dogs should not be permitted to run in brushy areas known to be infested with ticks, and upon their return from exercise in a place believed to harbor ticks, dogs should be carefully inspected for their presence.

If a dog's infestation is light, the ticks may be picked individually from his skin. To make tick release its grip, dab with alcohol or a drop of ammonia. If the infestation is heavy, it is easier and quicker to saturate his coat with a derris solution (one ounce of soap and two ounces of derris powder dissolved in one gallon of water). The derris should be of an excellent grade containing at least 3% of rotenone. The mixture may be used and reused, since it retains its strength for about three weeks if it is kept in a dark place.

If possible, the dip should be permitted to dry on the dog's coat. It should not get into a dog's eyes. The dip will not only kill the ticks that are attached to the dog, but the powder drying in the hair will repel further infestation for two or three days and kill most if not all the boarders. These materials act slowly, requiring sometimes as much as twenty-four hours to complete the kill.

If the weather is cold or the use of the dip should be otherwise inconvenient, derris powder may be applied as a dust, care being taken that it penetrates the hair and reaches the skin. Breathing or swallowing derris may cause a dog to vomit, but he will not be harmed by it. The dust and liquid should be kept from his eyes.

Since the dog is the principal host on which the adult tick feeds and since each female lays several thousand eggs after feeding, treating the dog regularly will not only bring him immediate relief but will limit the reproduction of the ticks. Keeping underbrush, weeds, and grass closely cut tends to remove protection favorable to the ticks. Burning vegetation accomplishes the same results.

Many of the ticks in an infested area may be killed by the thorough application of a spray made as follows: Four tablespoonfuls of nicotine sulphate (40% nicotine) in three gallons of water. More permanent results may be obtained by adding to this solution four ounces of sodium fluorides, but this will injure the vegetation.

Besides the ticks that attach themselves to all parts of the dog, there is another species that infests the ear specifically. This pest, the spinose ear tick, penetrates deep into the convolutions of the ear and often causes irritation and pain, as evidenced by the dog's scratching its ears, shaking its head or holding it on one side. One part derris powder (5% rotenone) mixed with ten parts medicinal mineral oil and dropped into the ear will kill spinose ear ticks. Only a few drops of the material is required, but it is best to massage the base of the ear to make sure the remedy penetrates to the deepest part of the ear to reach all the ticks.

72

FLIES

Flies can play havoc with dogs in outdoor kennels, stinging them and biting the ears until they are raw. Until recently the only protection against them was the screening of the entire kennel. The breeding places of flies, which are damp filth and stagnant garbage, are in most areas now happily abated, but the chief agent for control of the pest is DDT.

A spray of a 10% solution of DDT over all surfaces of the kennel property may be trusted to destroy all the flies that light on those surfaces for from two weeks to one month. It must, of course, be repeated from time to time when it is seen that the efficacy of the former treatment begins to diminish.

Intestinal Parasites and Their Control

THE varieties of worms that may inhabit the alimentary tract of the dog are numerous. Much misapprehension exists, even among experienced dog keepers, about the harm these parasites may cause and about the methods of getting rid of them. Some dog keepers live in terror of these worms and continually treat their dogs for them whether they are known to be present or not; others ignore the presence of worms and do nothing about them. Neither policy is justified.

Promiscuous dosing, without the certainty that the dog harbors worms or what kind he may have, is a practice fraught with danger for the well-being of the animal. All drugs for the expulsion or destruction of parasites are poisonous or irritant to a certain degree and should be administered only when it is known that the dog is infested by parasites and what kind. It is hardly necessary to say that when a dog is known to harbor worms he should be cleared of them, but in most instances there is no such urgency as is sometimes manifested.

It may be assumed that puppies at weaning time are more or less infested with intestinal roundworms or ascarids (*Toxocara canis*) and that such puppies need to be treated for worms. It is all but impossible to rear a litter of puppies to weaning age free from those parasites. Once the puppies are purged of them, it is amazing to see the spurt of their growth and the renewal of their thriftiness.

Many neglected puppies surmount the handicap of their worms and at least some of them survive. This, however, is no reason that good puppies—puppies that are worth saving—should go unwormed and neglected.

The ways to find out that a dog actually has worms are to see some of the worms themselves in the dog's droppings or to submit a sample of his feces to a veterinarian or to a biological laboratory for microscopic examination. From a report of such an examination, it is possible to know whether or not a dog is a host to intestinal parasites at all and intelligently to undertake the treatment and control of the specific kind he may harbor.

All of the vermifuges, vermicides, and anthelmintic remedies tend to expel other worms besides the kind for which they are specifically intended, but it is better to employ the remedy particularly effective against the individual kind of parasite the dog is known to have, and to refrain from worm treatment unless or until it is known to be needed.

ROUNDWORMS

The ascarids, or large intestinal roundworms, are the largest of the worm parasites occurring in the digestive tract of the dog, varying in length from 1 to 8 inches, the females being larger than the males. The name "spool worms," which is sometimes applied to them, is derived from their tendency to coil in a springlike spiral when they are expelled, either from the bowel or vomited, by their hosts. There are at least two species of them which frequently parasitize dogs: *Toxocara canis* and *Toxascaris leonina,* but they are so much alike except for some minor details in the life histories of their development that it is not practically necessary for the dog keeper to seek to distinguish between them.

Neither specie requires an intermediate host for its development. Numerous eggs are deposited in the intestinal tract of the host animal; these eggs are passed out by the dog in his feces and are swallowed by the same or another animal, and hatching takes place in its small intestine. Their development requires from twelve to sixteen days under favorable circumstances.

It has been shown that puppies before their birth may be infested by roundworms from their mother. This accounts for the occasional finding of mature or nearly mature worms in very young puppies. It cannot occur if the mother is entirely free from worms, as she should be.

These roundworms are particularly injurious to young puppies. The commonest symptoms of roundworm infestation are general unthriftiness, digestive disturbances, and bloat after feeding. The hair grows dead and lusterless, and the breath may have a peculiar sweetish odor. Large numbers of roundworms may obstruct the intestine, and many have been known to penetrate the intestinal wall. In heavy infestations the worms may wander into the bile ducts, stomach, and even into the lungs and upper respiratory passages where they may cause pneumonia, especially in very young animals.

The control of intestinal roundworms depends primarily upon prompt disposal of feces, keeping the animals in clean quarters and on clean ground, and using only clean utensils for feed and water. Dampness of the ground favors the survival of worm eggs and larvae. There is no known chemical treatment feasible for the destruction of eggs in contaminated soil, but prolonged exposure to sunlight and drying has proved effective.

Numerous remedies have been in successful use for roundworms, including turpentine, which has a recognized deleterious effect upon the kidneys; santonin, an old standby; freshly powdered betel nut and its derivative, arecoline, both of which tend to purge and sicken the patient; oil of chenopodium, made from American wormseed; carbon tetrachloride, widely used as a cleaning agent; tetrachlorethylene, closely related chemically to the former, but less toxic; and numerous other medicaments. While all of them are effective as vermifuges or vermicides, if rightly employed, to each of them some valid objection can be interposed.

In addition to the foregoing, there are other vermifuges available for treatment of roundworms. Some may be purchased without a prescription, whereas others may be procured only when prescribed by a veterinarian.

HOOKWORMS

Hookworms are the most destructive of all the parasites of dogs. There are three species of them—*Ancylostoma caninum, A. braziliense,* and *Uncinaria stenocephalia*—all to be found in dogs in some parts of the United States. The first named is the most widespread; the second found only in the warmer parts of the South and Southwest; the last named, in the North and in Canada. All are similar one to another and to the hookworm that infests mankind (*Ancylostoma uncinariasis*). For purposes of their eradication, no distinction need be made between them.

It is possible to keep dogs for many years in a dry and well drained area without an infestation with hookworms, which are contracted only on infested soils. However, unthrifty dogs shipped from infested areas are suspect until it is proved that hookworm is not the cause of their unthriftiness.

Hookworm males seldom are longer than half an inch, the females somewhat larger. The head end is curved upward, and is equipped with cutting implements, which may be called teeth, by which they attach themselves to the lining of the dog's intestine and suck his blood.

The females produce numerous eggs which pass out in the dog's feces. In two weeks or a little more these eggs hatch, the worms pass through various larval stages, and reach their infective stage. Infection of the dog may take place through his swallowing the organism, or by its penetration of his skin through some lesion. In the latter case the worms enter the circulation, reach the lungs, are coughed up, swallowed, and reach the intestine where their final development occurs. Eggs appear in the dog's feces from three to six weeks after infestation.

Puppies are sometimes born with hookworms already well developed in their intestines, the infection taking place before their birth. Eggs of the hookworm are sometimes found in the feces of puppies only thirteen days old. Assumption is not to be made that all puppies are born with hookworms or even that they are likely to become infested, but in hookworm areas the possibility of either justifies precautions that neither shall happen.

Hookworm infestation in puppies and young dogs brings about a condition often called kennel anemia. There may be digestive disturbances and blood streaked diarrhea. In severe cases the feces may be almost pure blood. Infested puppies fail to grow, often lose weight, and the eyes are sunken and dull. The loss of blood results in an anemia with pale mucous membranes of the mouth and eyes. This anemia is caused by the consumption of the dog's blood by the worms and the bleeding that follows the bites. The worms are not believed to secrete a poison or to cause damage to the dog except loss of blood.

There is an admitted risk in worming young puppies before weaning time, but it is risk that must be run if the puppies are known to harbor hookworms. The worms, if permitted to persist, will ruin the puppies and likely kill them. No such immediacy is needful for the treatment of older puppies and adult dogs, although hookworm infestation will grow steadily worse until it is curbed. It should not be delayed and neglected in the belief or hope that the dog can cure himself.

If treatment is attempted at home, there are available three fairly efficacious and safe drugs that may be used: normal butyl chloride, hexaresorcinal, and methyl benzine.

If a dog is visibly sick and a diagnosis of hookworm infestation has been made, treatment had best be under professional guidance.

Brine made by stirring common salt (sodium chloride) into boiling water, a pound and a half of salt to the gallon of water, will destroy hookworm infestation in the soil. A gallon of brine should be sufficient to treat eight square feet of soil surface. One treatment of the soil is sufficient unless it is reinfested.

TAPEWORMS

The numerous species of tapeworm which infest the dog may, for practical purposes, be divided into two general groups, the armed forms and the unarmed forms. Species of both groups resemble each other in their possession of a head and neck and a chain of segments. They are, however, different in their life histories, and the best manner to deal with each type varies. This is unfortunately not well understood, since to most persons a tapeworm is a tapeworm.

The armed varieties are again divided into the single pored forms of the genera *Taenia, Multiceps,* and *Echinococcus,* and the double pored tapeworm, of which the most widespread and prevalent among dogs in the United States is the so-called dog tapeworm, *Dipylidium caninum.* This is the variety with segments shaped like cucumber-seeds. The adult rarely exceeds a foot in length, and the head is armed with four or five tiny hooks. For the person with well cared for and protected dogs, this is the only tapeworm of which it is necessary to take particular cognizance.

The dog tapeworm requires but a single intermediate host for its development, which in most cases is the dog flea or the biting louse. Thus, by keeping dogs free from fleas and lice the major danger of tapeworm infestation is obviated.

The tapeworm is bi-sexual and requires the intermediate host in order to complete its life cycle. Segments containing the eggs of the tapeworm pass out with the stool, or the detached proglottid may emerge by its own motile power and attach itself to the contiguous hair. The flea then lays its eggs on this segment, thus affording sustenance for the larva. The head of the tapeworm develops in the lung chamber of the baby flea. Thus, such a flea, when it develops and finds its way back to a dog, is the potential carrier of tapeworm. Of course, the cycle is complete when the flea bites the dog and the dog, in biting the area to relieve the itching sensation, swallows the flea.

Since the egg of the tapeworm is secreted in the segment that breaks off and passes with the stool, microscopic examination of the feces is of no avail in attempting to determine whether tapeworms infest a dog. It is well to be suspicious of a finicky eater— a dog that refuses all but the choicest meat and shows very little appetite. The injury produced by this armed tapeworm to the dog that harbors it is not well understood. Frequently it produces no symptoms at all, and it is likely that it is not the actual cause of many of the symptoms attributed to it. At least, it is known that a dog may have one or many of these worms over a long period of time and apparently be no worse for their presence. Nervous symptoms or skin eruptions, or both, are often charged to the presence of tapeworm, which may or may not be the cause of the morbid condition.

Tapeworm-infested dogs sometimes involuntarily pass segments of worms and so soil floors, rugs, furniture, or bedding. The passage by dogs of a segment or a chain of segments via the anus is a frequent cause of the dog's itching, which he seeks to allay by sitting and dragging himself on the floor by his haunches. The segments or chains are sometimes mistakenly called pinworms, but pinworms are a kind of roundworm to which dogs are not subject.

Despite that they may do no harm, few dogs owners care to tolerate tapeworms in their dogs. These worms, it has been definitely established, are not transmissible from dog to dog or to man. Without the flea or the louse, it is impossible for the adult dog tapeworm to reproduce itself, and by keeping dogs free from fleas and lice it is possible to keep them also free from dog tapeworm.

The various unarmed species of tapeworm find their intermediate hosts in the flesh and other parts of various animals, fish, crustacians and crayfish. Dogs not permitted to eat raw meats which have not been officially inspected, never have these worms, and it is needless here to discuss them at length. Hares and rabbits are the intermediate hosts to some of these worms and dogs should not be encouraged to feed upon those animals.

Little is known of the effects upon dogs of infestations of the unarmed tapeworms, but they are believed to be similar to the effects (if any) of the armed species.

The prevention of tapeworm infestation may be epitomized by saying: Do not permit dogs to swallow fleas or lice nor to feed upon uninspected raw meats. It is difficult to protect dogs from such contacts if they are permitted to run at large, but it is to be presumed that persons interested enough in caring for dogs to read this book will keep their dogs at home and protect them.

The several species of tapeworm occurring in dogs are not all removable by the same treatment. The most effective treatment for the removal of the armed species, which is the one most frequently found in the dogs, is arecoline hydrobromide. This drug is a drastic purgative and acts from fifteen to forty-five minutes after its administration. The treatment should be given in the morning after the dog has fasted overnight, and food should be withheld for some three hours after dosing.

Arecoline is not so effective against the double-pored tapeworm as against the other armed species, and it may be necessary to repeat the dose after a few days waiting, since some of the tapeworm heads may not be removed by the first treatment and regeneration of the tapeworm may occur in a few weeks. The estimatedly correct dosage is not stated here, since the drug is so toxic that the dosage should be estimated for the individual dog by a competent veterinarian, and it is better that he should be permitted to administer the remedy and control the treatment.

WHIPWORMS

The dog whipworm (*Trichuris vulpis*) is so called from its fancied resemblance to a tiny blacksnake whip, the front part being slender and hairlike and the hinder part relatively thick. It rarely exceeds three inches in its total length. Whipworms in dogs exist more or less generally throughout the world, but few dogs in the United States are known to harbor them. They are for the most part confined to the caecum, from which they are hard to dislodge, but sometimes spill over into the colon, whence they are easy to dislodge.

The complete life history of the whipworm is not well established, but it is known that no intermediate host is required for its development. The eggs appear to develop in much the same way as the eggs of the large roundworm, but slower, requiring from two weeks to several months for the organisms to reach maturity.

It has not as yet been definitely established that whipworms are the true causes of all the ills of which they are accused. In many instances they appear to cause little damage, even in heavy infestations. A great variety of symptoms of an indefinite sort have been ascribed to whipworms, including digestive disturbances, diarrhea, loss of weight, nervousness, convulsions, and general unthriftiness, but it remains to be proved that whipworms were responsible.

To be effective in its removal of whipworms, a drug must enter the caecum and come into direct contact with them; but the entry of the drug into this organ is somewhat fortuitous, and to increase the chances of its happening, large doses of a drug essentially harmless to the dog must be used. Normal butyl chloride meets this requirement, but it must be given in large doses. Even then, complete clearance of whipworms from the caecum may not be expected; the best to be hoped is that their numbers will be reduced and the morbid symptoms will subside.

Before treatment the dog should be fasted for some eighteen hours, although he may be fed two hours after being treated. It is wise to follow the normal butyl chloride in one hour with a purgative dose of castor oil. This treatment, since it is not expected to be wholly effective, may be repeated at monthly intervals.

The only known means of the complete clearance of whipworms from the dog is the surgical removal of the caecum, which of course should be undertaken only by a veterinary surgeon.

HEART WORMS

Heart worms (*Dirofilaria immitis*) in dogs are rare. They occur largely in the South and Southeast, but their incidence appears to be increasing and cases have been reported along the Atlantic Seaboard as far north as New York. The various species of mosquitoes are known to be vectors of heart worms, although the flea is also accused of spreading them.

The symptoms of heart worm infestation are somewhat vague, and include coughing, shortness of breath and collapse. In advanced cases, dropsy may develop. Nervous symptoms, fixity of vision, fear of light, and convulsions may develop. However, all such symptoms may occur from other causes and it must not be assumed because a dog manifests some of these conditions that he has heart worms. The only way to be sure is a microscopic examination of the blood and the presence or absence of the larvae. Even in some cases where larvae have been found in the blood, post mortem examinations have failed to reveal heart worms in the heart.

Both the diagnosis and treatment of heart worm are functions of the veterinarian. They are beyond the province of the amateur. The drug used is a derivative from antimony known as fuadin, and many dogs are peculiarly susceptible to antimony poisoning. If proper treatment is used by a trained veterinarian, a large preponderance of cases make a complete recovery. But even the most expert of veterinarians may be expected to fail in the successful treatment of a percentage of heart worm infestations. The death of some of the victims is to be anticipated.

LESS FREQUENTLY FOUND WORMS

Besides the intestinal worms that have been enumerated, there exist in some dogs numerous other varieties and species of worms which are of so infrequent occurrence that they require no discussion in a book for the general dog keeper. These include, esophageal worms, lungworms, kidney worms, and eye worms. They are in North America, indeed, so rare as to be negligible.

COCCIDIA

Coccidia are protozoic, microscopic organisms. The forms to which the dog is a host are *Isospora rivolta, I. bigeminia* and *I. felis.* Coccidia eggs, called *oocysts,* can be carried by flies and are picked up by dogs as they lick themselves or eat their stools.

These parasides attack the intestinal wall and cause diarrhea. They are particularly harmful to younger puppies that have been weaned, bringing on fever, running eyes, poor appetite and debilitation as well as the loose stools.

The best prevention is scrupulous cleanliness of the puppy or dog, its surroundings and its playmates whether canine or human. Flies should be eliminated as described in the preceding chapter and stools removed promptly where the dog cannot touch it.

Infection can be confirmed by microscopic examination of the stool. Treatment consists of providing nourishing food, which should be force-fed if necessary, and whatever drug the veterinarian recommends. Puppies usually recover, though occasionally their teeth may be pitted as in distemper.

A dog infected once by one form develops immunity to that form but may be infected by another form.

Skin Troubles

THERE is a tendency on the part of the amateur dog keeper to consider any lesion of the dog's skin to be mange. Mange is an unusual condition in clean, well fed, and well cared for dogs. Eczema occurs much more frequently and is often more difficult to control.

MANGE OR SCABIES

There are at least two kinds of mange that effect dogs—sarcoptic mange and demodectic or red mange, the latter rare indeed and difficult to cure.

Sarcoptic mange is caused by a tiny spider-like mite (*Sarcoptes scabiei canis*) which is similar to the mite that causes human scabies or "itch." Indeed, the mange is almost identical with scabies and is transmissible from dog to man. The mite is approximately 1/100th of an inch in length and without magnification is just visible to acute human sight.

Only the female mites are the cause of the skin irritation. They burrow into the upper layers of the skin, where each lays twenty to forty eggs, which in three to seven days hatch into larvae. These larvae in turn develop into nymphs which later grow into adults. The entire life cycle requires from fourteen to twenty-one days for completion. The larvae, nymphs, and males do not burrow into the skin, but live under crusts and scabs on the surface.

86

The disease may make its first appearance on any part of the dog's body, although it is usually first seen on the head and muzzle, around the eyes, or at the base of the ears. Sometimes it is first noticed in the armpits, the inner parts of the thighs, the lower abdomen or on the front of the chest. If not promptly treated it may cover the whole body and an extremely bad infestation may cause the death of the dog after a few months.

Red points which soon develop into small blisters are the first signs of the disease. These are most easily seen on the unpigmented parts of the skin, such as the abdomen. As the female mites burrow into the skin, there is an exudation of serum which dries and scabs. The affected parts soon are covered with bran-like scales followed with grayish crusts. The itching is intense, especially in hot weather or after exercise. The rubbing and scratching favor secondary bacterial infections and the formation of sores. The hair may grow matted and fall out, leaving bare spots. The exuded serum decomposes and gives rise to a peculiar mousy odor which increases as the disease develops and which is especially characteristic.

Sarcoptic mange is often confused with demodectic (red) mange, ringworm, or with simple eczema. If there is any doubt about the diagnosis, a microscopic examination of the scrapings of the lesions will reveal the true facts.

It is easy to control sarcoptic mange if it is recognized in its earlier stages and treatment is begun immediately. Neglected, it may be very difficult to eradicate. If it is considered how rapidly the causative mites reproduce themselves, the necessity for early treatment becomes apparent. That treatment consists not only of medication of the dog but also of sterilization of his bedding, all tools and implements used on him, and the whole premises upon which he has been confined. Sarcoptic mange is easily and quickly transmissible from dog to dog, from area to area on the same dog, and even from dog to human.

In some manner which is not entirely understood, an inadequate or unbalanced diet appears to predispose a dog to sarcoptic mange, and few dogs adequately fed and cared for ever contract it. Once a dog has contracted mange, however, improvement in the amount of quality of his food seems not to hasten his recovery.

There are various medications recommended for sarcoptic mange, sulphur ointment being the old standby. However, it is messy, difficult to use, and not always effective. For the treatment of sarcoptic mange, there are available today such insecticides as lindane, chlordane, and DDT. The use of these chemicals greatly facilitates treatment and cure of the dogs affected with mange and those exposed to it.

A bath made by dissolving four ounces of derris powder (containing at least 5% rotenone) and one ounce of soap in one gallon of water has proved effective, especially if large areas of the surface of the dog's skin are involved. All crusts and scabs should be removed before its application. The solution must be well scrubbed into the skin with a moderately stiff brush and the whole animal thoroughly soaked. Only the surplus liquid should be taken off with a towel and the remainder must be permitted to dry on the dog. This bath should be repeated at intervals of five days until all signs of mange have disappeared. Three such baths will usually suffice.

The advantage of such all over treatment is that it protects uninfected areas from infection. It is also a precautionary measure to bathe in this solution uninfected dogs which have been in contact with the infected one.

Isolated mange spots may be treated with oil of lavender. Roll a woolen cloth into a swab with which the oil of lavender can be applied and rubbed in thoroughly for about five minutes. This destroys all mites with which the oil of lavender comes into contact.

Even after a cure is believed to be accomplished, vigilance must be maintained to prevent fresh infestations and to treat new spots immediately if they appear.

DEMODECTIC OR RED MANGE

Demodectic mange, caused by the wormlike mite *Demodex canis,* which lives in the hair follicles and the sebaceous glands of the skin, is difficult to cure. It is a baffling malady of which the prognosis is not favorable. The life cycle of the causative organism is not well understood, the time required from the egg to maturity being so far unknown. The female lays eggs which hatch into young of appearance similar to that of the adult, except that they are smaller and have but three pairs of legs instead of four.

One peculiar feature about demodectic mange is that some dogs appear to be genetically predisposed to it while others do not contract it whatever their contact with infected animals may be. Young animals seem to be especially prone to it, particularly those with short hair. The first evidence of its presence is the falling out of the hair on certain areas of the dog. The spots may be somewhat reddened, and they commonly occur near the eyes, on the hocks, elbows, or toes, although they may be on any part of the dog's body. No itching occurs at the malady's inception, and it never grows so intense as in sarcoptic mange.

In the course of time, the hairless areas enlarge, and the skin attains a copper hue; in severe cases it may appear blue or leadish gray. During this period the mites multiply and small pustules develop. Secondary invasions may occur to complicate the situation. Poisons are formed by the bacteria in the pustules, and the absorption of toxic materials deranges the body functions and eventually affects the whole general health of the dog, leading to emaciation, weakness, and the development of an acrid, unpleasant odor.

This disease is slow and subtle in its development, runs a casual course, and frequently extends over a period of two or even three years. Unless it is treated, it usually terminates in death, although spontaneous recovery occasionally occurs, especially if the dog has been kept on a nourishing diet. As in other skin diseases, correct nutrition plays a major part in recovery from demodectic mange, as it plays an even larger part in its prevention.

It is possible to confuse demodectic mange with sarcoptic mange, fungus infection, acne, or eczema. A definite diagnosis is possible only from microscopic examination of skin scrapings and of material from the pustules. The possibility of demodectic mange, particularly in its earlier stages, is not negated by the failure to find the mites under the microscope, and several examinations may be necessary to arrive at a definite diagnosis.

The prognosis is not entirely favorable. It may appear that the mange is cured and a new and healthy coat may be re-established only to have the disease manifest itself in a new area, and the whole process of treatment must be undertaken afresh.

In the treatment of demodectic mange, the best results have been obtained by the persistent use of benzine hexachloride, chlordane, rotenone, and 2-mercapto benzothiazole. Perseverance is necessary, but even then failure is possible.

EAR MITES OR EAR MANGE

The mites responsible for ear mange (*Ododectes cynotis*) are considerably larger than the ones which cause sarcoptic mange. They inhabit the external auditory canal and are visible to the unaided eye as minute, slowly moving, white objects. Their life history is not known, but is probably similar to that of the mite that causes sarcoptic mange.

These mites do not burrow into the skin, but are found deep in the ear canal, near the eardrum. Considerable irritation results from their presence, and the normal secretions of the ear are interfered with. The ear canal is filled with inflammatory products, modified ear wax, and mites, causing the dog to scratch and rub its ears and to shake its head. While ear mange is not caused by incomplete washing or inefficient drying of the ears, it is encouraged by such negligence.

The ear mange infestation is purely local and is no cause for anxiety. An ointment containing benzine hexachloride is very effective in correcting this condition. The ear should be treated every third or fourth day.

ECZEMA

Eczema is probably the most common of all ailments seen in the dog. Oftentimes it is mistaken for mange or ringworm, although there is no actual relationship between the conditions. Eczema is variously referred to by such names as "hot spots," "fungitch," and "kennel itch."

Some years ago there was near-unanimity of opinion among dog people that the food of the animal was the major contributing factor of eczema. Needless to say, the manufacturers of commercial dog foods were besieged with complaints. Some research on the cause of eczema placed most of the blame on outside environmental factors, and with some help from other sources it was found that a vegetative organism was the causative agent in a great majority of the cases.

Some dogs do show an allergic skin reaction to certain types of protein given to them as food, but this is generally referred to as the "foreign protein" type of dermatitis. It manifests itself by raising numerous welts on the skin, and occasionally the head, face, and ears will become alarmingly swollen. This condition can be controlled by the injection of antihistamine products and subsequent dosage with antihistaminic tablets or capsules such as chlortrimenton or benedryl. Whether "foreign protein" dermatitis is due to an allergy or whether it is due to some toxin manufactured and elaborated by the individual dog is a disputed point.

Most cases of eczema start with reddening of the skin in certain parts. The areas most affected seem to be the region along the spine and at the base of the tail. In house dogs this may have its inception from enlarged and plugged anal glands. The glands when full and not naturally expressed are a source of irritation. The dog will rub his hind parts on the grass in order to alleviate the itching sensation. Fleas, lice, and ticks may be inciting factors, causing the dog to rub and roll in the grass in an attempt to scratch the itchy parts.

In hunting dogs, it is believed that the vegetative cover through which the dogs hunt causes the dermatitis. In this class of dogs the skin becomes irritated and inflamed in the armpits, the inner surfaces of the thighs, and along the belly. Some hunting dogs are bedded down in straw or hay, and such dogs invariably show a general reddening of the skin and a tendency to scratch.

As a general rule, the difference between moist and dry eczema lies in the degree to which the dog scratches the skin with his feet or chews it with his teeth. The inflammation ranges from a simple reddening of the skin to the development of papules, vesicles, and pustules with a discharge. Crusts and scabs like dandruff may form, and if the condition is not treated, it will become chronic and then next to impossible to treat with any success. In such cases the skin becomes thickened and may be pigmented. The hair follicles become infected, and the lesions are constantly inflamed and exuding pus.

When inflammation occurs between the toes and on the pads of the feet, it closely resembles "athletes foot" in the human. Such inflammation generally causes the hair in the region to turn a reddish brown. The ears, when they are affected, emit a peculiar moldy odor and exude a brownish black substance. It is thought that most cases of canker of the ear are due to a primary invasion of the ear canal by a vegetative fungus. If there is a pustular discharge, it is due to the secondary pus-forming bacteria that gain a foothold after the resistance of the parts is lowered by the fungi.

Some breeds of dogs are more susceptible to skin ailments than are others. However, all breeds of dogs are likely to show some degree of dermatitis if they are exposed to causative factors.

Most cases of dermatitis are seen in the summer time, which probably accounts for their being referred to as "summer itch" or "hot spots." The warm moist days of summer seem to promote the growth and development of both fleas and fungi. When the fleas bite the dog, the resulting irritation causes the dog to scratch or bite to alleviate the itch. The area thus becomes moist and makes a perfect place for fungi spores to propagate. That the fungi are the cause of the trouble seems evident, because most cases respond when treated externally with a good fungicide. Moreover, the use of a powder containing both an insecticide and a fungicide tends to prevent skin irritation. Simply dusting the dog once or twice a week with a good powder of the type mentioned is sound procedure in the practice of preventive medicine.

(Editor's note: I have had some success with hydrogen peroxide in treating mild skin troubles. Saturate a cotton pad with a mixture of 2 parts 3% hydrogen peroxide to 1 part boiled water. Apply, but do NOT rub, to affected skin. Let dry naturally and when *completely* dry apply an antiseptic talcum powder like Johnson & Johnson's Medicated Powder. When this treatment was suggested to my veterinarian, he confirmed that he had had success with it. If the skin irritation is not noticeably better after two of these treatments, once daily, the case should be referred to a veterinarian.)

RINGWORM

Ringworm is a communicable disease of the skin of dogs, readily transmissible to man and to other dogs and animals. The disease is caused by specific fungi, which are somewhat similar to ordinary molds. The lesions caused by ringworm usually first appear on the face, head, or legs of the dog, but they may occur on any part of the surface of his body.

The disease in dogs is characterized by small, circular areas of dirty gray or brownish-yellow crusts or scabs partially devoid of hair, the size of a dime. As the disease progresses, the lesions increase both in size and in number and merge to form larger patches covered with crusts containing broken off hair. A raw, bleeding surface may appear when crusts are broken or removed by scratching or rubbing to relieve itching. In some cases, however, little or no itching is manifested. Microscopic examination and culture tests are necessary for accurate diagnosis.

If treatment of affected dogs is started early, the progress of the disease can be immediately arrested. Treatment consists of clipping the hair from around the infected spots, removing the scabs and painting the spots with tincture of iodine, five percent salicylic acid solution, or other fungicide two or three times weekly until recovery takes place. In applying these remedies it is well to cover the periphery of the circular lesion as well as its center, since the spots tend to expand outward from their centers. Scabs, hair, and debris removed from the dog during his treatments should be burned to destroy the causative organisms and to prevent reinfection. Precautions in the handling of animals affected with ringworm should be observed to preclude transmission to man and other animals. Isolation of affected dogs is not necessary if the treatment is thorough.

COAT CARE

Skin troubles can often be checked and materially alleviated by proper grooming. Every dog is entitled to the minimum of weekly attention to coat, skin and ears; ideally, a daily stint with brush and comb is highly recommended. Frequent examination may catch skin disease in its early stages and provide a better chance for a quick cure.

The outer or "guard" hairs of a dog's coat should glint in the sunlight. There should be no mats or dead hair in the coat. Wax in the outer ear should be kept at a minimum.

It is helpful to stand the dog on a flat, rigid surface off the floor at a height convenient to the groomer. Start at the head and ears brushing briskly *with* the lay of short hair, *against* the lay of long hair at first then with it. After brushing, use a fine comb with short teeth on fine, short hair and a coarse comb with long teeth on coarse or long hair. If mats cannot be readily removed with brush or comb, use barber's thinning shears and cut into the matted area several times until mat pulls free easily. Some mats can be removed with the fingers if one has the patience to separate the hair a bit at a time.

After brushing and combing, run your palms over the dog's coat from head to tail. Natural oils in your skin will impart sheen to your dog's coat.

The ears of some dogs secrete and exude great amounts of wax. Frequent examination will determine when your dog's ears need cleaning. A thin coating of clean, clear wax is not harmful. But a heavy accumulation of dirty, dark wax needs removal by cotton pads soaked in diluted hydrogen peroxide (3% cut in half with boiled water), or alcohol or plain boiled water if wax is not too thick.

There are sprays, "dry" bath preparations and other commercial products for maintaining your dog's coat health. Test them first, and if they are successful, you may find them beneficial time-savers in managing your dog's coat.

First Aid

J OHN STEINBECK, the Nobel Prize winning author, in *Travels with Charley in Search of America* bemoans the lack of a good, comprehensive book of home dog medicine. Charley is the aged Poodle that accompanies his illustrious author-owner on a motor tour of the U.S.A.

As in human medicine, most treatment and dosing of dogs are better left in the experienced, trained hands and mind of a professional—in this case, the veterinarian. However, there are times and situations when professional aid is not immediately available and an owner's prompt action may save a life or avoid permanent injury. To this purpose, the following suggestions are given.

The First Aid Kit

For instruments keep on hand a pair of tweezers, a pair of pliers, straight scissors, a rectal thermometer, a teaspoon, a tablespoon, and swabs for cotton.

For dressings, buy a container of cotton balls, a roll of cotton and a roll of 2″ gauze. Strips of clean, old sheets may come in handy.

For medicines, stock ammonia, aspirin, brandy, 3% hydrogen peroxide, bicarbonate of soda, milk of bismuth, mineral oil, salt, tea, vaseline, kaopectate, baby oil and baby talcum powder.

Handling the Dog for Treatment

Approach any injured or sick dog calmly with reassuring voice and gentle, steady hands. If the dog is in pain, slip a gauze or sheet strip noose over its muzzle tying the ends first under the throat and then back of the neck. Make sure the dog's lips are not caught between his teeth, but make noose around muzzle *tight*.

If the dog needs to be moved, grasp the loose skin on the back of the neck with one hand and support chest with the other hand. If the dog is too large to move in this manner, slide him on a large towel, blanket or folded sheet which may serve as a stretcher for two to carry.

If a pill or liquid is to be administered, back the dog in a corner in a sitting position. For a pill, pry back of jaws apart with thumb and forefinger of one hand and with the same fingers of your other hand place pill as far back in dog's throat as possible; close and hold jaws, rubbing throat to cause swallowing. If dog does not gulp, hold one hand over nostrils briefly; he will gulp for air and swallow pill. For liquids, lift the back of the upper lip and tip spoon into the natural pocket formed in the rear of the lower lip; it may be necessary to pull this pocket out with forefinger. Do not give liquids by pouring directly down the dog's throat; this might choke him or make the fluid go down the wrong way.

After treatment keep dog quiet, preferably in his bed or a room where he cannot injure himself or objects.

Bites and Wounds

Clip hair from area. Wash gently with pure soap and water or hydrogen peroxide. If profuse bleeding continues, apply sheet strip or gauze tourniquet between wound and heart but nearest the wound. Release tourniquet briefly at ten-minute intervals. Cold water compresses may stop milder bleeding.

For insect bites and stings, try to remove stinger with tweezers or a dab of cotton, and apply a few drops of ammonia. If dog is in pain, give aspirin at one grain per 10 pounds. (An aspirin tablet is usually 5 grains.)

Burns

Clip hair from area. Apply strong, lukewarm tea (for its tannic acid content) on a sheet strip compress. Vaseline may be used for slight burns. Give aspirin as recommended if dog is in pain. Keep him warm if he seems to be in shock.

Constipation

Give mineral oil: one-quarter teaspoon up to 10 pounds; half teaspoon from 10 to 25 pounds; full teaspoon from 25 to 75 pounds; three-quarters tablespoon over 75 pounds.

Diarrhea

Give kaopectate in same doses by size as indicated for mineral oil above, but repeat within four and eight hours.

Fighting

Do not try forcibly to separate dogs. If available throw a pail of cold water on them. A sharp rap on the rump of each combatant with a strap or stick may help. A heavy towel or blanket dropped over the head of the aggressor, or a newspaper twisted into a torch, lighted and held near them, may discourage the fighters. If a lighted newspaper is used, be careful that sparks do not fall or blow on dogs.

Fits

Try to get the dog into a room where he cannot injure himself. If possible, cover him with a towel or blanket. When the fit ends, give aspirin one grain for every 10 pounds.

Nervousness

Remove cause or remove the dog from the site of the cause. Give the recommended dose of aspirin. Aspirin acts as a tranquilizer.

97

Poisoning

If container of the poison is handy, use recommended antidote printed thereon. Otherwise, make a strong solution of household salt in water and force as much as possible into the dog's throat using the lip pocket method. Minutes count with several poisons; if veterinarian cannot be reached immediately, try to get dog to an MD or registered nurse.

Shock

If dog has chewed electric cord, protect hand with rubber glove or thick dry towel and pull cord from socket. If dog has collapsed, hold ammonia under its nose or apply artificial respiration as follows: place dog on side with its head low, press on abdomen and rib cage, releasing pressure at one- or two-second intervals. Keep dog warm.

Stomach Upsets

For mild stomach disorders, milk of bismuth in same doses as recommended for mineral oil under *Constipation* will be effective. For more severe cases brandy in the same doses but diluted with an equal volume of water may be helpful.

Swallowing Foreign Objects

If object is still in mouth or throat, reach in and remove it. If swallowed, give strong salt solution as for *Poisoning*. Some objects that are small, smooth or soft may not give trouble.

Porcupines and Skunks

Using tweezers or pliers, twist quills one full turn and pull out. Apply hydrogen peroxide to bleeding wounds. For skunk spray, wash dog in tomato juice.

WARNING! Get your dog to a veterinarian *soonest* for severe bites, wounds, burns, poisoning, fits and shock.

Internal Canine Diseases and Their Management

THE word *management* is employed in this chapter heading rather than *treatment,* since the treatment of disease in the dog is the function of the veterinarian, and the best counsel it is possible to give the solicitous owner of a sick dog is to submit the case to the best veterinarian available and to follow his instructions implicitly. In general, it may be said, the earlier in any disease the veterinarian is consulted, the more rapid is the sick animal's recovery and the lower the outlay of money for the services of the veterinarian and for the medicine he prescribes.

Herein are presented some hints for the prevention of the various canine maladies and for their recognition when they occur. In kennel husbandry, disease is a minor problem, and, if preventive methods are employed, it is one that need not be anticipated.

DISTEMPER

Distemper, the traditional bugbear of keeping dogs, the veritable scourge of dog-kind, has at long last been well conquered. Compared with some years ago when "over distemper" was one of the best recommendations for the purchase of a dog, the incidence of distemper in well-bred and adequately cared for dogs is now minimal.

The difference between then and now is that we now have available preventive sera, vaccines, and viruses, which may be employed to forestall distemper before it ever appears. There are valid differences of opinion about which of these measures is best to use and at what age of the dog they are variously indicated. About the choice of preventive measures and the technique of administering them, the reader is advised to consult his veterinarian and to accept his advice. There can be no doubt, however, that any person with a valued or loved young dog should have him immunized.

For many years most veterinarians used the so-called "three-shot" method of serum, vaccine and virus, spaced two weeks apart after the puppy was three or four months old, for permanent immunization. For temporary immunization lasting up to a year, some veterinarians used only vaccine; this was repeated annually if the owner wished, though since a dog was considered most susceptible to distemper in the first year of his life, the annual injection was often discontinued. Under both these methods, serum was used at two-week intervals from weaning to the age when permanent or annual immunization was given.

Until 1950 living virus, produced by the methods then known to and used by laboratories, was considered too dangerous to inject without the preparation of the dog for it by prior use of serum or vaccine (killed virus). Then, researchers in distemper developed an attenuated or weakened live virus by injecting strong virus into egg embryos and other intermediate hosts. The weakened virus is now often used for permanent, one-shot distemper immunization of puppies as young as eight weeks.

Today certain researchers believe that the temporary immunity given by the bitch to her young depends on her own degree of immunity. If she has none, her puppies have none; if she has maximum immunity, her puppies may be immune up to the age of 12 weeks or more. By testing the degree of the bitch's immunity early in her pregnancy, these researchers believe they can determine the proper age at which her puppies should receive their shots.

The veterinarian is best qualified to determine the method of distemper immunization and the age to give it.

Canine distemper is an acute, highly contagious, febrile disease caused by a filterable virus. It is characterized by a catarrhal inflammation of all the mucous membranes of the body, frequently accompanied by nervous symptoms and pustular eruptions of the skin. Its human counterpart is influenza, which, though not identical with distemper, is very similar to it in many respects. Distemper is so serious and complicated a disease as to require expert attention; when a dog is suspected of having it, a veterinarian should be consulted immediately. It is the purpose of this discussion of the malady rather to describe it that its recognition may be possible than to suggest medication for it or means of treating it.

Distemper is known in all countries and all parts of the United States in all seasons of the year, but it is most prevalent during the winter months and in the cold, damp weather of early spring and late autumn. No breed of dogs is immune. Puppies of low constitutional vigor, pampered, overfed, unexercised dogs, and those kept in overheated, unventilated quarters contract the infection more readily and suffer more from it than hardy animals, properly fed and living in a more natural environment. Devitalizing influences which decrease the resistance of the dog, such as rickets, parasitic infestations, unsanitary quarters, and especially an insufficient or unbalanced diet, are factors predisposing to distemper.

While puppies as young as ten days or two weeks have been known to have true cases of distemper, and very old dogs in rare instances, the usual subjects of distemper are between two months (after weaning) and full maturity at about eighteen months. The teething period of four to six months is highly critical. It is believed that some degree of temporary protection from distemper is passed on to a nursing litter through the milk of the mother.

As was first demonstrated by Carré in 1905 and finally established by Laidlaw and Duncan in their work for the Field Distemper Fund in 1926 to 1928, the primary causative agent of distemper is a filterable virus. The clinical course of the disease may be divided into two parts, produced respectively by the primary Carré filterable virus and by a secondary invasion of bacterial organisms which produce serious complicating conditions usually associated with the disease. It is seldom true that uncomplicated Carré distemper would cause more than a fever with malaise and indisposition if the secondary bacterial invasion could be avoided. The primary disease but prepares the ground for the secondary invasion which produces the havoc and all too often kills the patient.

Although it is often impossible to ascertain the source of infection in outbreaks of distemper, it is known that the infection may spread from affected to susceptible dogs by either direct or indirect contact. The disease, while highly infectious throughout its course, is especially easy to communicate in its earliest stages, even before clinical symptoms are manifested. The virus is readily destroyed by heat and by most of the common disinfectants in a few hours, but it resists drying and low temperatures for several days, and has been known to survive freezing for months.

The period of incubation (the time between exposure to infection and the development of the first symptoms) is variable. It has been reported to be as short as three days and as long as two weeks. The usual period is approximately one week. The usual course of the disease is about four weeks, but seriously complicated cases may prolong themselves to twelve weeks.

The early symptoms of distemper, as a rule, are so mild and subtle as to escape the notice of any but the most acute observer. These first symptoms may be a rise in temperature, a watery discharge from the eyes and nose, an impaired appetite, a throat-clearing cough, and a general sluggishness. In about a week's time the symptoms become well marked, with a discharge of mucus or pus from the eyes and nose, and complications of a more or less serious nature, such as broncho-pneumonia, hemorrhagic inflammation of the gastro-intestinal tract, and disturbances of the brain and spinal cord, which may cause convulsions. In the early stages of distemper the body temperature may suddenly rise from the normal 101°F. to 103°. Shivering, dryness of the nostrils, a slight dry cough, increased thirst, a drowsy look, reluctance to eat, and a desire to sleep may follow. Later, diarrhea (frequently streaked with blood or wholly of blood), pneumonia, convulsions, paralysis, or chorea (a persistent twitching condition) may develop. An inflammation of the membranes of the eye may ensue; this may impair or destroy the sight through ulceration or opacity of the cornea. Extreme weakness and great loss of body weight occur in advanced stages.

All, any, or none of these symptoms may be noticeable. It is believed that many dogs experience distemper in so mild a form as to escape the owner's observation. Because of its protean and obscure nature and its strong similarity to other catarrhal affections, the diagnosis of distemper, especially in its early stages, is difficult. In young dogs that are known to have been exposed to the disease,

102

a rise of body temperature, together with shivering, sneezing, loss of appetite, eye and nasal discharge, sluggishness, and diarrhea (all or any of these symptoms), are indicative of trouble.

There is little specific that can be done for a dog with primary distemper. The treatment is largely concerned with alleviating the symptoms. No drug or combination of drugs is known at this time that has any specific action on the disease. Distemper runs a definite course, no matter what is done to try to cure it.

Homologous anti-distemper serum, administered subcutaneously or intravenously by the veterinarian, is of value in lessening the severity of the attack. The veterinarian may see fit to treat the secondary pneumonia with penicillin or one of the sulpha drugs, or to allay the secondary intestinal infection with medication. It is best to permit him to manage the case in his own way. The dog is more prone to respond to care in his own home and with his own people, if suitable quarters and adequate nursing are available to him. Otherwise, he is best off in a veterinary hospital.

The dog affected with distemper should be provided with clean, dry, warm but not hot, well ventilated quarters. It should be given moderate quantities of nourishing, easily digested food—milk, soft boiled eggs, cottage cheese, and scraped lean beef. The sick dog should not be disturbed by children or other dogs. Discharges from eyes and nose should be wiped away. The eyes may be bathed with boric acid solution, and irritation of the nose allayed with greasy substances such as petrolatum. The dog should not be permitted to get wet or chilled, and he should have such medication as the veterinarian prescribes and no other.

When signs of improvement are apparent, the dog must not be given an undue amount of food at one meal, although he may be fed at frequent intervals. The convalescing dog should be permitted to exercise only very moderately until complete recovery is assured.

In the control of distemper, affected animals should be promptly isolated from susceptible dogs. After the disease has run its course, whether it end in recovery or death, the premises where the patient has been kept during the illness should be thoroughly cleaned and disinfected, as should all combs, brushes, or other utensils used on the dog, before other susceptible dogs are brought in. After an apparent recovery has been made in the patient, the germs are present for about four weeks and can be transmitted to susceptible dogs.

CHOREA OR ST. VITUS DANCE

A frequent sequela of distemper is chorea, which is characterized by a more or less pronounced and frequent twitching of a muscle or muscles. There is no known remedy for the condition. It does not impair the usefulness of a good dog for breeding, and having a litter of puppies often betters or cures chorea in the bitch. Chorea is considered a form of unsoundness and is penalized in the show ring. The condition generally becomes worse.

ECLAMPSIA OR WHELPING TETANY

Convulsions of bitches before, during, or shortly after their whelping are called eclampsia. It seldom occurs to a bitch receiving a sufficient amount of calcium and vitamin D in her diet during her pregnancy. The symptoms vary in their severity for nervousness and mild convulsions to severe attacks which may terminate in coma and death. The demands of the nursing litter for calcium frequently depletes the supply in the bitch's system.

Eclampsia can be controlled by the hypodermic administration of calcium gluconate. Its recurrence is prevented by the addition to the bitch's ration of readily utilized calcium and vitamin D.

RICKETS, OR RACHITIS

The failure of the bones of puppies to calcify normally is termed rickets, or more technically rachitis. Perhaps more otherwise excellent puppies are killed or ruined by rickets than by any other disease. It is essentially a disease of puppies, but the malformation of the skeleton produced by rickets persists through the life of the dog.

The symptoms of rickets include lethargy, arched neck, crouched stance, knobby and deformed joints, bowed legs, and flabby muscles. The changes characteristic of defective calcification in the puppy are most marked in the growth of the long bones of the leg, and at the cartilaginous junction of the ribs. In the more advanced stages of rickets the entire bone becomes soft and easily deformed or broken. The development of the teeth is also retarded.

Rickets results from a deficiency in the diet of calcium, phosphorus, or vitamin D. It may be prevented by the inclusion of sufficient amounts of those substances in the puppy's diet. It may also be cured, if not too far advanced, by the same means, although distortions in the skeleton that have already occurred are seldom rectified. The requirements of vitamin D to be artificially supplied are greater for puppies raised indoors and with limited exposure to sunlight or to sunlight filtered through window glass.

(It is possible to give a dog too much vitamin D, but very unlikely without deliberate intent.)

Adult dogs that have had rickets in puppyhood and whose recovery is complete may be bred from without fear of their transmission to their puppies of the malformations of their skeletons produced by the disease. The same imbalance or absence from their diet that produced rickets in the parent may produce it in the progeny, but the disease in such case is reproduced and not inherited.

The requirements of adult dogs for calcium, phosphorus, and vitamin D are much less than for puppies and young dogs, but a condition called osteomalacia, or late rickets, is sometimes seen in grown dogs as the result of the same kind of nutritional deficiency that causes rickets in puppies. In such cases a softening of the bones leads to lameness and deformity. The remedy is the same as in the rickets of puppyhood, namely the addition of calcium, phosphorus, and vitamin D to the diet. It is especially essential that bitches during pregnancy and lactation have included in their diets ample amounts of these elements, both for their own nutrition and for the adequate skeletal formations of their fetuses and the development of their puppies.

BLACKTONGUE

Blacktongue (the canine analogue of pellagra in the human) is no longer to be feared in dogs fed upon an adequate diet. For many years, it was a recognized scourge among dogs, and its cause and treatment were unknown. It is now known to be caused solely by the insufficiency in the ration of vitamin B complex and specifically by an insufficiency of nicotinic acid. (Nicotinic acid is vitamin B_2, formerly known as vitamin G.)

Blacktongue may require a considerable time for its full development. It usually begins with a degree of lethargy, a lack of appetite for the kind of food the dog has been receiving, constipation, often with spells of vomiting, and particularly with a foul odor from the mouth. As the disease develops, the mucous membranes of the mouth, gums, and tongue grow red and become inflamed, with purple splotches of greater or lesser extent, especially upon the front part of the tongue, and with ulcers and pustules on the lips and the lining of the cheeks. Constipation may give way to diarrhea as the disease develops. Blacktongue is an insidious malady, since its development is so gradual.

This disease is unlikely to occur except among dogs whose owners are so unenlightened, careless, or stingy as to feed their dogs exclusively on a diet of cornmeal mush, salt pork, cowpeas, sweet potatoes, or other foodstuffs that are known to be responsible for the development of pellagra in mankind. Blacktongue is not infectious or contagious, although the same deficiency in the diet of dogs may produce the malady in all the inmates throughout a kennel.

Correct treatment involves no medication as such, but consists wholly in the alteration of the diet to include foods which are good sources of the vitamin B complex, including nicotinic acid; such food as the muscles of beef, mutton, or horse, dried yeast, wheat germ, milk, eggs, and especially fresh liver. As an emergency treatment, the hypodermic injection of nicotinic acid may be indicated. Local treatments of the mouth, its cleansing and disinfection, are usually included, although they will avail nothing without the alteration in the diet.

LEPTOSPIROSIS OR CANINE TYPHUS

Leptospirosis, often referred to as canine typhus, is believed to be identical with Weil's disease (infectious jaundice) in the human species. It is not to be confused with non-infectious jaundice in the dog, which is a mere obstruction in the bile duct which occurs in some liver and gastric disorders. Leptospirosis is a comparatively rare disease as yet, but its incidence is growing and it is becoming more widespread.

It is caused by either of two spirocheates, *Leptospira canicola* or *Leptospira icterohenorrhagiae*. These causative organisms are found in the feces or urine of infected rats, and the disease is transmitted to dogs by their ingestion of food fouled by those rodents. It is therefore wise in rat infested houses to keep all dog food in covered metal containers to which it is impossible for rats to gain access. It is also possible for an ill dog to transmit the infection to a well one, and, it is believed, to man. Such cases, however, are rare.

Symptoms of leptospirosis include a variable temperature, vomiting, loss of appetite, gastroenteritis, diarrhea, jaundice and depression. Analysis of blood and urine may be helpful toward diagnosis. The disease is one for immediate reference to the veterinarian whenever suspected.

Prognosis is not entirely favorable, especially if the disease is neglected in its earlier stages. Taken in its incipience, treatment with penicillin has produced excellent results, as has antileptospiral serum and vaccine.

Control measures include the extermination of rats in areas where the disease is known to exist, and the cleaning and disinfection of premises where infected dogs have been kept.

INFECTIOUS HEPATITIS

This is a virus disease attacking the liver. Apparently it is not the same virus that causes hepatitis in humans. Symptoms include an unusual thirst, loss of appetite, vomiting, diarrhea, pain causing the dog to moan, anemia and fever. The afflicted dog may try to hide.

The disease runs a fast course and is often fatal. A dog recovering from it may carry the virus in his urine for a long period, thus infecting other dogs months later.

Serum and vaccine are available to offer protection. A combination for distemper and hepatitis is now offered.

TURNED-IN OR TURNED-OUT EYELIDS

When the eyelid is inverted, or turned-in, it is technically termed entropion. When the eyelid is turned-out, it is referred to as extropion. Both conditions seem to be found in certain strains of dogs and are classified as being heritable. Both conditions may be corrected by competent surgery. It is possible to operate on such cases and have complete recovery without scar formation. However, cognizance should be taken of either defect in a dog to be used for breeding purposes.

CONJUNCTIVITIS OR INFLAMMATION OF THE EYE

Certain irritants, injuries or infections, and many febrile diseases, such as distemper, produce conjunctivitis, an inflammation of the membranes lining the lids of the dog's eyes. At first there is a slight reddening of the membranes and a watery discharge. As the condition progresses, the conjunctivae become more inflamed looking and the color darkens. The discharge changes consistency and color, becoming muco-purulent in character and yellow in color. The eyelids may be pasted shut and granulation of the lids may follow.

When eye infection persists for an extended period of time, the cornea sometimes becomes involved. Ulcers may develop, eventually penetrating the eyeball. When this happens, the condition becomes very painful and, even worse, often leads to the loss of vision.

Home treatment, to be used only until professional care may be had, consists of regular cleaning of the eye with a 2% boric acid solution and the application of one of the antibiotic eye ointments.

When anything happens to the dog's eye, it is always best to seek professional help and advice.

RABIES

This disease, caused by a virus, is transmissible to all warm blooded animals, and the dog seems to be the number one disseminator of the virus. However, outbreaks of rabies have been traced to wild animals—the wolf, coyote, or fox biting a dog which in turn bites people, other dogs, or other species of animals.

The virus, which is found in the saliva of the rabid animal, enters the body only through broken skin. This usually is brought about by biting and breaking the skin, or through licking an open cut on the skin. The disease manifests itself clinically in two distinct forms. One is called the "furious type" and the other the "dumb type." Both types are produced by the same strain of virus.

The disease works rather peculiarly on the dog's disposition and character. The kindly old dog may suddenly become ferocious; just the reverse may also occur, the mean, vicious dog becoming gentle and biddable. At first the infected dog wants to be near his master, wants to lick his hand or his boots; his appetite undergoes a sudden change, becoming voracious, and the animal will eat anything—stones, bits of wood, even metal. Soon there develops a sense of wanderlust, and the dog seems to wish to get as far away as possible from his owner.

In all rabid animals there is an accentuation of the defense mechanisms. In other words, the dog will bite, the cat will hiss and claw, the horse will bite and kick, and the cow will attack anything that moves.

An animal afflicted with rabies cannot swallow because there is usually a paralysis of the muscles of deglutinition. The animal, famished for a drink, tries to bite the water or whatever fluid he may be attempting to drink. The constant champing of the jaws causes the saliva to become mixed and churned with air, making it appear whipped and foamy. In the old days when a dog "frothed at the mouth," he was considered "mad." There is no doubt but what some uninfected dogs have been suspected of being rabid and shot to death simply because they exhibited these symptoms.

One of the early signs of rabies in the dog is the dropping of the lower jaw. This is a sign of rabies of the so-called "dumb type." The animal has a "faraway" look in his eyes, and his voice or bark has an odd pitch. Manifesting these symptoms, the dog is often taken to the clinic by the owner, who is sure the dog has a bone in the throat. The hind legs, and eventually the whole hindquarters, subsequently become paralyzed, and death ensues.

Many commonwealths have passed laws requiring that all dogs be vaccinated against rabies, and usually, a vaccination certificate must be presented before a dog license may be issued. The general enforcement of this law alone would go a long way toward the eradication of rabies.

Some will ask why a dog must be impounded as a biter when he has taken a little "nip" at someone and merely broken the skin—if this must be done, they cannot understand the "good" of the vaccination. But the vaccination does not give the dog the right to bite. Statistics show that rabies vaccination is effective in about 88% of the cases. All health authorities wish it were 100% effective, thus eliminating a good deal of worry from their minds. Because the vaccination is not 100% effective, we cannot take a chance on the vaccine alone. The animal must be impounded and under the daily supervision of a qualified observer, generally for a period of fourteen days. It is pretty well recognized that if the bite was provocated by rabies, the biting animal will develop clinical symptoms in that length of time; otherwise, he will be released as "clinically normal."

THE SPAYING OF BITCHES

The spaying operation, technically known as an ovariectomy, is the subject of a good deal of controversy. It is an operation that has its good and its bad points.

Spayed bitches cannot be entered in the show ring, and of course can never reproduce their kind. However, under certain circumstances, the operation is recommended by veterinarians. If the operation is to be performed, the bitch should preferably be six to eight months of age. At this age, she has pretty well reached the adolescent period; time enough has been allowed for the endocrine balance to become established and the secondary sex organs to develop.

Mechanical difficulties sometimes arise in the urinary systems of bitches that have been operated on at three or four months of age. In a very small percentage of the cases, loss of control of the sphincter muscles of the bladder is observed. But this can readily be corrected by an injection of the female hormone stilbestrol.

There are many erroneous ideas as to what may happen to the female if she is spayed. Some people argue that the disposition will be changed, that the timid dog may become ferocious, and, strangely enough, that the aggressive animal will become docile. Some breeders say that the spayed bitch will become fat, lazy, and lethargic. According to the records that have been kept on bitches following the spaying operation, such is not the case. It is unjust to accuse the spaying operation when really the dog's owner is at fault—he just feeds the dog too much.

THE CASTRATION OF DOGS

This operation consists of the complete removal of the testes. Ordinarily the operation is not encouraged. Circumstances may attenuate the judgment, however. Castration may be necessary to correct certain pathological conditions such as a tumor, chronic prostatitis, and types of perineal troubles. Promiscuous wetting is sometimes an excuse for desexing.

It must be remembered that as with the spayed bitch, the castrated dog is barred from the show ring.

ANAL GLANDS

On either side of the anus of the dog is situated an anal gland, which secretes a lubricant that better enables the dog to expel the contents of the rectum. These glands are subject to being clogged, and in them accumulates a fetid mass. This accumulation is not, strictly speaking, a disease—unless it becomes infected and purulent. Almost all dogs have it, and most of them are neglected without serious consequences. However, they are better if they are relieved. Their spirits improve, their eyes brighten, and even their coats gradually grow more lively if the putrid mass is occasionally squeezed out of the anus.

This is accomplished by seizing the tail with the left hand, encircling its base with the thumb and forefinger of the right hand, and pressing the anus firmly between thumb and finger. The process results in momentary pain to the dog and often causes him to flinch, which may be disregarded. A semi-liquid of vile odor is extruded from the anus. The operation should be repeated at intervals of from one week to one month, depending on the rapidity of glandular accumulation. No harm results from the frequency of such relief, although there may be no apparent results if the anal glands are kept free of their accumulations.

If this process of squeezing out of the glands is neglected, the glands sometimes become infected and surgery becomes necessary. This is seldom the case, but, if needful at all, it must be entrusted to a skillful veterinary surgeon.

METRITIS

Metritis is the acute or chronic inflammation of the uterus of the bitch and may result from any one of a number of things. Perhaps the most common factor, especially in eight- to twelve-year-old bitches, is pseudocyesis, or false pregnancy. Metritis often follows whelping; it may be the result of a retained placenta, or of infection of the uterus following the manual or instrument removal of a puppy.

The term pyometria is generally restricted to cases where the uterus is greatly enlarged and filled with pus. In most such cases surgery must be resorted to in order to effect a cure.

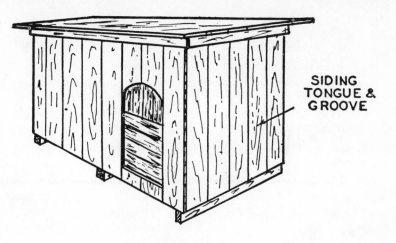

SIDING
TONGUE &
GROOVE

ASSEMBLED VIEW

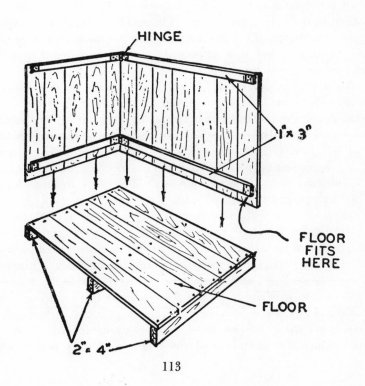

HINGE

1"x 3"

FLOOR
FITS
HERE

FLOOR

2" x 4"

Housing for Dogs

EVERY owner will have, and will have to solve, his own problems about providing his dog or dogs with quarters best suited to the dog's convenience. The special circumstances of each particular owner will determine what kind of home he will provide for his dogs. Here it is impossible to provide more than a few generalities upon the subject.

Little more need be said than that fit quarters for dogs must be secure, clean, dry, and warm. Consideration must be given to convenience in the care of kennel inmates by owners of a large number of dogs, but by the time one's activities enlarge to such proportions one will have formulated one's own concept of how best to house one's dogs. Here, advice will be predicated upon the maintenance of not more than three or four adult dogs with accommodations for an occasional litter of puppies.

First, let it be noted that dogs are not sensitive to aesthetic considerations in the place they are kept; they have no appreciation of the beauty of their surroundings. They do like soft beds of sufficient thickness to protect them from the coldness of the floors. These beds should be secluded and covered to conserve body heat. A box or crate of adequate size to permit the dog to lie full length in it will suffice. The cushion may be a burlap bag stuffed with shredded paper, *not straw, hay, or grass*. Paper is recommended, for its use will reduce the possibility of the dog's developing skin trouble.

114

Most dogs are allergic to fungi found on vegetative matter such as straw, hay, and grass. Wood shavings and excelsior may be used with impunity.

The kennel should be light, except for a retiring place; if sunshine is available at least part of the day, so much the better. Boxes in a shed or garage with secure wire runs to which the dogs have ready access suffice very well, are very inexpensive, and are easy to plan and to arrange. The runs should be made of wire fencing strong enough that the dogs are unable to tear it with their teeth and high enough that the dogs are unable to jump or climb over it. In-turning flanges of wire netting at the tops of the fences tend to obviate jumping. Boards, rocks, or cement buried around the fences forestall burrowing to freedom.

These pens need not be large, if the dogs are given frequent respites from their captivity and an opportunity to obtain needed exercise. However, they should be large enough to relieve them of the aspect of cages. Concrete floors for such pens are admittedly easy to keep clean and sanitary. However, they have no resilience, and the feet of dogs confined for long periods on concrete floors are prone to spread and their shoulders to loosen. A further objection to concrete is that it grows hot in the summer sunshine and is very cold in winter. If it is used for flooring at all, a low platform of wood, large enough to enable the dogs to sprawl out on it full length, should be provided in each pen.

A well drained soil is to be preferred to concrete, if it is available; but it must be dug out to the depth of three inches and renewed occasionally, if it is used. Otherwise, the accumulation of urine will make it sour and offensive. Agricultural limestone, applied monthly and liberally, will "sweeten" the soil.

Gates, hinges, latches, and other hardware must be trustworthy. The purpose of such quarters is to confine the dogs and to keep them from running at large; unless they serve such a purpose they are useless. One wants to know when one puts a dog in his kennel, the dog will be there when one returns. An improvised kennel of old chicken wire will not suffice for one never knows whether it will hold one's dogs or not.

Frequently two friendly bitches may be housed together, or a dog housed with a bitch. Unless one is sure of male friendships, it is seldom safe to house two adult male dogs together. It is better, if possible, to provide a separate kennel for each mature dog. But, if the dogs can be housed side by side with only a wire fence between them, they can have companionship without rancor. Night barking can be controlled by confining the dogs indoors or by shutting them up in their boxes.

Adult dogs require artificial heat in only the coldest of climates, if they are provided with tight boxes placed under shelter. Puppies need heat in cold weather up until weaning time, and even thereafter if they are not permitted to sleep together. Snuggled together in a tight box with shredded paper, they can withstand much cold without discomfort. All dogs in winter without artificial heat should have an increase of their rations—especially as pertains to fat content.

Whatever artificial heat is provided for dogs should be safe, foolproof, and dog-proof. Caution should be exercised that electric wiring is not exposed, that stoves cannot be tipped over, and that it is impossible for sparks from them to ignite the premises. Many fires in kennels, the results of defective heating apparatus or careless handling of it, have brought about the deaths of the inmates. It is because of them that this seemingly unnecessary warning is given.

No better place for a dog to live can be found than the home of its owner, sharing even his bed if permitted. So is the dog happiest. There is a limit, however, to the number of dogs that can be tolerated in the house. The keeper of a small kennel can be expected to alternate his favorite dogs in his own house, thus giving them a respite to confinement in a kennel. Provision must be made for a place of exercise and relief at frequent intervals for dogs kept in the house. An enclosed dooryard will serve such a purpose, or the dog may be exercised on a lead with as much benefit to the owner as to the dog.

That the quarters of the dog shall be dry is even more important than that they shall be warm. A damp, drafty kennel is the cause of much kennel disease and indisposition. It is harmless to permit a dog to go out into inclement weather of his own choice, if he is provided with a sheltered bed to which he may retire to dry himself.

By cleanness, sanitation is meant—freedom from vermin and bacteria. A little coat of dust or a degree of disorder does not discommode the dog or impair his welfare, but the best dog keepers are orderly persons. They at least do not permit bedding and old

116

bones to accumulate in a dog's bed, and they take the trouble to spray with antiseptic or wash with soap and water their dog's house at frequent intervals. The feces in the kennel runs should be picked up and destroyed at least once, and better twice, daily. Persistent filth in kennels can be counted on as a source of illness sooner or later. This warning appears superfluous, but it isn't; the number of ailing dogs kept in dirty, unsanitary kennels is amazing. It is one of the axioms of keeping dogs that their quarters must be sanitary or disease is sure to ensue.

GOOD DOG KEEPING PRACTICES

Pride of ownership is greatly enhanced when the owner takes care to maintain his dog in the best possible condition at all times. And meticulous grooming not only will make the dog look better but also will make him feel better. As part of the regular, daily routine, the grooming of the dog will prove neither arduous nor time consuming; it will also obviate the necessity for indulging in a rigorous program designed to correct the unkempt state in which too many owners permit their dogs to appear. Certainly, spending a few minutes each day will be well worth while, for the result will be a healthier, happier, and more desirable canine companion.

THAT DOGGY ODOR

Many persons are disgusted to the point of refusal to keep a dog by what they fancy is a "doggy odor." Of course, almost everything has a characteristic odor—everyone is familiar with the smell of the rose. No one would want the dog to smell like a rose, and, conversely, the world wouldn't like it very well if the rose smelled doggy. The dog must emit a certain amount of characteristic odor or he wouldn't be a dog. That seems to be his God-given grant. However, when the odor becomes too strong and obnoxious, then it is time to look for the reason. In most cases it is the result of clogged anal glands. If this be the case, all one must do to rid the pet of his odor is to express the contents of these glands and apply to the anal region a little soap and water.

If the odor is one of putrefaction, look to his mouth for the trouble. The teeth may need scaling, or a diseased root of some one or two teeth that need to be treated may be the source of the odor. In some dogs there is a fold or a crease in the lower lip near the lower canine tooth, and this may need attention. This spot is favored by fungi that cause considerable damage to the part. The smell here is somewhat akin to the odor of human feet that have been attacked by the fungus of athlete's foot.

The odor may be coming from the coat if the dog is heavily infested with fleas or lice. Too, dogs seem to enjoy the odor of dead fish and often roll on a foul smelling fish that has been cast up on the beach. The dog with a bad case of otitis can fairly "drive you out of the room" with this peculiar odor. Obviously, the way to rid the dog of odor is to find from whence it comes and then take steps to eliminate it. Some dogs have a tendency toward excessive flatulence (gas). These animals should have a complete change of diet and with the reducing of the carbohydrate content, a teaspoon of granular charcoal should be added to each feeding.

BATHING THE DOG

There is little to say about giving a bath to a dog, except that he shall be placed in a tub of warm (not hot) water and thoroughly scrubbed. He may, like a spoiled child, object to the ordeal, but if handled gently and firmly he will submit to what he knows to be inevitable.

The water must be only tepid, so as not to shock or chill the dog. A bland, unmedicated soap is best, for such soaps do not irritate the skin or dry out the hair. Even better than soap is one of the powdered detergents marketed especially for this purpose. They rinse away better and more easily than soap and do not leave the coat gummy or sticky.

It is best to begin with the face, which should be thoroughly and briskly washed with a cloth. Care should be taken that the cleaning solvent does not get into the dog's eyes, not because of the likelihood of causing permanent harm, but because such an experience is unpleasant to the dog and prone to prejudice him against future baths. The interior of the ear canals should be thoroughly cleansed until they not only look clean but also until no unpleasant odor comes from them. The head may then be rinsed and dried before proceeding to the body. Especial attention should be given to the drying of the ears, inside and outside. Many ear infections arise from failure to dry the canals completely.

With the head bathed and the surplus water removed from that part, the body must be soaked thoroughly with water, either with a hose or by dipping the water from the bath and pouring it over the dog's back until he is totally wetted. Thereafter, the soap or detergent should be applied and rubbed until it lathers freely. A stiff brush is useful in penetrating the coat and cleansing the skin. It is not sufficient to wash only the back and sides—the belly, neck, legs, feet, and tail must all be scrubbed thoroughly.

If the dog is very dirty, it may be well to rinse him lightly and repeat the soaping process and scrub again. Thereafter, the dog must be rinsed with warm (tepid) water until all suds and soil come away. If a bath spray is available, the rinsing is an easy matter. If the dog must be rinsed in standing water, it will be needful to renew it two or three times.

When he is thoroughly rinsed, it is well to remove such surplus water as may be squeezed with the hand, after which he is enveloped with a turkish towel, lifted from the tub, and rubbed until he is dry. This will probably require two or three dry towels. In the process of drying the dog, it is well to return again and again to the interior of the ears.

THE DOG'S TEETH

The dog, like the human being, has two successive sets of teeth, the so-called milk teeth or baby teeth, which are shed and replaced later by the permanent teeth. The temporary teeth, which begin to emerge when the puppy is two and a half to three weeks of age, offer no difficulty. The full set of milk teeth (consisting usually of six incisors and two canines in each jaw, with four molars in the upper jaw and six molars in the lower jaw) is completed usually just before weaning time. Except for some obvious malformation, the milk teeth may be ignored and forgotten about.

At about the fourth month the baby teeth are shed and gradually replaced by the permanent teeth. This shedding and replacement process may consume some three or four months. This is about the most critical period of the dog's life—his adolescence. Some constitutionally vigorous dogs go through their teething easily, with no

119

seeming awareness that the change is taking place. Others, less vigorous, may suffer from soreness of the gums, go off in flesh, and require pampering. While they are teething, puppies should be particularly protected from exposure to infectious diseases and should be fed on nutritious foods, especially meat and milk.

The permanent teeth normally consist of 42—six incisors and two canines (fangs) in each jaw, with twelve molars in the upper jaw and fourteen in the lower jaw. Occasionally the front molars fail to emerge; this deficiency is considered by most judges to be only a minor fault, if the absence is noticed at all.

Dentition is a heritable factor in the dog, and some dogs have soft, brittle and defective permanent teeth, no matter how excellent the diet and the care given them. The teeth of those dogs which are predisposed to have excellent sound ones, however, can be ruined by an inferior diet prior to and during the period of their eruption. At this time, for the teeth to develop properly, a dog must have an adequate supply of calcium phosphate and vitamin D, besides all the protein he can consume.

Often the permanent teeth emerge before the shedding of the milk teeth, in which case the dog may have parts of both sets at the same time. The milk teeth will eventually drop out, but as long as they remain they may deflect or displace the second teeth in the process of their growth. The incisors are the teeth in which a malformation may result from the late dropping of the baby teeth. When it is realized just how important a correct "bite" may be deemed in the show ring, the hazards of permitting the baby teeth to deflect the permanent set will be understood.

The baby teeth in such a case must be dislodged and removed. The roots of the baby teeth are resorbed in the gums, and the teeth can usually be extracted by firm pressure of thumb and finger, although it may be necessary to employ forceps or to take the puppy to the veterinarian.

The permanent teeth of the puppy are usually somewhat overshot, by which is meant that the upper incisors protrude over and do not play upon the lower incisors. Maturity may be trusted to remedy this apparent defect unless it is too pronounced.

An undershot mouth in a puppy, on the other hand, tends to grow worse as the dog matures. Whether or not it has been caused by the displacement of the permanent teeth by the persistence of the milk teeth, it can sometimes be remedied (or at least bettered) by frequent hard pressure of the thumb on the lower jaw, forcing the lower teeth backward to meet the upper ones. Braces on dog teeth have seldom proved efficacious, but pressure and massage are worth trying on the bad mouth of an otherwise excellent puppy.

High and persistent fevers, especially from the fourth to the ninth month, sometimes result in discolored, pitted, and defective teeth, commonly called "distemper teeth." They often result from maladies other than distemper. There is little that can be done for them. They are unpleasant to see and are subject to penalty in the show ring, but are serviceable to the dog. Distemper teeth are not in themselves heritable, but the predisposition for their development appears to be. At least, at the teething age, the offspring from distemper toothed ancestors seem to be especially prone to fevers which impair their dentition.

Older dogs, especially those fed largely upon carbohydrates, tend to accumulate more or less tartar upon their teeth. The tartar generally starts at the gum line on the molars and extends gradually to the cusp. To rectify this condition, the dog's teeth should be scaled by a veterinarian.

The cleanliness of a dog's mouth may be brought about and the formation of tartar discouraged by the scouring of the teeth with a moist cloth dipped in a mixture of equal parts of table salt and baking soda.

A large bone given the dog to chew on or play with tends to prevent tartar from forming on the teeth. If tartar is present, the chewing and gnawing on the bone will help to remove the deposit mechanically. A bone given to puppies will act as a teething ring and aid in the cutting of the permanent teeth. So will beef hide strips you can buy in pet shops.

CARE OF THE NAILS

The nails of the dog should be kept shortened and blunted right down to the quick—never into the quick. If this is not done, the toes may spread and the foot may splay into a veritable pancake. Some dogs have naturally flat feet, which they have inherited. No pretense is made that the shortening of the nails of such a foot will obviate the fault entirely and make the foot beautiful or serviceable.

It will only improve the appearance and make the best of an obvious fault. Short nails do, however, emphasize the excellence of a good foot.

Some dogs keep their nails short by digging and friction. Their nails require little attention, but it is a rare dog whose foot cannot be bettered by artificially shortening the nails.

Nail clippers are available, made especially for the purpose. After using them, the sides of the nail should be filed away as much as is possible without touching the quick. Carefully done, it causes the dog no discomfort. But, once the quick of a dog's nail has been injured, he may forever afterward resent and fight having his feet treated or even having them examined.

The obvious horn of the nail can be removed, after which the quick will recede to permit the removal of more horn the following week. This process may be kept up until the nail is as short and blunt as it can be made, after which nails will need attention only at intervals of six weeks or two months.

Some persons clip the nails right back to the toes in one fell swoop, disregarding injury to the quick and pain of the dog. The nails bleed and the dog limps for a day or two, but infection seldom develops. Such a procedure should not be undertaken without a general anesthetic. If an anesthetic is used, this forthright method does not prejudice the dog against having his feet handled.

NAIL TRIMMING ILLUSTRATED

The method here illustrated is to take a sharp file and stroke the nail downwards in the direction of the arrow, as in Figure 24, until it assumes the shape in Figure 25, the shaded portion being the part removed, a three-cornered file should then be used on the underside just missing the quick, as in Figure 26, and the operation is then complete, the dog running about quickly wears the nail to the proper shape.

Care for
the Old Dog

FIRST, how old is old, in a dog? Some breeds live longer than others, as a general rule. The only regularity about dog ages at death is their irregularity breed to breed and dog to dog.

The dog owner can best determine senility in his canine friend by the dog's appearance and behavior. Old dogs "slow down" much as humans do. The stairs are a little steeper, the breath a little shorter, the eye dimmer, the hearing usually a little harder.

As prevention is always better than cure, a dog's life may be happily and healthfully extended if certain precautionary steps are taken. As the aging process becomes quite evident, the owner should become more considerate of his dog's weaknesses, procrastinations and lapses. A softer, drier, warmer bed may be advisable; a foam rubber mattress will be appreciated. If a kennel dog has been able to endure record-breaking hot or cold, torrential or desert-dry days, he may in his old age appreciate spending his nights at least in a warm, comfy human house. And if the weather outside is frightful during the day, he should—for minimum comfort and safety—be brought inside before pneumonia sets in.

The old dog should NOT be required or expected to chase a ball, or a pheasant, or one of his species of different sex. The old bitch should not continue motherhood.

If many teeth are gone or going, foods should be softer. The diet should be blander—delete sweet or spicy or heavy tidbits—and there should be less of it, usually. The older dog needs less fat, less carbohydrate and less minerals unless disease and convalescence dictate otherwise. DON'T PERMIT AN OLD DOG TO GET FAT! It's cruel. The special diet known as PD or KD may be in order, if the dog has dietary troubles or a disease concomitant with old age. The veterinarian should be asked about PD or KD diets. Vitamin B-12 and other vitamin reinforcements may help.

The dog diseases of old age parallel many of the human illnesses. Senior male dogs suffer from prostate trouble, kidney disease and cancer. Senior bitches suffer from metritis and cancer. Both sexes suffer blindness, deafness and paralysis. Dogs suffer from heart disease; I know one old dog that is living an especially happy old age through the courtesy of digitalis. If the symptoms of any disease manifest themselves in an old dog the veterinarian MUST be consulted.

Many dog owners are selfish about old dogs. In their reluctance to lose faithful friends, they try to keep their canine companions alive in terminal illnesses, such as galloping cancer. If the veterinarian holds little or no promise for recovery of a pet from an illness associated with old age, or if the pet suffers, the kindest act the owner can perform is to request euthanasia. In this sad event, the kindest step the owner may take in *his* interest is to acquire a puppy or young dog of the same breed immediately. Puppies have a wonderful way of absorbing grief!

Glossary of Dog Terms

Achilles tendon: The large tendon attaching the muscle of the calf in the second thigh to the bone below the hock; the hamstring.

A.K.C.: The American Kennel Club.

Albino: An animal having a congenital deficiency of pigment in the skin, hair, and eyes.

American Kennel Club: A federation of member show-giving and specialty clubs which maintains a stud book, and formulates and enforces rules under which dog shows and other canine activities in the United States are conducted. Its address is 221 Park Avenue South, New York 3, N. Y.

Angulation: The angles of the bony structure at the joints, particularly of the shoulder with the upper arm (front angulation), or the angles at the stifle and the hock (rear angulation).

Anus: The posterior opening of the alimentary canal through which the feces are discharged.

Apple head: A rounded or domed skull.

Balance: A nice adjustment of the parts one to another; no part too big or too small for the whole organism; symmetry.

Barrel: The ribs and body.

Bitch: The female of the dog species.

Blaze: A white line or marking extending from the top of the skull (often from the occiput), between the eyes, and over the muzzle.

Brisket: The breast or lower part of the chest in front of and between the forelegs, sometimes including the part extending back some distance behind the forelegs.

Burr: The visible, irregular inside formation of the ear.

Butterfly nose: A nose spotted or speckled with flesh color.

Canine: (Noun) Any animal of the family *Canidae,* including dogs, wolves, jackals, and foxes.
(Adjective) Of or pertaining to such animals; having the nature and qualities of a dog.

Canine tooth: The long tooth next behind the incisors in each side of each jaw; the fang.

Castrate: (Verb) Surgically to remove the gonads of either sex, usually said of the testes of the male.

Character: A combination of points of appearance, behavior, and disposition

125

contributing to the whole dog and distinctive of the individual dog or of its particular breed.

Cheeky: Having rounded muscular padding on sides of the skull.

Chiseled: (Said of the muzzle) modeled or delicately cut away in front of the eyes to conform to breed type.

Chops: The mouth, jaws, lips, and cushion.

Close-coupled: Short in the loins.

Cobby: Stout, stocky, short-bodied; compactly made; like a cob (horse).

Coupling: The part of the body joining the hindquarters to the parts of the body in front; the loin; the flank.

Cowhocks: Hocks turned inward and converging like the presumed hocks of a cow.

Croup: The rear of the back above the hind limbs; the line from the pelvis to the set-on of the tail.

Cryptorchid: A male animal in which the testicles are not externally apparent, having failed to descend normally, not to be confused with a castrated dog.

Dentition: The number, kind, form, and arrangement of the teeth.

Dewclaws: Additional toes on the inside of the leg above the foot; the ones cn the rear legs usually removed in puppyhood in most breeds.

Dewlap: The pendulous fold of skin under the neck.

Distemper teeth: The discolored and pitted teeth which result from some febrile disease.

Down in (or on) pastern: With forelegs more or less bent at the pastern joint.

Dry: Free from surplus skin or flesh about mouth, lips, or throat.

Dudley nose: A brown or flesh-colored nose, usually accompanied by eye-rims of the same shade and light eyes.

Ewe-neck: A thin sheep-like neck, having insufficient, faulty, or concave arch.

Expression: The combination of various features of the head and face, particularly the size, shape, placement and color of eyes, to produce a certain impression, the outlook.

Femur: The heavy bone of the true thigh.

Fetlock or Fetlock joint: The joint between the pastern and the lower arm; sometimes called the "knee," although it does not correspond to the human knee.

Fiddle front: A crooked front with bandy legs, out at elbow, converging at pastern joints, and turned out pasterns and feet, with or without bent bones of forearms.

Flews: The chops; pendulous lateral parts of the upper lips.

Forearm: The part of the front leg between the elbow and pastern.

Front: The entire aspect of a dog, except the head, when seen from the front; the forehand.

Guard hairs: The longer, smoother, stiffer hairs which grow through the undercoat and normally conceal it.

Hackney action: The high lifting of the front feet, like that of a Hackney horse, a waste of effort.

Hare-foot: A long, narrow, and close-toed foot, like that of the hare or rabbit.

Haw: The third eyelid, or nictitating membrane, especially when inflamed.

Height: The vertical distance from withers at top of shoulder blades to floor.

Hock: The lower joint in the hind leg, corresponding to the human ankle; sometimes, incorrectly, the part of the hind leg, from the hock joint to the foot.

Humerus: The bone of the upper arm.

Incisors: The teeth adapted for cutting; specifically, the six small front teeth in each jaw between the canines or fangs.

126

Knuckling over: Projecting or bulging forward of the front legs at the pastern joint; incorrectly called knuckle knees.

Leather: Pendant ears.

Lippy: With lips longer or fuller than desirable in the breed under consideration.

Loaded: Padded with superfluous muscle (said of such shoulders).

Loins: That part on either side of the spinal column between the hipbone and the false ribs.

Molar tooth: A rear, cheek tooth adapted for grinding food.

Monorchid: A male animal having but one testicle in the scrotum; monorchids may be potent and fertile.

Muzzle: The part of the face in front of the eyes.

Nictitating membrane: A thin membrane at the inner angle of the eye or beneath the lower lid, capable of being drawn across the eyeball. This membrane is frequently surgically excised in some breeds to improve the expression.

Occiput or occiputal protuberance: The bony knob at the top of the skull between the ears.

Occlusion: The bringing together of the opposing surfaces of the two jaws; the relation between those surfaces when in contact.

Olfactory: Of or pertaining to the sense of smell.

Out at elbow: With elbows turned outward from body due to faulty joint and front formation, usually accompanied by pigeon-toes; loose-fronted.

Out at shoulder: With shoulder blades loosely attached to the body, leaving the shoulders jutting out in relief and increasing the breadth of the front.

Overshot: Having the lower jaw so short that the upper and lower incisors fail to meet; pig-jawed.

Pace: A gait in which the legs move in lateral pairs, the animal supported alternatively by the right and left legs.

Pad: The cushion-like, tough sole of the foot.

Pastern: That part of the foreleg between the fetlock or pastern joint and the foot; sometimes incorrectly used for pastern joint or fetlock.

Period of gestation: The duration of pregnancy, about 63 days in the dog.

Puppy: Technically, a dog under a year in age.

Quarters: The two hind legs taken together.

Roach-back: An arched or convex spine, the curvature rising gently behind the withers and carrying over the loins; wheel-back.

Roman nose: The convex curved top line of the muzzle.

Scapula: The shoulder blade.

Scissors bite: A bite in which the incisors of the upper jaw just overlap and play upon those of the lower jaw.

Slab sides: Flat sides with insufficient spring of ribs.

Snipey: Snipe-nosed, said of a muzzle too sharply pointed, narrow, or weak.

Spay: To render a bitch sterile by the surgical removal of her ovaries; to castrate a bitch.

Specialty club: An organization to sponsor and forward the interests of a single breed.

Specialty show: A dog show confined to a single breed.

Spring: The roundness of ribs.

Stifle or stifle joint: The joint next above the hock, and near the flank, in the hind leg; the joint corresponding to the knee in man.

Stop: The depression or step between the forehead and the muzzle between the eyes.

Straight hocks: Hocks lacking bend or angulation.

Straight shoulders: Shoulder formation with blades too upright, with angle greater than 90° with bone of upper arm.

Substance: Strength of skeleton, and weight of solid musculature.

Sway-back: A spine with sagging, concave curvature from withers to pelvis.

Thorax: The part of the body between the neck and the abdomen, and supported by the ribs and sternum.

Throaty: Possessing a superfluous amount of skin under the throat.

Undercoat: A growth of short, fine hair, or pile, partly or entirely concealed by the coarser top coat which grows through it.

Undershot: Having the lower incisor teeth projecting beyond the upper ones when the mouth is closed; the opposite to overshot; prognathous; underhung.

Upper arm: The part of the dog between the elbow and point of shoulder.

Weaving: Crossing the front legs one over the other in action.

Withers: The part between the shoulder bones at the base of the neck; the point from which the height of a dog is usually measured.

(End of Part II. Please see Contents page for total number of pages in book.)